DATE DUE

Apr 7 '75			
Aug 9 '77			
Mar28 79			
Apr26 79			
Aug15 79			
Mar 4 '83			

With This Ring

WITH THIS RING

LOUIS H. BURKE

Judge of the Superior Court, Los Angeles County

with

THE GORDONS

Psychological consultant,

DR. EVERETT L. SHOSTROM

Co-director, Institute of Juridical Psychotherapy

McGraw-Hill Book Company, Inc.

New York Toronto London

To Ruth

WITH THIS RING

Printed in the United States of America.

Library of Congress Catalog Card Number: 58-7413

First Edition

Contents

This book is based upon the actual procedures and practices of the Conciliation Court, a department of the Superior Court of Los Angeles County, which deals with the problems of marriage. Of necessity, the names, characters, and stories used are entirely fictional and any similarity to actual persons or incidents is purely coincidental. The problems encountered and related, however, are as old as marriage itself.

chapter one

Little Jacob

The case was entitled "McQuarrie *v.* McQuarrie" and the charge was adultery.

As I mounted the bench, I saw a woman in her mid-thirties give final admonitions to three children lined up in the first row of the spectators' section, and then hurry to take her place beside her attorney at the plaintiff's table. She was a slender, pretty blonde, short of stature, with a sober, intelligent face.

At the other table, her husband sat with two attorneys. He was a big, rawboned man, handsome in a rugged way, although the lines were digging deeper into his face than in most men his age. His jaw was bull-set.

Neither glanced the other's way. It was as though already the other didn't exist.

Their gaze instead was fixed on my tanned and weather-beaten face, the product of salt spray, wind, and sun. If they had expected a portly, old white-haired judge, clothed in black poplin and severity, they must have been disappointed. Even my robe cannot disguise my tall thin frame, nor am I white haired, although only that morning Ruth, my wife, had commented that I was beginning to acquire a bit of "distinction" about the temples.

They could not possibly know, I kept reminding myself, that this was my first trial after being discharged from military service, nor that it was my first domestic relations case in twenty-six years.

As the plaintiff's attorney rose, my eyes ran down the divorce complaint that lay before me until they came to the names of the children: a boy six, another boy ten, and a girl twelve. There they sat, almost immediately behind their mother's lawyer. The six-year-old, a pudgy little fellow, was squirming, trying to see better what was going on. The boy of ten sat as though petrified. The girl's eyes caught and held mine briefly. Never before, not even during the closing days of the war in Germany, had I seen such shock and hurt.

Only thirty minutes before, I had been sworn in and enrobed as a superior-court judge in Los Angeles for the state of California. As Presiding Judge W. Turney Fox handed me a well-worn file, he informed me that litigants, lawyers, and witnesses were already in Department 21 awaiting immediate trial. He expressed regret that he had to hurry me to the bench within minutes after my induction, but the case load for the county was so heavy he had no choice.

And thus it was that I suddenly found myself in the midst of a bitterly contested divorce action. During the years I had been away from domestic relations cases, I had served as city attorney in my home town of Montebello, California, as general counsel for the League of California Cities, and during part of my stint in the Army during World War II, as a military government trial judge in Germany.

Now, before the first witness took the stand, I called the lawyers to the bench for a whispered conference. Could they arrange to remove the children? Surely, with the kind of evidence that would be introduced . . . ?

The wife's lawyer said he had already discussed the matter with her, and she was adamant. She wanted the children to know what kind of man their father was.

It was an old story, of course. The children, born of love, were now being sacrificed on an altar of hatred.

The witnesses came forth and were sworn. All the lurid details were recited . . . the husband's dates with other women . . . the motels they visited . . . the exact hour they arrived and when they left, as recorded by private detectives. During portions of the testimony I ordered the children excluded, but I couldn't save them the ordeal of being called as witnesses.

A perfect judge, I suppose, would be one unhampered by emotions, completely objective, hearing a case only on its cold legal basis. But that morning I was probably as emotionally disturbed as either the husband or wife. Here were two people once deeply in love, whispering all the little nothings that we all say, feeling good with each other, high with hopes and plans, with their hearts pounding as they said, "with this ring . . . I thee wed."

Exactly what had happened? At what point had their marriage begun to break up, at what point still later on had the husband turned to other women, and why? Couldn't someone perhaps have done something at that crucial moment that would have held these two together, and the 330,000 other couples in these United States who each year, with varying degrees of bitterness, wind up their marriages in tragedy?

And even now, was it too late? Wasn't there something more that the courts could do than was being done? Some step that would save some of these marriages, at least those that deserved to be saved, where man and wife, deep down, still wanted each other but had gone so far in rancor and a basic failure to understand human nature, their own included, that they weltered in a bog of emotion?

And couldn't something be worked out that would help those couples who were just buying the engagement ring to know and understand the sicknesses that befall marriage, so they might successfully avoid them?

The case of "McQuarrie *v.* McQuarrie" dragged on for four miserable days in the dark, old courtroom with the air conditioning wheezing and the stenotype chattering faintly as it recorded the sordid details. At the mother's insistence, the twelve-year-old girl eventually took the stand to tell of a telephone conversation she had overheard between her father and one of the women named in the complaint. She spoke so low she could scarcely be heard, and at times the words had to be prodded out by the attorney. Looking at her suffering there in the witness chair, I felt a knife wrench deep inside me; so, I imagine, did everyone else in the court that afternoon.

At last, the time came to grant the divorce to the wife, give her custody of the children, set the alimony, and decide the amount the husband should pay each month for the children's care. I had scarcely finished when the wife, smiling in vindictive triumph, rose and glanced for the first time at the defendant.

That evening I drove home completely depressed that human beings could treat each other with such inhumanity, even their very own children, who would never forget what they had experienced this day.

I parked the car for the night in the garage which I always catch myself calling the barn to the delight of our children. I wandered then to the kitchen where Ruth, my bride of 1933, was busy getting dinner. I did not feel much like talking about my first day as a judge, and, sensing this, she began telling me what the children had been doing: Michael and Kathleen, then in their late teens; Sheila Ann and Mary Eileen, in their early teens; and Patrick, nine and all boy.

Afterwards I drifted to the piano and began picking out a tune, proud that I could at least read the right hand. Soon I was conscious of someone from the other room softly shutting the door on my music, a cause-effect situation that has been going on for years without ever discouraging me in the slightest, although I confess it hurts a little.

Shortly afterwards, I found I was playing out-of-season Christmas carols in a vain effort to cheer myself up. My thoughts slipped back to many years before, to a case I handled as a young attorney, one of my first, a case that was to mold my feelings toward divorce long before I went to the bench, and one that was to turn me at that time to branches of the law which did not exact such a high toll of one's emotions.

At the time I was just out of Loyola University in Los Angeles, and also had been graduated *cum laude*—I like to believe—from a brickyard where I had worked summers and vacations. So I had been with men who labored at rough, hard work, and could understand the feelings and thoughts of this man I shall call Hans who walked into my office one morning. He was short and stocky, beginning to go bald, and his beaten-up, gnarled hands spoke of the kind of work he did on a ranch.

This is the story he told me that day. He was from Europe originally, but once in the United States and making a little money as a ranch hand, he began thinking about buying a small farm and settling down with a wife. He never had forgotten a girl named Anna back in his little village, although at the time he left she was only twelve.

He remembered her as straight of back, sturdy legged, with long brown hair, braided and falling below her waist. So he arranged with his brother, still living in the village, to talk to her about marriage.

Anna's memory of Hans, of course, was dim, but the lure of America plus her parents' wishes decided her, and she set forth for a country she did not know and a man twice her age whom she knew even less. She arrived in New York bewildered, lost, homesick, and frightened. Somehow she made her way to Hans in California, where he had arranged for her to work as a cook on the ranch.

Her first day would have broken the spirit of many, but she pitched into the work with a will. It helped to dull the pangs of disappointment which tore at her. Hans was not even as she remembered him. Years of hard work had taken their toll. His hair had thinned to partial baldness, the skin of his hands was cracked, calloused, and rough. He had appeared tall to a child of twelve, but from the vantage point of a young woman of nineteen standing five feet six in her stocking feet, he was short and stocky.

He already had their "home" fixed up. Before she arrived, he converted a harness shed into a large bedroom with a little dressing room off to the side. He whitewashed the building outside and painted it inside. It was rough, to be sure, but it showed a lot of thoughtfulness for the feelings of his young bride.

He was quick to note her disappointment in him. While she was getting acquainted with the boss's wife, he excused himself and went to rearrange things. He placed a camp cot in the corner where it was partially obscured by the dressing room. It would serve as his bed. Things would take time with Anna. But he was both understanding and patient. What the ranch hands didn't know wouldn't hurt them.

When he thought of Anna, his heart almost pounded through the coarse wool shirt. To him she was beautiful beyond belief.

In time, Anna became a dutiful wife to Hans. But love him she could not. Hans maintained the pretense that all was well between them, and when Anna was carrying Little Jacob, he truly believed that his dreams of happiness on a farm of his own with Anna were really on their way. Anna had a way with her—so full of vitality, good cheer, and good health.

On the heels of Little Jacob's arrival, a new hand came down from the city. Franz was a mechanic, a recent graduate of a trade school, and this was his first outside job in his chosen field. His parents had come from Europe, too. He had learned the old language from them but disdained to speak it. "This is America, not the old country. Here we should speak English." He started a crusade to substitute it for the old language at the table. Anna loved this, for it gave her a chance to practice her school English. With the older hands, including Hans, it was different. English was difficult for them.

Months rolled by, and one day Franz, Anna, and Little Jacob disappeared. Hans ran to the village to talk with the police. He believed Franz had kidnapped his wife and son. The others at the ranch said little or nothing. None dared to suggest what was in his mind, for Hans had a temper which was very slow to excite but terrible to behold once it built up.

The fateful day Anna's letter reached the ranch, everyone debated who should take it to him. Finally, the boss waited until late at night to slip it under his door where he would find it in the morning. But in the dark room, Hans was not asleep. He lit the oil lamp and saw the white envelope. It was the first and only word he was to have of her for a whole year. In it, she asked him to forgive her.

Two hours before the other hands would be stirring, Hans left the ranch, on foot as he had come. Sensing that Franz would go to a city, Hans went from one area to another as far as his savings would take him. At the end of a year, a former friend he chanced to meet told him where they were living. Hans fought off his desire to kill Franz and, at the friend's insistence, went to see a lawyer instead.

It was Little Jacob he wanted, since he could not have Anna, and he was prepared to fight for him. The month that followed, however, contained bitter disappointment for Hans. The judge gave temporary custody to the mother pending a full hearing on the case.

"There is no justice in America," Hans muttered to himself. In the following weeks he took a room near the cottage where Franz and Anna lived, and bided his time. One day she left the boy in the yard unattended for a few minutes. That was the last she saw of Little Jacob for many years.

Under an assumed name, and with Little Jacob back to live and work for, Hans drove himself to get ahead, working from sunup to long after sundown. Eventually he bought a small farm, and there they lived alone. It was strictly a man's world that Little Jacob grew up in, and he was all farm boy, from the unruly mesh of hair on top of his head to the hard-toed boots on his feet.

When they came into my law office for the first time, Jacob was ten and in the fifth grade. Hans was middle-aged and stooped from years of hard labor, and he spoke English with the greatest difficulty.

They handed me a blue-covered legal document which had been served on Hans by a deputy sheriff, an order to show cause why Hans should not be found in contempt of court for violating the nine-year-old order restraining him from removing the child from the custody of the mother. A second portion ordered him to produce Jacob in court at a given time and place.

We journeyed north, Hans, Little Jacob, and I. After two days of trial we were totally unprepared for the jolting court order that Hans surrender Jacob to Anna, now "Ann," for a period of three weeks so that she could become reacquainted with him. The judge, in his chambers, got a promise out of Jacob that he would go along quietly and give his mother a chance to know him, with the understanding that when he returned to court the judge would ask Jacob what he wished done about his future custody.

On the courthouse steps, a sorrowful Hans and I watched Little Jacob get into the big Cadillac that Franz, now "Frank," owned.

When we entered the courthouse three weeks later, I got quite a shock. I hardly knew "Little" Jacob. He had a short haircut, a new suit which replaced the clean but well broken-in overalls, a pair of new oxfords, sport socks, and an open-collared sport shirt.

Jacob rushed to Hans with justifiable pride in his appearance. The two embraced but in Hans's brimming eyes, pride in the boy was struggling with hate for everything which bore the stamp of Franz and his money. For Franz had done very well. A small garage had mushroomed into a chain of service stations.

Jacob's change in appearance, I could see, made an impression on the judge. But as the trial progressed, I kept reminding myself that the judge had said he would let Jacob tell him what he wanted done about his own custody. Somehow I felt certain these three weeks of movies, candy, clothes, trips, and his mother's genuine love could not prevail over the boy's strong devotion to his father.

The moment came when the whole courtroom hung on the words of the boy. The judge said, "Jacob, you now have had the opportunity to meet your mother and be with her. Has she been good to you?"

"Yes, sir."

"Do you feel that your mother loves you?"

"Yes, sir."

"And do you love her?"

The answer was slow in coming. A boy's heart was being pried open in full view.

"Yes, sir." He had been taught honesty, having learned it at the knee of the tense man beside me. "But I love my father, too," he quickly added.

"But, son," the heavy voice of the judge went on, "your father has had you for ten years. It was a wrong thing for him to do, and your mother is entitled to have you, too."

So that was the way the wind blew. At the risk of incurring the displeasure of the judge, who was still questioning the boy, I reminded his honor that this woman had deserted her husband and run away with another man, that she had been guilty of keeping the child's whereabouts from his father for over a year. The pent-up emotion that this case aroused in me was finding its way into words and demeanor. The judge, finding my manner offensive, ordered me seated. When I insisted on the right to finish, the bailiff and a deputy sheriff started converging on me.

"Young man, you are in contempt of court! Mr. Bailiff, seat the gentleman!" He did.

The judge's questioning continued. Finally he asked, "Tell me, son, what would you have the court do—give your custody to your mother or your father?"

Everyone in the court forgot to breathe, waiting for the boy's words. Jacob said, "To my father, if you please, sir."

A look of obvious displeasure crossed the judge's face.

The boy hurried on. "My father, I'm all he has, all he lives for. He needs me. I write his letters, help him on the farm. You heard him. He doesn't speak good English. How could he get along if I weren't there to help him?"

Hans was overcome. His head went down on the table, and seeing him, the boy, too, started to cry. The mother was already sobbing.

The judge said abruptly, "The law places final responsibility in these matters upon the judge, to determine in his own mind what is in the best interests of the child." He granted custody to the mother and stepfather, who would be able to give him "every advantage by way of education and training."

I jumped to my feet and in an excited voice reminded him of his promise to the boy to consider and be guided by the boy's wishes.

My interference infuriated the judge. Looking as if he were about to jump right down on me from the bench, he said, in measured words, "You know better than that, counsel. You *should* know, at least, that a court may not divest itself of its judicial discretion and vest it in anyone else, least of all a ten-year-old child. I made a promise to the boy and I kept it. I told him that upon his return I would ask him his wishes. However, the court is not *bound* by the wishes of children, as you must know."

Everyone's stock pile of emotion had suddenly been released on me; particularly the judge's, who fined me $10 for contempt of court.

It was a strange little procession the next morning to the railroad station, where the father and I were to leave on the

11 o'clock train for Los Angeles. I walked ahead with Hans by the arm. Half a block behind, the boy followed. Disdaining a ride with her husband, Anna trailed by a few yards. The shiny black Cadillac moved slowly along the curb, bringing up the rear.

After Hans bade his son good-by, telling him to remember all he had taught him and to be a good boy to his mother, I hurried him into the train and pushed him into a double seat. He looked through the window for a last view of his son. A moment later he erupted, throwing me violently into the aisle. A glance through the window indicated what had triggered him. The boy had been trying to follow his father and Franz was having a hard time holding him back.

By the time I reached him, Hans had "poleaxed" Franz for the second time with his large hamlike fist, slamming him against the building. I couldn't break the viselike grip around Franz's throat.

"I'm an officer," I shouted to the attendant. "Help me put this man on the train." Between the two of us, we pried his hands loose and rushed him toward the train and up the steps.

As the train started its preliminary shudders, I took a last look at the station. The attendant was helping Franz to his feet, Little Jacob was crying his heart out, and Anna was doing her best to comfort him.

When we got to Los Angeles, I drove Hans to his farm. We turned into the drive, and he said one word, the first since we had boarded the train—"Wait." I saw him light a lantern and go into a little tool shed. He came out with an ax. I reached for the switch and starter, thinking perhaps this was his way of settling with unsuccessful lawyers. But no, he went into the barn. He came out in a few minutes with a large bundle in his arms. He handed it to me. It was warm and soft.

"Big turkey," he said. "Was saving for when Little Jacob come home." He swallowed. "Now, you take, please, home to family." Neither of us could speak. He turned to the house.

A year and a half later he had lost his battle to keep his little farm above water. He left the area and I never heard from him again.

Little Jacob? Three years later I heard he had disappeared and no trace had been found.

I always hoped that somewhere, somehow, Little Jacob had found his father again and helped make his dream of a farm of his own come true.

chapter two

Quicksand

Little Jacob sat beside me during those early months on the bench. I never heard a divorce case in which the custody of children was being decided without having him in my mind.

Other kinds of cases, too, were assigned, but more and more divorce was beginning to shadow me, until at last it caught up with me. I was assigned to an "order to show cause" department, better known around the courthouse as the "Little War Department."

This court heard only the preliminary steps in contested divorce cases, deciding on a temporary basis the custody of children, the support of the wife and children, and a score of other matters that could not wait until the final hearing, which would be set for perhaps months hence.

The small courtroom was packed every morning with litigants in the first stages of shock and anger resulting from the impact of the filing of the action. A wife, angry and crying by turns, fighting to keep her two children; and her husband, swearing she had consorted with other men in their presence. Another woman, sweet-eyed and shy, declaring her mate had threatened to kill her and the baby, and asking for a court order to restrain him from molesting them. A husband storming that he couldn't even get into the house to get his shaving equipment. An aggressive, hard-bitten girl demanding $80 out of her husband's $100 weekly salary. Another woman, in her fifties, seeking an order to evict her husband from their home, and the husband threatening to shoot on sight any deputy who tried to oust him. A gum-chewing girl who wanted the television set and her baby, in that order. A quiet, little man in his forties, red-eyed and distraught, charging that his bride of two months was spending everything he had in an effort to ruin him.

And so it went, from five to twenty cases every morning. I found myself dreading to walk from the peace of my chambers to the bench to begin another long day of settling complaints as equitably as I could. The two most difficult and common were the custody of children and finances. They called for the wisdom of Solomon and the patience of Job, and no human being can measure up to that.

Occasionally after a court decision the rancor was so deep or irresponsibility so gross that the parties would be summoned to show cause why they should not be found guilty of contempt for violations of court orders. Some welcomed jail or the road camp, rather than submit to the tyranny of a vindictive wife armed with an order for support.

With some 2,500 divorce actions being instituted in Los Angeles County alone each month, the impossibility of my department's doing anything more constructive than providing an armed truce lay like a weight on me. It was like another time, back in World War II, when I sat in the half blown-up city hall of Bardenberg in Germany, with artillery shells screaming over the village, which was caught between the fire of the American and German forces. At a given hour each day, both armies would cease fire to give the villagers time to hurry to food points for water and potatoes, or to the city hall, where we would consider requests for emergency aid for babies being born and people dying. Most requests had to be refused. One day my German interpreter posted a notice in German above the door to my office. Some time later I learned he had printed: ABANDON HOPE ALL YE WHO ENTER HERE!

Just as those were very real people who emerged in the deadly quiet of the daily armistice, so were those who came before me in the courtroom. They were not statistics compiled by some far-off census bureau. They were basically decent people for the most part, like my own friends and neighbors.

With some, of course, the roots of their troubles went deep, and for them to continue to live together would have been worse than any prison sentence. But with others, perhaps the majority, there was still love. These were the marriages that could be salvaged—and many of them were being rescued by clergymen to whom the couples had turned, by psychologists, psychiatrists, and social workers in private practice, and by the Conciliation Court.

But wasn't there some bridge I might help build, a bridge that would provide a way back for couples still in love who didn't know how to reconcile their differences? Even if it were a rickety bridge, that would be something.

So it was a bridge I was searching for when I migrated from the Little War Department to a branch court situated in an area that promised its share of divorce problems. Most of the cases now were default ones, taking only five to ten minutes to hear. Only one side of the story was told, and only one witness was required to substantiate the bare essentials of proof necessary. Usually, the wife would charge extreme mental cruelty and bring a friend to testify that the husband would disappear for days at a time, or would yell at her before friends, or would taunt her endlessly about her shortcomings. Sometimes she would charge grievous bodily injury, and then the friend would swear the husband had slapped the wife, or perhaps beaten her.

After hearing this brief evidence, I would ask if all efforts at reconciliation had been explored. The breathless quiet that fell over all parties was usually the only answer. It was a fearful quiet, fearful that the court might take some unforeseen step to block the divorce.

About this time I began to realize that the very mechanics of the divorce process—the lawyers, the papers filed, the courtroom itself, the charges, and countercharges—only widened the breach between the husband and wife. Perhaps their rift had started with no more than a quarrel. One of them had threatened divorce, and the other in the heat of anger had said, "All right, if that's the way you feel." So the wife had hurried to an attorney, who proceeded to draw up papers in legal language, the kind a semantics professor would call "fighting language," in which a slap becomes "grievous bodily injury." The husband, served with this paper by a process deputy, would naturally grow furious as he read the document. So this was how his wife regarded him? He would remember little things out of the past, and in the light of these charges, they would take on great importance. His friends and relatives would side with him and perhaps egg him on. He would answer the charges, of course, through his attorney, and there would be more "fighting language." By the day they arrived in court, they would be inflamed and ready for battle.

All this I was mulling over when, one day in December, 1953, I learned that a veteran California judge, the much beloved Georgia Bullock, planned to resign from the Conciliation Court. In spite of my acquaintanceship with the army adage, "Never volunteer," I did just that. Shortly afterwards, Presiding Judge Philip H. Richards granted my request. It was a department no one else really wanted.

Although Christmas was upon us, I found little yuletide spirit as I began my new assignment. Some wives and husbands were outright hostile to me, some heard me out patiently but considered their situation so hopeless they didn't care to talk about it, and some were only going through the motions of reconciliation to satisfy friends and relatives.

Briefly, this was how the Court functioned: Any wife or husband whose marriage was in trouble could file a petition for a conciliation hearing. He, or she, would swear to an affidavit setting forth the problem and the background facts. Neither the affidavit nor the counseling that followed cost anything. Upon receiving the petition, the court clerk would notify the other spouse to come in for an informal hearing. If that person refused, he could be compelled to do so. From that point on, however, the proceedings were entirely voluntary, and either party could drop out at any time.

On the day appointed, a trained counselor would talk over their differences with them, first separately and then with the two together. Generally, the problem would be resolved in one or two conferences, and a reconciliation effected or refused. Quite often the couple would be referred to a family counseling agency of their choice, either a private or a community one, or to their pastors, or to a psychologist or psychiatrist if they required such treatment.

From its start in 1939, the Court was both praised and damned. Many attorneys and judges entertained serious doubts over whether the results justified its existence. They cited the statistics. In the first year of its operation, one in ten couples sought help. Five years later, only one in one hundred did so—in a year when 33,000 divorce actions were filed.

Many other lawyers and judges foresaw the possibilities and thought it was a sound, constructive step. They appreciated that human relations cannot be measured by figures, that even if only one family in hundreds could be kept intact, a boy or girl might grow into a fine person who otherwise might have drifted into juvenile delinquency and eventually crime. They knew the other side of the statistics: that seven out of ten children in trouble with the police come from broken homes.

Eventually, the percentage that suggested success was brought up. In 1953, the case load increased to 100 a month. This increase was due largely to the devoted efforts of Commissioner Margaret Harpstrite, Counselor Josephine Maxon who assisted her, and the good will of a small segment of the Los Angeles bar.

Now the responsibility was mine. Every night I sank down into my old chair in the living room, with my wife across the way sewing, to read everything I could find about reconciliation. Most of the articles, including many in technical journals, took a disturbing view of the Court. They pointed out that about all it did was afford the parties an opportunity to discuss their troubles with an impartial third person who would attempt to reconcile their differences. In other words, the Conciliation Court had no real power, no authority, and in some corners, no respect. Some attorneys were using it as a legal means of stalling divorce proceedings for thirty days.

Disturbed by all this and hoping to find an answer, I decided to put aside my "severity and black poplin" for a while and become a counselor myself. The result was a trying year. For more than twelve months I sat in a small counseling room, looking across the desk at faces of all ages, from seventeen up into the sixties, putting in the most nerve-racking labor I have ever attempted. The task called for a tremendous amount of patience, self-restraint, and natural sympathy for the problems of others. It wasn't easy to remain impartial while mates spoke from a life's store of hatred, or to sublimate your own feelings when a man spoke of his wife as though she were a chattel he was through with and now wanted to discard. Hardest was simply to listen and restrain all impulse to deliver a lecture.

Some of the faces I remember vividly. One belonged to a girl of nineteen, pretty in a chubby way, intelligent but extremely sensitive. She said her husband didn't "understand" her and criticized her constantly, and her nerves couldn't take it any longer. When he told me his side of the story, he said she irritated him and he couldn't help flaring up. He was a big, robust fellow who had played football in high school and now had a good job in an aircraft factory.

Their problem seemed small compared with the future of their year-old baby, a girl they both adored. But it had grown to the explosion point. Yet they listened attentively, and after many hours of counseling they came in one afternoon to tell me he was moving back into their apartment.

It was a good, joyous feeling I experienced, but short-lived. She returned two weeks later, saying he had broken his promises. When he drifted in shortly afterward, they got into a violent argument in my office over what each had promised, or hadn't. The one thing they did agree upon was divorce, and no argument would change their minds. It was a tragic thing—two swell kids, who had everything to offer each other except forgiveness and understanding.

As I pulled the door of the Conciliation Court shut that evening, perhaps more discouraged than I had ever been, I muttered to myself, "Well, I can't say I didn't ask for it." I vented my frustration by a sharp jab at the elevator button.

"How's it going, Louis?" a deep, vibrant voice asked.

I turned to greet a judge many years my senior, now presiding over a juvenile court. "Mighty slow. I've had three rugged case failures in a row."

As we stepped into the elevator, the operator grinned at me. "You must've had an exciting day, Judge," he said. "That last couple was still going strong all the way down to the street."

The humor missed me. All I could muster was a weak "Good night, George."

I fell in step with my colleague on the way to the parking lot. "Something's wrong with our approach," I said.

He took a deep breath. "I just wish some of your husbands and wives could sit in juvenile court for a day and see what may happen to their children if they split up." He turned to me. "You've at least got a chance to help a family, and if you succeed in one out of a hundred times, well, that's something. But with us—the harm's been done by the time the youngsters reach us."

As he started to get into his car, I said, "Do you know what struck me after reviewing hundreds of these cases?"

"What's that?"

"It's that so many people don't seem to know what's expected of them as husbands and wives. They enter into marriage as they'd buy a new suit. If it turns out they don't like it, they can always get another. The idea that marriage is a *contract* from which obligations arise, as well as *rights* flow, has never been brought home to them."

"I know. It's a what's-in-it-for-me attitude."

He paused. "One thought occurs to me, Louis. Never underestimate the power of influence of a judge or court. We who are in court all the time seldom think about the impact that contact with a judge has on most people. More often than not it's the first they've had. It might be helpful if somehow you could use this impact—this influence for good—in your reconciliation work."

He started the motor. "Don't get discouraged, Louis." He added, "Good night," as he drove away.

I scarcely heard him. A thought was beginning to churn about and take shape.

chapter three

A Bridge Is Built

As I threaded my course through the heavy evening traffic, these thoughts kept coming to the surface: Fundamentally, ours is a job of educating or reeducating couples about their "obligations" toward each other and their children. They must realize that marriage is a contract, the most important they will ever sign. But how can the court best bring its "good influence" to bear?

After dinner that evening, I could scarcely keep my mind on the high school algebra course I was retaking for the fourth time, this time with my fourth youngster, Mary Eileen. She deserted me eventually to work out the equation on her own, and I settled down to read a book whose pages I never once turned. Over and over, the day's cases filed by, what the husband had said, what the wife had told me, how they had acted, the chances for bringing them together.

There was the couple in their early thirties who had found happiness in their marriage—until the baby arrived. Now, with the child four, they bickered constantly over its rearing. He was from an easygoing home, and she from a very strict one. Each now projected that earlier home, and because neither would surrender that "home image," they wanted out.

But marriage is a contract . . . a contract.

And then, the second case. The husband was an electronics worker in his late twenties who doled out $10 a week for grocery money to his wife, and not a cent for anything else. She told me, "He said that was all I was worth—that he could get a woman off the street for that." He had a different story. She had quit talking to him, never cooked breakfast, and wasn't home half the time when he returned evenings.

Ours is a job of educating couples about their obligations . . .

But time and again my thoughts reverted to the nineteen-year-olds with their year-old baby—the husband who didn't "understand" her, the wife who "irritated" him. What had happened to the "good influence" of the Court with them? They had pledged promises in my presence, promises made with so much love they could scarcely take their eyes from each other to listen to me. And yet two weeks later, they were back. They couldn't even remember the promises.

They couldn't remember the promises.

An idea began to root itself and grow. We had lost with them. But there had been another couple that afternoon, about their ages and equally immature. They would be coming back tomorrow. Perhaps, with them. . . .

Their names were Amy and Rex Bulland. Their pastor, who had persuaded them to file a petition with the Conciliation Court, had telephoned early in the morning to brief me. They had been seventeen and in the midst of a whirlwind romance when Amy became pregnant. Both sets of parents descended upon the bewildered youngsters. A hasty marriage ensued, followed by the mechanics of covering up the true date of the ceremony so as to bring conception within the all-important mathematical computation. That had been two years ago, and now at nineteen, with two babies, Amy was through.

The two came in together, a little strained with each other but at least civil. She was small and shy but at the same time slightly on the defiant side, too. He was a tall, lanky, awkward fellow with tousled red hair, and he was scared. It took only a glance to tell that he was still very much a teen-ager. Their pastor had said: "He had to quit high school when they were married and get a job. But it never seemed to help him much, and when the baby came, he was just floored. He was at that age, Judge, when the most important thing was getting 'pipes' for his jalopy."

They stood hesitantly as I indicated the chairs across from my desk. "We're not formal here," I began. "It's not like most courts. We simply talk, and sometimes by talking we can discover the basic causes of the problem and do something about them. You're to feel free to say anything you want to, or not to say anything. No one is going to make any demands on either of you. I hope you will be honest with me, though, because that's the only way we can get anywhere."

They both nodded but avoided looking at each other. "Now," I said, "I'd like to talk to you separately and then, afterwards, together. Which one wants to be first?"

Rex glanced hesitantly at her. "Do you want to go first, Amy?"

She whispered, "Okay," and he left, to sit in the small reception room outside.

She swallowed once or twice and nervously toyed with her charm bracelet. During the next few minutes I did most of the talking, not saying anything vital but attempting to make her feel at ease.

Eventually, she said, "I think I should tell you, Judge, we . . . we had to get married. He got me pregnant."

It was an accusation, as though the fault were all his.

"And then last year he got me pregnant again, and that did it, Judge. I want out, before I have any more babies. Not only do I have to look after them, Judge, but him, too. He's nothing but a kid. I have to do everything, and it's too much to ask anyone my age. I'm only nineteen. My girl friends are all out having fun, going to dances, and swimming, and I'm sitting home washing diapers. Not that I mind too much, because I wouldn't give the babies up for anything."

Carefully, I explained that it was normal to have such divided feelings when one marries so young, that many young couples feel proud of their marriage one day, and then something happens, and immediately they want to call it quits.

"Your girl friends probably feel the same about you," I said. "They take a look at you and think they are the ones missing out on life. They're thinking how wonderful it would be to have a husband and babies and a home."

She saw the logic and smiled faintly. "I know. Maybe it's me. Maybe the whole trouble's me. I . . . I don't know how to say it, but sometimes I do want Rex. I want him so badly I can hardly wait for him to come home, and then the next day I can't bear for him to touch me, and I'm mean to him, and make him sleep in the guest room."

She took a deep breath. "He doesn't love me any more, not like he used to. He just comes home and plops in front of the television and doesn't pay any attention to me. And when he makes love . . . well, he doesn't make love. You know what I mean? He forces himself on me, and it doesn't matter how I feel or what I want to do, and it's every night of the world, and I just can't take it, and I don't care what my mom says about it."

"What did your mother say?"

"Well, I talked to her about getting a divorce, and she said I'd made my bed and I had to lie in it. But that's old-fashioned talk and I'm not going to."

For a moment I sat silent. Here were two youngsters who had been brought up with a minimum of training in morality, self-restraint, and sacrifice. Intercourse had taken place before they knew whether they were suited for each other. Then their parents had taken hold, and as a result, a second child had been brought into the "family," a family in name only. I couldn't help thinking, although I know many will disagree with me, that it would have been better had the first child been placed for adoption in a good home with a deserving couple.

"I want you to think about something," I said. "A great philosopher pointed out once that love can be influenced considerably by acts of the will. You can will to love someone, and by keeping ever present in your mind the good things about that person—such as his kindness and unselfishness and other good qualities—it may be possible to capture and build up a warmth of feeling toward him. Then perhaps in time you will want to do things for him, to give of yourself to him—and you'll be on your way to the kind of love that sustains marriage."

She listened attentively but left the room without comment. Rex came in then, passing her without a word. He showed the effects of waiting. An hour had given him time for thought, and perhaps thought of a quiet, more penetrating kind than he had had before.

"Did she tell you I struck her a couple nights ago?"

"No, she didn't."

"Well, I did. I've been drinking some since this trouble started, and I'd had a few. I didn't mean to slap her, and I'm real upset about it. I tried to tell her, but she wouldn't listen. Do you think it's all my fault?"

"I'm not here to decide who is at fault," I told him. "I don't think it matters as much as what is causing the trouble, getting at the basic reasons, and trying to do something about them."

"Well, I'm to blame," he blurted. He added, "I love her so much I'd never get over it if she walks out on me. I want to get things fixed up. She's always telling me I'm a kid—and I guess I am. But I'm going to grow up in a hurry, if she'll take me back."

Unlike his wife, he had no ambivalent views toward the marriage, no regrets about not being out with his friends.

"But I can't understand her, Judge. She comes up one evening and snuggles—and then a couple nights later, she won't even let me kiss her when I come home. I don't get it—I just don't get it at all. . . ."

That was the scene that replayed itself as I sat there that evening holding a book I never read. Amy and Rex were coming back the next afternoon. I could persuade them to make promises to each other, I was sure. But there had been promises with the other couple, promises so meaningless that in two weeks' time neither remembered them.

But this time there would be more than promises.

The next day I bided the hours until they arrived. At two o'clock they came in together, which was a good sign, and in the outer reception room, she reached up matter of factly to arrange his tie.

"You tell him," he said.

"We . . . we talked things over last night," she began.

"We talked about what you said about the will to love. We want to love each other. We honestly do."

She hesitated. "He . . . he promised me. . . ."

As she related what he had promised, I wrote the points down: that he would discuss finances with her and live on a budget, that he would be more attentive, that he would care for the children three evenings a week, and that he would consult her wishes about sexual intercourse. On her part, she promised she would forget about the "good times" she thought she was missing out on, that she would quit seeing one particular girl friend who was urging her to get a divorce, that she would try to act the same toward her husband each day, and that she wouldn't refuse his love-making without good reason.

"I'm going to have this typed up," I told them, "and if you want to, you may sign. No one will persuade you to sign, or coerce you. It must be your own decision. But if you do sign, then this becomes a formal contract, the same as any other contract, and if you fail to live up to its terms, the Court may find you in contempt and may even sentence you to jail."

Amy shot Rex a questioning glance. He hesitated but a second. "Sure," he said. "I mean it. I'll sign."

At long last the thing that had been in my mind had crystallized. I had begun my bridge, my bridge of words. That night I held in my hands the first slender, tenuous strand, the contract Amy and Rex had signed—our first Reconciliation Agreement.

Now if only I could anchor it firmly, make it stick. It would take many more such strands to complete my bridge, I realized, because this one covered only one angle of the many-faceted problem, but perhaps with God's help, in time . . .

The thought born of my mental turmoil the night before was simply this: if a court can enforce contracts of all types, including those whereby property is divided in a divorce case, and the custody of children decided, and a husband or wife evicted from a home or enjoined from seeing each other, then surely a court may enforce a contract whereby the parties agree to live together in marriage and behave toward each other in certain specific ways.

A court order is an integral part of the judicial process. Every petition to a court ends with the court making some kind of an order. So, is it not fair that the court should demand something of the parties to a conciliation proceeding who have invoked aid to assist them in the reestablishment of their homes? And why shouldn't that demand be that they keep their promises to the court? Once such an order has been made, does it not inevitably follow that if one of the persons commits a serious and willful violation of a promise made in writing, such a violation should carry with it some penalty?

Amy and Rex put their names in effect to a formal contract, and I made an order based on it which would continue in force "until further order of the Court." Marriage for them, in fact, had become a contract. What my colleague, the veteran judge, had mentioned—the dignity and influence for good of the court—had been brought to bear.

That was several years ago, and many troubled waters have since flowed under my bridge. It is in common use, although it could bear much more traffic. It is still unfinished. Like anything in constant use, there is always need for repair, for remodeling. And that is good.

I can take no true pride of authorship for the construction of the span. That must go to the couples who came for counsel that first year. They themselves, out of their desperation and struggle to solve their specific problems, wrote the Agreement. It has grown until it now fills many pages, runs into thousands of words, and covers everything from the problems of sex and in-laws and jealousy and alcoholism to such matters as the weekly budget. If a new paragraph seemed to help one couple, that paragraph became a permanent part of the Agreement. Sometimes a paragraph was rewritten scores of times as we sought for simple, effective English that anyone might understand. We avoided legal phraseology, and attempted to substitute warmth for "fighting words."

As the Agreement grew, it became more than a contract. We found it developing into a document on marriage rather than divorce. More and more, we discovered that we needed to set forth the basic philosophy of a good marriage—to incorporate into it the methods of adapting to each other, the means of perfecting a union—all the threads that bind a husband and wife together.

From the beginning, the Agreement proved effective. The reasons were simple: A promise gains dignity when set forth in writing, and a contract will not be broken so lightly as a pledge given glibly during an emotional moment. A couple couldn't be expected to remember everything said in a conference, but if they had this matter in printed form, they could read it in the quiet and privacy of their homes. They could refer to it as a "working document" when troubles arose. It served, moreover, as a means of educating or reeducating people about their responsibilities.

In time, we began sending letters to reconciled parties, usually at the end of the first month, congratulating them. We would advise them that if for any reason they were unable to live together under their agreement, they should not violate its provisions and the court order but should request a further hearing. They were informed that if it appeared at such a hearing that their reconciliation attempt had failed, the court order would be terminated.

We utilized the contempt powers of the Court very carefully. Obviously, to warrant the Court's imposing a penalty, the violation must be serious and willful. If the husband agreed not to strike his wife again, or if he and his paramour promised not to see each other again, and they violated the order, the Court felt that such a flagrant violation should not go ignored.

In the first two-year period, contempt proceedings were instituted in only twenty instances, and in ten of these, seven husbands and three wives were sentenced to serve jail terms.

The results in the first two years were heart-warming. Amy and Rex became the first of 887 couples reconciled out of the 2,074 who appeared before the Court. To put it another way, we were successful in 43 per cent of our cases—cases which involved more than 2,000 children.

We were more successful, of course, with those couples who had not yet filed divorce papers but were seriously contemplating such a step. Sixty out of every hundred were in that group, and here the Court's percentage was 65. The other forty out of every one hundred cases were where divorce actions were already pending, and the reconciliations in this group totaled 24 per cent.

We are often asked, "But do these reconciliations last—or are the couples back in the divorce courts right away?" We conducted a survey which showed 75 per cent of the parties still living together one year after their reconciliation. We estimate that over a longer period 66 per cent would still be wed.

The figures themselves reflect that the Reconciliation Agreement, and the process by which it is reached, is not the final solution to marital problems. We think of it as one more span we have built across the chasm separating wives and husbands, and naturally it has structural defects as well as strength. Nevertheless, since its inception in 1953, its workability has been such that it has won wide recognition from judges, law schools, bar associations, psychologists and psychiatrists, and social service agencies in this and many other countries.

Even more rewarding are letters such as this one:

> This is just a note to let you know how happy we are. During the first six months, we found it difficult to live up to our agreement, but we stayed with it and are very grateful to you. The shadow of the last year has passed and I often shudder to think how narrowly we escaped a permanent break-up of our home.... We certainly needed a firm set of rules to go by....

chapter four

Help Wanted

Many people believe that only they can really understand and do something about their marital problems. . . . One has but to ask himself this question: "If I can solve my own problems, why haven't I done so? . . . To admit that there is a problem, and ask for help with it, is a sign of strength, not weakness.

—RECONCILIATION AGREEMENT

Even though Amy and Rex Bulland were in full accord about their plan to try living together again, they continued to sit stiffly as I drew up the terms of the Reconciliation Agreement. Although not more than a half-hour ago she had said that she wanted to keep her husband's love and her marriage, it was evident now that she wasn't so certain. It was as though she were two people, one a grown-up woman who saw values clearly, the other a petulant child.

He asked softly, "Can I move back in tonight, Amy?"

She tensed and started to shake her head, then caught herself, and nodded. It was a long step she had taken, one that called for considerable courage.

While the Agreement was being typed, I took them to talk with one of our counselors, Meyer "Mike" Elkin, a husky, kindly man in his late thirties, a graduate of the University of California with a Master's Degree. He was deeply religious, but quietly so, an inspired person who approached each day with the freshness and enthusiasm of his first. He earned $575 a month, a modest sum certainly for his education, experience, and work done. He was one of three court counselors chosen by a committee of judges which, as a result of our study, required that applicants have a Master's Degree and two years' experience in counseling, or in lieu of a Master's Degree, four years of supervised experience.

From the outset I recognized the worth of professionally trained counselors. Although I spent almost one year acting as a counselor in my study of the Court, I soon realized that the counseling operations would suffer greatly if I or any other judge not trained in such matters were to so function. I would go home deeply burdened, especially by the coarseness and cruelty shown by some people to whom human dignity was meaningless. "How do you reach these people?" I would ask myself. A trained counselor would know.

Aside from the fact that a judge does not have the specialized education or the experience needed for counseling, he may be completely unsuited by personality for a job that calls for such patience and understanding and is such a drain on the emotions. And besides, in most large cities, judges are transferred from one department to another at regular intervals, and a conciliation court needs a permanent staff. Hence, a judge should confine himself to the supervision of the staff and the legal work of the court.

Amy was still torn as Counselor Elkin talked along slowly and easily.

"You're not alone in your problems," Mike Elkin said. This was often the hardest part, getting over to a couple that many others had been caught up in the same circumstances—and had come through their desperation to find happiness. As in a serious illness, the patient takes hope when he learns others have been cured.

"I don't want you to think I'm trying to minimize your problems—because they are serious. You need help—help to find your true selves and to adapt to each other."

He suggested they go to one of the many family counseling agencies in the Los Angeles area. As in most metropolitan centers, some of these agencies function under the Community Chest, and others are private enterprises. Some are staffed with psychiatrists, psychologists, and medical men as well as family counselors.

As he talked with Amy and Rex, I thought of how most of the cases which come before the Court fall into two major categories, one where the difficulties come from "without" the family, the other where they come from "within" the individuals. In the first category, a couple may run into sudden financial hardships, or may have a long sickness, or third persons may interfere. Very often troubles originating "without" the family may be remedied through the conciliation process, with no need for further counseling.

In the second category, however, the difficulties are more deeply seated within one or both of the individuals, such as in situations where alcoholism, insecurity, emotional instability, gross immaturity, mental illness, and the like are present—or where one mate simply lacks the inner resources to cope with the problems of everyday living. Many problems in marriage involve an analysis of unconscious motives and feelings which require longer-term counseling or psychotherapy. Since the Conciliation Court obviously cannot render such services, we have enlisted the aid of various counseling agencies to supply long-term assistance. Actually, in the very limited time a court counselor has for each case, he can do little more than explore the surface trouble, or as a psychologist might put it, attempt to probe for the "precipitating cause," the immediate problems that have brought the situation to an explosive point. Usually he doesn't have time to explore for the historic or "predisposing" causes.

Counselor Elkin reviewed with the Bullands a list of available counseling agencies. "They won't try to tell you what to do," he told them, "because advice never benefits much. But they will help you to think through your own problems, so you can reach your own decisions, and so you can understand yourselves emotionally as well as intellectually. If you are going to adjust your way of living, you must *feel* it as well as think it out in words."

He explained that most agencies charge a fee in accord with the couple's ability to pay. A Community Chest agency will charge from $5 to $10 a week if the couple earns $100, and a private agency from $10 to $20. "You won't have to take time off from work," he said. "You can arrange for evening or Saturday appointments."

"I don't know," Amy said halfheartedly. "I could do a lot with that money. . . ."

"Yeah," Rex said, thinking it over, "but we oughta. We just oughta—if we're going to get any place."

"Maybe one of us could go. We have the babies to worry about."

"It won't help much unless you both go," Mike Elkin said.

Amy took a deep breath and straightened up. It was coming hard, being a woman, but she was trying. "I suppose you're right."

They chose a counseling service of their own church

affiliation, and gave the Court consent to notify the agency and to release information developed from our talks with them.

From our experience with the Bullands, and from scores of other couples whose cases we handled in the months that followed, we felt the need to begin the Reconciliation Agreement with a discussion of marital counseling. Eventually the pertinent points shaped up in this fashion:

> The ability of a husband and wife to meet each other's basic needs as human beings is important to a successful marriage. When these needs are not being met... each party begins to pull in the opposite direction... and the marriage has become sick.
>
> When we are sick most people go to a doctor. When a marriage is sick we should go to a professionally trained person for help....
>
> The marital counselor helps people to discuss and analyze the problems which are interfering with their marriage. He does not blame, judge, or take sides. Information given to him is held in strict confidence.
>
> The relationship between counselor and client is a voluntary one which is started by the client and can be ended at any time by him. To be effective, however, it requires some time to give it a fair trial. Often, for example, it is necessary to understand the past in order to deal more adequately with the problems and pressures of the present and future. The time and money spent for counseling is, in a way, an investment in the future....

We always filled in the name of the agency chosen so that the husband and wife might avoid those psycho quacks who flourish in every large city and advertise themselves as marriage counselors with quick cures. Usually this type of "psychologist" is by self-appointment only, with little if any training and a degree bought from a diploma mill for $50 to $100. No reputable psychologist advertises, nor does he hold forth any promises about the time the treatment may require, which may run from twelve to eighteen months. Many outstanding psychologists among the 16,200 who belong to the American Psychological Association devote themselves to marital problems. About half hold doctorates and have served internships, just as medical men do. Some work in clinics and with Community Chest agencies, and some are in private practice, often in association with a physician.

Lest I paint a picture that marriages may be saved only by payment of counseling fees, I want to emphasize that such counseling was the exception rather than the rule. At least 50 per cent of the cases reconciled in our Court did not require follow-up counseling. Forty per cent used family service agencies, and the remaining 10 per cent went to psychologists or psychiatrists in private practice.

Not all couples, of course, were as amenable to our suggestion of continued counseling as were the Bullands. One couple, Edna and Ken Burns, stand out. She was a small, hesitant woman approaching thirty. Her petition disclosed that she and her husband were childless, that each accused the other of sterility although neither had gone to a physician for examination. The husband dated other women occasionally and sometimes drank to excess. He had already filed divorce papers.

She told me a little about herself. Her mother had had three husbands and a child by each. Edna Burns's half sisters had known their fathers, but she had only a faint recollection of a big, broad-shouldered man carrying her to the gate in their front yard, setting her down, kissing her good-by, and then walking out of her life completely. For years she had held to the hope that he would return. Eventually she had come to hate him for abandoning her.

She wasn't bitter toward her husband but only hopeful that she could work out some arrangement to save her marriage. "He can be very kind and thoughtful," she said. "He's a terribly tense person. He can't seem to let go and take things easy. He can't even sleep, and he won't go to the doctor to see what's wrong. Maybe it's because he doesn't have any outside interest. He just works, comes home, eats, and goes to bed.

"When I try to talk to him about it he gets mad, tells me it's none of my business what he does, and that's when he may go off on a drinking bout or pick up some woman."

Considerable immaturity and insecurity showed through in her conversation, but unlike her husband, she was able to discuss her problems freely. He was a big, broad-shouldered, rugged fellow, and he came in bristling.

"Let's get something straight right now," he said, "this isn't my idea and I'm not having any of it."

His record showed that he was the oldest of seven children. When he was sixteen his widowed mother had married again and his stepfather had pushed him out of the home. With a more experienced youth he had held up a market, and had served three years in a reformatory. Upon his release a parole officer took him in hand, got him a job, and he had made good.

"We don't need anybody else's help. If Edna and me have got anything to talk about we'll talk about it ourselves."

After the Burnses were gone the counselor wrote a report in which he concluded that Ken Burns probably would always refuse help, because unconsciously he felt that to seek help would be an admission of failure on his part. In his eyes, to ask for or even listen to counsel would betray to the world that he was a weak individual, incapable of making his own decisions.

Two months later, as we had feared, his attorney asked that conciliation proceedings be closed. His client had instructed him to proceed with the divorce.

Ken Burns's refusal to accept help introduced us to a concept psychologists call "unconscious motivation." By this is meant that the *reasons* or motives for our behavior are often not accessible to our awareness. In other words, we do not always know *why* we think and feel and act as we do. The psychotherapist or counselor helps people such as Ken Burns to ferret out some of these underlying motives or needs which exist within all of us.

A common reason for refusing to seek help is cost. People say they cannot afford $10 a week or whatever the fee may be, although they spend more than this on their automobile for depreciation and upkeep alone. In reality, they are unconsciously afraid they will have to reevaluate their own behavior and, worst of all, may have to change. And so they continue to project all the blame onto the other partner.

I should mention that the word "blame" is never used in counseling or psychotherapy. Instead, the counselor seeks to find *causes*, and he will find them in both parties' situations. Often these causes are due to early experiences in the lives of both which have contributed to their marital behavior but which have long since been forgotten. In therapy, these forgotten experiences are brought out from the unconscious mind and sometimes found to be the roots of the trouble.

One partner, for example, found through therapy that he had learned unconsciously from his divorced parents that marriage need not be regarded as permanent, that wives can be traded in like old cars when they no longer function well.

A young wife discovered that she had learned early in life to "take her dollies and run home" whenever things got rough. She had been doing exactly that in her marriage, running home to mother rather than facing and working through her difficulties.

Often people take a too legalistic view of human behavior. They blame the "guilty" party for an act of unfaithfulness, not realizing that they may be the underlying cause themselves by acting in ways which encourage such behavior.

Finally, a major cause of refusal to seek help lies in unexpressed hostility. Some people are angry but refuse to talk about it. They think their hostility will just go away if they are left alone. In reality, however, such hostile feelings simply pile up in the unconscious and, unless expressed, get worse and cause more serious trouble. Just thinking positive thoughts won't help. In such persons it is as if the unconscious mind were a pitcher of dirty water. No matter how much clean water is added to it, it stays dirty. Likewise, hostile feelings have to be expressed and cleaned out before good feelings can come in.

For some, finding reality is the most difficult of all steps. There will always be those like Ken Burns who refuse to face what is in their own minds and hearts. For these, to seek counseling means to admit being weak and having failed. Fortunately, more and more every year are coming to realize that seeking assistance signifies strength. Last year, 150,000 men and women on the verge of divorce applied to the country's 265 family service agencies for help, an increase of 50,000 in the last seven years.

"I didn't know it at the time," one man told me, "but the day I brought myself to ask for help, half of the battle was already won."

chapter five

He Doesn't Love Me

When people say they are "falling out of love," they usually mean out of romantic or passionate love. Often it is just the beginning of real love.

—RECONCILIATION AGREEMENT

One of the most common complaints psychologists and marriage counselors hear is this one, "We have fallen out of love."

Amy had told me, "He doesn't love me any more, not like he used to. He just comes home and plops in front of the television and doesn't pay any attention to me."

If Rex had struck her, she couldn't have been hurt more. She could scarcely get the words out. "He used to buy me flowers, and every week end, he'd get me a box of candy, and any time we had a reason to celebrate, he'd bring me some little thing."

Rex had been guilty of thoughtlessness, of taking his wife for granted. On the surface, her complaint sounded trivial. Yet the insecurity and hostility that result in such instances may completely destroy a marriage. Usually this feeling of being unloved stems from deep immaturity, from failing to adjust emotionally to reality. And when I mention immaturity, I am not speaking of any age group; a couple of fifty may be more immature than seventeen-year-olds. Immaturity is a condition of mind, not an age classification.

"Look, Amy," I said, "every marriage goes through a period like adolescence. The adolescent has to revise his idealized image of his parents and see them as ordinary human beings with faults such as we all have, so that he can develop his own individuality. Likewise, in marriage we idealize the loved one before marriage and often for a long time afterward. Psychologists call it a temporary delusionary state.

"Eventually we come to see each other's failings, to realize that we are all human beings, that we have weaknesses as well as strengths. That's why we have to say to ourselves: 'This is the man I married, he's not perfect, but I love him for both his weaknesses and strengths. He is my husband and I'm going to stand by him.' We have then made a most important step. We have substituted the temporary infatuation of romantic love for mature love. And the first you know, you are loving him all the more.

"You're loving him through the experiences that you're sharing together, which never can be shared with anyone else—that first home you buy, that first long trip, the time one of the children almost died and you were pulled so closely together that it seemed you'd never really loved before. Then you'll look back, and while you'll always think fondly of those months of romantic love, still you'll know that mature love is more than dates and good times and flowers, that mature love is giving of yourself, and sacrificing for your loved one."

Amy was convinced intellectually—but not deep down. Romantic love had been an emotional experience for her, as it is for all of us, and while her mind accepted my explanation, her feelings refused to go along. I was reminded of

Keats's line, "I have met with women who I really think would like to be married to a poem."

We began to draft a section of the Reconciliation Agreement which eventually bore the heading, "Falling out of Love." We kept it brief, hoping to plant one single idea. We quoted the French philosopher, Jean Guitton:

> The process of love consists in the gift of oneself to another ... [and] there is no real gift without a sacrifice of self.... The loftiest act of love is therefore not receiving, but in giving. Here, moreover, lies the difference between love and passion; the latter is nothing but love without sacrifice and consequently without gift.*

Aristotle discussed this matter of sacrifice, although he didn't use the word as we know it today. He divided marriages into three categories. In the first, based on utility, one partner, or both, marries for definite advantages—money, security, escape. If something happens and the utility advantages disappear, the marriage will likely fail. In the second group, one partner, or both, marries to gain pleasure. When the glamour and excitement fade, pleasure diminishes and the marriage fails. In both these categories, the motivating force is to *gain* something. In the third category, the objective is a *gift*—one of self—a desire to sacrifice for the other with its resultant gain to both. These are the marriages that survive adversity, since the greater the adversity the greater the opportunity for giving of oneself to one's loved one.

In the weeks that followed my meeting with Amy and Rex, I often wanted to ask other couples: What have you given of yourself to your wife? What have you given your

* Jean Guitton, *Essay on Human Love,* Philosophical Library, Inc., New York, 1951, p. 80.

husband? What sacrifice have you made for him? Because if each had brought a gift of self, then surely they never would have "fallen out of love."

Romantic love has added beauty and joy to most of our lives at one time or another—but it has also wrecked many marriages in which one partner or the other, like Amy, refused to grow into a more enduring and mature love.

While Amy's basic trouble was immaturity, there were other factors. They had failed to adjust sexually, a problem we will discuss in the next chapter. They had had premarital relations resulting in pregnancy, and she had been literally forced into marriage. Moreover, he was immature, and the entire burden of living had fallen on her. These all played a part in her feeling that "he doesn't love me."

From Amy and Rex, and other couples in those first months, I learned what every counselor knows: that no one specific cause is ever responsible solely for a marriage breakup. The problem always has many causes, and often the one that appears to the eye hides others far more rancorous.

So whenever any of us heard that expression about falling out of love, we would begin to probe. Sometimes we found causes entirely different from those in Amy's situation, causes that went back to childhood.

Such was the case with the Ryans—Thomas and Susan. The woman clerk couldn't take her eyes from this beautiful woman of twenty-six who approached, carrying a baby whose dark head was in striking contrast to the mother's amber blond.

"Please, would you look at these? Have I filled them out right?" she asked the clerk. The corners of her lips lifted in the faintest suggestion of a smile, but the large eyes retained their somber, hurt look.

Years of dealing with people in trouble had taught the clerk to guard against taking a personal interest in them. "If you do that, it takes too much out of you," she would say. But in spite of her resolution, she found herself studying the girl, who had seated herself on the other side of the room. Then she glanced down at the papers before her:

> Thomas Ryan. Age, 27. College graduate. Occupation, industrial design engineer with an aircraft company. Salary, $650 per month. Married, 2 years. Separated, 3 months. Cause of separation, "incompatibility."

She turned to the page giving the statistics concerning the wife:

> Susan Ryan. Age, 26. High school and business college. Secretary, now housewife. One child, Janice, age 2 months. Cause of separation, "My husband doesn't love me."

The front door opened and a tall, black-haired young man entered. "I'm Tom Ryan," he said to the clerk. Seeing his wife, he walked over to her. They exchanged the briefest of greetings, followed by a charged silence.

A few minutes later, the clerk ushered them into my chambers. "Mr. and Mrs. Ryan, Judge."

To put them at ease, I explained the concern of the Court over the breakup of marriages and particularly those in which children were involved. Even if the reconciliation effort failed, I said, it might result in reaching a better understanding with one another in the discharge of their joint obligations to their child.

The young wife said, "It's no use. He just doesn't love me any more and I won't live with him."

Tom Ryan protested, "Judge, if that's the way she feels, we shouldn't be taking up your time. You see, sir, I'd hoped that a short separation might make her realize how much we really do care for one another, but it's just made things worse." He glanced at Susan, but there was no change in her determined expression.

He continued, "She says I don't love her any more. I just don't get it! I work hard every day for her and the baby, six days a week and overtime. Every Friday I get my check and turn it over to her, except about $10 a week for gas, oil, and my pocket money. I've never stayed out late, gambled, or done any running around, and yet she says I don't love her! It beats me, I just don't get it!"

She nodded quickly. "What Tom says is true enough but he just doesn't love me—and I'm not going to have his charity either. He can have the house, car, furniture, everything. I just want the baby and enough to get along on until she's old enough for me to go to work. After that I don't want anything. The baby and I'll do all right. . . ."

Tears washed out the rest of what she was saying. To calm her, I took her into an adjoining office where she could lay the baby down on a couch while I talked with her husband.

Tom Ryan explained he had come from a large, closely knit family. He met Susan, a secretary, when he went to work at the aircraft factory as engineer. It had been love at first sight for him; his first and only attachment.

"We couldn't've been happier those first few months we were married," he said, "and I still don't know what happened. All of a sudden I woke up to the fact that she was finding all kinds of excuses to stall me when I wanted to make love to her, and in a short time she had me sleeping on the couch in the living room."

His eyes became misty. "Judge, I don't care if she doesn't want to live with me as husband and wife. If she'd only let me stay at home with her and the baby, I wouldn't ask anything else. I just can't stand living away from her. . . ." His voice started to break.

It was Susan's turn then. The baby was sound asleep in her arms. I encountered the same reserve her husband had spoken about. The troubled waters lay deep, I thought. I gave her plenty of time while I spoke of the problems facing her and the child who would be from a broken home.

"Broken home?" She nodded thoughtfully, "I know something about that. I'm from one myself."

Somehow, this much I had guessed. She said she had been shifted back and forth between her parents and relatives so much that every attachment she formed was always being abruptly broken off, to the point where she was frightened of loving anything or anyone, for fear of being hurt.

And then she met Tom. "He was so gentle and kind. His folks were as nice as anyone could be. I guess I envied a little the way the Ryans loved each other. There was a sort of family spirit which took you in and made you feel you 'belonged.' It was something I had never known. As for Tom, his every thought seemed for me."

Her mood changed, "But now I know he doesn't *really* love me and maybe never did." The barriers were going back up.

"What makes you think that?"

"It's hard to explain. I guess a woman just knows when a man really loves her."

"Try and think of things that gave you that feeling," I suggested, "no matter how insignificant they may seem."

"Well, to begin with, he has never once told me he loved me since the first month of our marriage. In the early days he used to—you know—pet me by the hour in his car, or at the show. And after we got married, he'd never leave home without holding me a moment or two and kissing me good-by. When he'd come back it was always a big bear hug and kiss. He used to open doors for me and carry in the heavy groceries, and he was always noticing my clothes and commenting on how nice they looked. But now he doesn't even know it when he kisses me, and he never really looks at me at all."

She paused and then began again, "Shortly after we were married, I just ceased to exist except when he wanted me ... physically. I ... I began to hurt inside, just like I had when I was little."

She gave a small shudder. She was weighing whether she should say more.

"This ... this ... is hard for me to say. ..."

"Try," I said. "I'm sure I'll understand."

"Well, one time I felt so starved for his love—the tender little things he used to do—I felt so shut out—that I decided to see for myself if it was all dead in him. I went into the bedroom, slipped out of my clothes and into a negligee I hadn't worn since our honeymoon. The lights were low in the living room, and Tom was seated in his big chair buried deep in a TV program he likes. I just slid over the arm of the chair into his lap. I put my head on his shoulder and ruffled the back of his neck with my hand.

"It all surprised him so, I guess, because we had had a quarrel only a little while before. He said, 'What's this? Does little Susan want her daddy?' "

"With that, he swept me up in his arms and said, 'Let's go to bed and make up.' "

Suddenly the tears welled over. She had hungered that night for tenderness and affection. By a natural progression of events, she would have engaged eventually in the marital act. But he was insensitive to her feelings and had by-passed what she wanted most—to feel loved for herself alone. It became evident as she talked that intercourse was a happy experience when she was convinced of his love and when it was associated with tenderness and little affectionate gestures, but without these it was something so ugly in her mind that she rebelled.

The baby commenced to stir in her arms. "I can't tell you how much it's meant to tell you these things. I've had them within me so long. I've never had anyone really close I could talk to. How is it, Judge, that Tom and I can talk about anything under the sun but never the things inside us? I can't tell you how many times the words have started to come, only to be choked off in trying to say them . . . then later, what comes out are cruel things I never meant to say."

There was a long pause while I gathered my thoughts. "Susan," I began, "you're making a mistake in thinking Tom doesn't love you, because I'm positive, to use his own words, he worships the ground you walk on. True, he hasn't done a good job of reassuring you, and he needs some counseling in this phase of your relationship.

"But as in all cases, the causes for what has happened lie on both sides. Much of our adjustment in marriage goes back to what we learn from our own parents and to our lives as children. Surely you must see how your background influences you to feel the way you do." I advised a period of psychotherapy so that she could discover whether she really wanted a divorce.

She said, "But I can't help the way I feel. I can't bear to have him make love to me. How can I live with him under those circumstances? It wouldn't be fair to either of us."

"I'm sure Tom would promise not to make any demands upon you until you yourself welcome them. In the meantime, you could continue living in the same house but under an agreement in writing which would include that promise."

She finally agreed, and I asked her to step out while I talked to her husband.

"Tom," I said, "you married a girl who has battled insecurity all her life. She was attracted to you because both you and your family represented what she had never known but always wanted—to love and be loved in return."

I sat silent a moment, gazing out the window, thinking that that was what all of us want, no matter how simple or sophisticated we may be—to love and to be loved in return.

I continued, "She weighed your love by all the countless little things you did for her and by the abundance of affection you bestowed on her. They convinced her that she was the one girl in your life, and as long as she had that feeling, she could give herself completely to you. However, little by little she noticed you didn't kiss her the way you once had, nor do affectionate things for her. As a result, doubts began to assail her, *just as they had when she was a little girl.*"

He nodded in understanding as I continued, "Had you been married to a person from a happy home, she would have found ways to satisfy herself that you still loved her, or she would have done something about the situation. But not Susan, because these were deep hurts that one didn't let anybody see. So she crawled into her shell. With each additional 'proof' that you did not *really* love her, a part of her froze and rebelled. In this mental state, sexual intercourse first became difficult and then impossible.

"So you see, Tom, it wasn't things that you *did*, but rather things that you *failed* to do. To make her happy you're going to have to devote a lot of thought all your life to the problem of furnishing her the moral support, encouragement, and the tremendous amount of love which she didn't get earlier in her life."

His head lifted. He was beginning to see wherein he had failed her.

"I... I just thought she knew I loved her." He added, "Our family's never been real demonstrative, Judge. We're a tight little group, and it's always gone without saying how we feel about each other."

"I understand that—but she doesn't. She's got to be shown. We must never take each other for granted, Tom. Little things mean a lot. Most of us—and some more than others—need to be reassured repeatedly that we are loved. And it's not just in marriage alone that we seek this assurance. We want our friends to show that they like us, and our boss to say we're doing a good job.

"But we have to feel these expressions of affection are *honest* and not just tricks."

The clerk then brought in two sets of agreements. In signing them, the Ryans agreed to seek aid at once from a professional counsel or psychotherapist. In addition, Tom Ryan promised to occupy the guest room of their home and to forego marital relations until such time as she herself proposed that they resume. He promised, furthermore, to show her the normal affection that should exist between a husband and wife. One such clause set forth:

> ... the love between a husband and wife is so strong a force for developing all that is good in human nature that wise couples will not suffer their mutual attachment to become casual and commonplace under the spell of monotony, or to languish with neglect, or to degenerate into mere selfish passion; for they will realize that in this life they possess nature's most valued treasure—the loyal love of a human heart.

Susan Ryan, in turn, promised to make every effort to understand their problem and to forget the past.

This clause, "Forgetting the Past," which has become a standard part of the Reconciliation Agreement, reads:

> We agree that we will not accuse, blame or nag each other about things which have happened in the past. Each agrees to start afresh. . . . We realize that love deepens just because it has survived a crisis in which it might possibly have perished.

It was amazing to see the change in the two as they stood across the desk and extended their hands to me for a final handshake. The tension was gone. They each had a definite goal. Susan handed the baby to Tom to hold while she gathered her belongings, and the baby and Tom eyed each other with wonder.

This matter of "promises," "forgetting the past," and "the will to love" is predicated on my earnest conviction that many individuals by will power alone may bring about great changes within themselves. This is neither a blind nor a whimsical conviction but one that has grown out of my experiences as a judge and counselor dealing with scores of conciliation cases.

My psychologist friend, Dr. Everett Shostrom, points out that there are limitations to this line of reasoning. A sincere man devoted to his profession, with quick, penetrating eyes, he often sits across from me in my chambers, and stirs up a lot of thought.

One night when we were discussing in confidence the case of Susan and Tom Ryan, he said, "In my experience, Louis, promises to do better seldom work alone. Each must change his perceptions before any *real* change in behavior is possible. Then these contractual agreements develop real, personal meaning for each spouse."

He added, "When Susan and Tom consult a psychologist, he will assist them in seeing that understanding and helpfulness must come from a central *relationship* which will be developed only through a thorough analysis of each other and their marriage."

I agreed with him that this was a very valid point in regard to deep-seated difficulties which require a complete overhaul of the individual. But many times, I said, the problems are such that treatment to this extent is not necessary and illnesses in marriage may be cured by the exercise of intelligence and will power. In one Conciliation Court case, a man promised to stay out of bars and kept that promise. Another, in a triangle affair, agreed he never would see his girl friend again; he has lived up to his pledge now for three years. Husbands have promised to show their wives more attentiveness and to go out more often socially. Wives have agreed to allocation of television programs that had been a bone of contention, and some have promised to take better care of themselves, to dress more attractively, and to diet. In none of these situations, it should be noted, were the problems deep-seated or rooted in the historic past.

Dr. Shostrom also felt that this matter of "forgetting the past" should be studied carefully. "I think you should make it very clear to your couples, Louis," he said, "that forgetting the past is not always accomplished just by a new resolution to do so. If we simply *try* forgetting, we don't really forget at all but suppress our hostile feelings about the past into our unconscious minds."

He grew very intent about this. "In psychotherapy, the Ryans will clean out of their unconcious minds all the hatred and ill will which exists between them. Real forgiveness requires forgetting the past. But forgetting can really take place only when the full *facing* of all the realities of their situation takes place with their counselors. This is often a difficult and painful process, but a rewarding one. It is because of a failure to look at *all* our negative feelings that forgiveness often fails."

Here again we agreed that our differences were one of degree. Suppression of a very intense hostile feeling, in an effort to "forget the past," could easily result only in further discord. But there are many, many little episodes from the past which the husband or wife keeps bringing up and throwing into the face of the other—episodes that could be forgotten by the exercise of mental discipline, or at least could be held in silence to spare the other one hurt. For example, the time the wife drove through the garage door, that time at a party when the husband became inebriated and embarrassed his wife, the flirtation at another party that one of them carried on in all innocence, the unkind words one said about the other's relatives in a moment of anger, or the occasion when the husband pushed his wife roughly out of the way in a fit of anger. These are matters which should be forgiven and then forgotten but which sometimes build up through the years in combination with other episodes and causes to wreck a marriage.

And then, lastly, Dr. Shostrom would clarify and define the "will to love." Again, he believes that *will* or a *desire* to love is only one step, that there must again come a change in *feelings* and that this change will result only from a basic understanding of one's self and the other person.

On this particular evening, I asked him to set down exactly what he had in his mind, and this is what he wrote:

> The will to love can only function when the path is clear to will *freely*. Fears, inhibitions, hostilities: there must first be

a willingness to look at all of these roadblocks to perceiving our partner as lovable. By "will to love" is meant a willingness to look at the factors which distort our perceptions.

Willing to love in the sense of merely trying harder often creates the opposite effect. Psychologists call this the law of reversed effort. By this is meant that an unusual conscious effort often brings about the opposite effect. For example, the bicyclist who strives to avoid a stone will often hit it because of his fear that he may be unable to avoid it. Likewise, the person who *wills* (tries hard) too strongly to love another may fail because his anger or fear distorts his ability to love. These hostilities and fears have come from past experiences. Until he willingly examines the basis for his angers and fear, he will never be able to love freely.

Several days later, Dr. Shostrom and I discussed what makes a marriage grow and endure—what are the elements that strengthen the bond of love—the tensile strands so strong they can stand up under any amount of stress and weathering.

Obviously they would not be the same for every couple. Sacrifice, or call it devotion, will suffice for one couple to offset any number of serious flaws in each. For another, devotion may prove insufficient in itself. Marriage is such a complex state of being, often meaning different things to different persons, depending on their backgrounds, their attitudes, their talent for adjusting, all the facets that make up a human being.

What are the elements, though, that are common to most happy marriages? Could I find them in the cases before the Court by looking for what was most lacking, by turning the negatives of those couples into positives?

As a boy I had collected turtles, stamps, coins, and most anything imaginable. Now, I thought, as I sat down that night at home, playing the piano in the deserted living room, I would collect these elements common to sturdy marriages. I would clear out my bottom desk drawer at the office and whenever I came across one, I would write it out and drop it in. I would call them my sailing directions, since I have a fondness for the sea and its terms. And someday I would bring them all together to try to find out what makes a marriage strong.

chapter six

Taboo

Sexual intercourse provides a safe and healthy outlet for passion and preserves each party from temptations. . . . Moderation and considerateness should be observed. . . . The amount of sexual activity that constitutes moderation differs with persons. . . . Love and consideration for the other partner will operate to find the right balance.

—RECONCILIATION AGREEMENT

Amy's and Rex's sex problems were complex, but no more so than many others that couples have brought to the Conciliation Court. The marital act itself is complex, involving as it does emotions that may run the gamut from tender love and passion to antagonism, and physical reactions that may range from the pleasurable to the painful.

Amy had said that Rex insisted on engaging in intercourse every night, sometimes to the point of almost attacking her if she refused.

"Did you talk with him about it?" I asked, studying her. She had been forthright and honest about the problem.

She looked at me strangely and hesitated a long moment. "He knew I didn't want to every night."

"But did you discuss it with him?"

She shook her head. "I . . . I wanted to . . . but I never got around to it."

"So he still doesn't know your reasons and your feelings.

You see, Amy, he wanted something, and you put up a roadblock, and being the kind of fellow he is, he crashed it. You should have sat down some time, and talked quietly to him, and explained how you were thinking and how you felt. A psychologist may help him somewhat, but in this matter, it's going to be partly up to you."

She took a deep breath. "I know it sounds crazy and all —but I can't talk with him about it. I've tried, and something happens. I just don't get it out."

"I understand," I said. "Many couples have told me the same thing—wives who are sitting where you are now."

Over and over I had heard it. A husband would say, "I wish you'd talk to my wife about this, and tell her what you've been telling me." And a wife would say, "I'd appreciate it, Judge, if you would let my husband know how I feel."

Paradoxically, they could confide their most intimate feelings and thoughts to a third party, but they could not bring themselves to discuss such matters with the one they loved. With some, they did not wish to talk about their sex problem at the time they were engaged in the marital act, and the rest of the time it was a verboten subject. They had been reared in the belief that sex should never be mentioned. They had been hushed by shocked parents when they had brought the topic up as children. Even those whose intelligence told them better had feelings of guilt, a hangover from the Victorian Era when sex had an evil connotation.

One husband said, "We just didn't have time to talk about it." And a wife told me, "What good would it have done? He won't listen to anything." Another young wife confided, "I never even talked with my mother about it. So how could I with my husband?"

These were only excuses. They were hiding the fact that this was a subject which had been taboo all their lives and which, even after marriage, still was. So strong was the barrier that had been built up during childhood that not even the commission of the sex act itself could tear it down.

"You must talk it out," I told Amy. "You must talk until you know each other and have understanding, and then you'll be solicitous of each other, and being normal people you won't want to do anything that disturbs or injures the other one."

But how can a person so inhibited help himself? A third party may be the key, a psychologist, a marriage counselor, a family service agency, the family doctor or pastor, or perhaps a lifelong confidant. They may prove an effective sounding board. The troubled person may find himself reaching a solution, merely by putting every fact out where he can see it. Or the third person may assist simply by suggesting that the husband and wife should give the subject the same kind of discussion they would give a knotty financial matter. Oddly, many couples have never thought of "talking it out."

Group therapy, one of the newer approaches to handling complex marriage problems, has been tried in some cities. Couples with difficulties meet together with a trained psychologist, psychiatrist, or social worker and discuss their concerns openly and frankly. By doing so, they break down the artificial verbal barriers which so often exist. By mutually exploring their problems, they help each other to understand the causes of their difficulties. They free themselves of the taboos which contribute to a lack of understanding. One of the prime requisites for success of this kind of work is the confidentiality of the group. Another requirement, of course, is that members do not socialize outside group meetings.

With Amy, the sex act was associated closely with a feeling of guilt. She had carried on relations with Rex on dates during high school and eventually become pregnant. Because of that pregnancy, she had been hurried into marriage. Before she could adjust to a new life, she was again pregnant. In time, she blamed all her troubles simply on the sex act itself.

"We'd heard a lot of conversation about premarital relations," she said, "and Rex and I got to talking one night. We decided it was the only way to know whether we were suited for each other. But it didn't work out that way, Judge. We were trapped, even before I became pregnant. I told him I wouldn't let him do it unless I loved him, and he told me he wouldn't be doing it if he didn't love me. So later, when we might have dated others, we found ourselves so tied to each other we just couldn't break off."

The story was one that I had heard often. Aside from the moral issue, many couples become so emotionally involved that they feel a compulsion to marry, even when they realize that their love was only something physical and that they are totally unsuited for each other. One wife in her twenties told me, "What was I to do? I didn't want to marry my husband, but we had been having an affair all through college, and I felt I had sealed the pact. He felt the same way, I know, although he couldn't say so."

Others develop a guilt complex that shadows them throughout their married life. It is a secret they hide from their husbands. Even when they marry the boy of their premarital experiences, like Amy, they still feel it.

I asked Amy, "How often do you think you should engage in the marital act—thinking of it in all fairness to your husband and to yourself?"

She thought about twice a week, and later when I discussed it with Rex and attempted to explain his wife's feelings in the matter, he nodded in assent. So we drew up an agreement which, revised many times in the months that followed, was eventually to read:

> The parties have agreed that ________ a ________ on an average, under normal conditions, should not be considered excessive. They further agree that it should not be necessary for one to urge or insist that the other shall indulge in an act of sexual intercourse; because the other does not have the right to refuse, except for serious reasons. They further agree that it would be quite selfish and unjust for one to manufacture excuses or put difficulties in the way of granting the other's request. Mere inconvenience or disinclination are not sufficient reasons for refusing. The attitude of continual unwillingness or of reluctant and uncooperative acquiescence is a common cause of marital unhappiness. On the contrary, to anticipate the other's wishes—while sparing the other having to request—is proof of a love that is thoughtful, as well as genuine.

We were cognizant that by setting forth the subject of the frequency of the sex act, we laid ourselves open to criticism. Numerous psychologists believe that intercourse is an "expression of love" on the part of a couple and that the couple should so engage only when they want to express this love. The timing, hence, may vary widely. Others hold that the male builds up to the act at intervals that are fairly cyclical.

But frequently we found ourselves dealing with individuals whose marriages were about to dissolve over this factor of frequency. If neither raised the issue after reading the paragraph, we simply struck it out. By having it there, it served the purpose of bringing the subject into the open. If the problem existed, one or the other would mention it. But if we had left it out of the agreement, the old taboos might have prevented either from mentioning the matter and the trouble would have continued to provoke and irritate the one who felt he or she was being taken advantage of by the other. As I have said, the Court used only those sections of the Reconciliation Agreement that applied in each instance.

This matter of timing often entered a case in which the husband charged that his wife was unresponsive without any apparent reason. In one such hearing, the wife admitted as much. She suggested no reason herself, nor did she blame her husband in any way. We referred them to a counseling service, and the reports sent us bared the usual cause. The woman had carried guilt feelings into her marriage from a childhood that had been implanted with the historic conception that sex was evil. She thought it unnatural and sinful that a woman should have any desire for a man.

The frequency factor, of course, was only one phase of Amy's and Rex's problem. She had said that he occasionally forced himself on her, without regard to her wishes.

"Sometimes he'd treat me like I was a prostitute," she said, "and sometimes he'd hurt me. I don't think he meant to—but he wasn't considerate and gentle like he'd been when we were dating each other. After we were married, he seemed to think he could do anything he wanted to with me."

When I talked with Rex alone, he was surprised that she felt this way. "I didn't know I ever treated her like that. I didn't mean to, honest."

"I believe you," I said. He was so upset his lips were trembling. "You didn't know any better. Both of you needed knowledge."

Slowly I talked along, watching him as understanding came into his eyes, and regret, too.

"We know two kinds of love," I said, "the carnal or animal kind, and that which we call the spiritual. The spiritual encompasses the tenderness and respect we have for the other person, and which we show in a hundred little ways. It is, actually, the spiritual sense in which we love the other one. The most rewarding love in marriage develops when these two, the carnal and the spiritual, are fused. The carnal satisfies us physically, and the spiritual satisfies our mind and soul.

"Many men, though, separate the two. They keep them pigeonholed. They may engage in intercourse with a prostitute purely on an animal level and, at the same time, bestow a spiritual love on their girl friend. They may weld the two early in their marriage and then later, when marriage has become commonplace, forget the spiritual and expect their wives to function on a carnal level.

"But women never can separate the two. At least, the majority cannot. The woman must feel that she is being loved, and loved for herself alone, that she is not merely an animal to serve a man. She associates tenderness and affection with the sex act, the saying of sweet nothings, the kisses, the caresses, and all the little thoughtful gestures that show the respect and the love the man holds for her. When these are removed, she may turn against her husband.

"That's what happened with Amy," I continued. "You were so anxious to satisfy your own feelings that you forgot hers. You never gave her time to adjust mentally to your approaches—and to a woman, this is tremendously important.

"You yourself will find far more pleasure and satisfaction in your relations with Amy if you think of them as spiritual, something wonderful and fine—if you think that here God has given me this girl to look after and care for and to love. And you'll be surprised what it will do for Amy—and for you."

We drew up a section which we called, "The Importance of Lovemaking," for such persons as Rex, who had such little understanding of the sex relationship. In part, it read:

> The importance of "lovemaking" in the first stages of intercourse must not be ignored. Unfortunately, this occurs quite often between husband and wife after a few years of marriage. . . .
>
> Lovemaking as a prelude to sexual intercourse takes into account the difference in the nature of love in man and woman. In man, the physical or passion side is generally quickly and strongly aroused by the slightest stimulation and desire and by appropriate actions he quickly reaches the climax of physical satisfaction. In woman, it is the emotional and mental side that is most in evidence; for her, love is meaningless unless it be manifested in a profusion of loving attentions. Consequently, her passion side is slow to make its appearance, generally speaking; nor will it become strongly enough aroused except after an abundance of appropriate lovemaking. . . . Unless she has been properly prepared for it, the few minutes of union will not be sufficient to bring her to the necessary climax and consequent release of nervous tension.

A few phrases should be underlined, among them: "*The importance of lovemaking . . . should not be ignored. . . .*

This occurs quite often between husband and wife after a few years of marriage."

For many, the sex relationship in time becomes commonplace. This is true of any repetitious act unless we guard against it. A wife in her mid-thirties once told me, "My husband thinks so little of love that sometimes he'll discuss a business deal while we're having relations." Husbands, too, complained about wives who would bring up troubles the children had gotten into that day. Unknowingly, they were driving a wedge between themselves and their mates. They were destroying all semblance of love which must be thought about and nurtured as a very precious part of our lives.

We continued to add paragraphs to this section on marital relations as couples came with common problems. One paragraph grew out of the husband's tendency to insist upon sexual intercourse as a part of "making up" after a quarrel.

This was the paragraph that resulted:

> Many husbands feel that this is the one big way to make up. This ignores the importance of the time needed for the wife to forget and forgive and to get herself mentally in hand so that she feels kindly and lovingly disposed toward her husband. The suggestion of intercourse, until this mental attitude has been adjusted, is generally very repulsive to her.

Another situation was the one in which the wife or husband for organic reasons either was unable to have intercourse or suffered discomfort or pain during it. This was not a common situation, but it did enter into a number of cases. The parties promised jointly, in these instances, to discuss the matter with their physician and to make no physical demands on each other until the trouble had been remedied.

In the meantime they agreed to occupy separate bedrooms.

During those first months, we waited as anxiously as any politician for the closing of the polls to learn what results, if any, we were getting. Would this section on love-making and intercourse help couples whose basic problem was sex relationship?

By the end of six months, we knew. A substantial percentage had been aided. Notable was one couple with five children who dismissed a divorce action four months after signing the Reconciliation Agreement. The husband told us, "It started my wife and me thinking, and that was all we needed." His thought was echoed by many others.

Yet we failed more often than we succeeded. By the time some of the couples reached us, their problem had assumed such proportions in their minds that nothing could have shaken their determination to divorce. Other couples sincerely tried and failed to adjust to each other. And of course, some were so unsuited by temperament, breeding, sensitivity, and other factors, that no amount of understanding or endeavor could help their sexual relations to any extent. Usually in these instances, the wife was undersexed physically, or burdened with taboos, and her husband was strongly sexed. Even with these, psychotherapy or counseling sometimes remedied the situation. Others forgot divorce for the sake of their children.

Out of conferences with hundreds of wives and husbands, one fact repeated itself: Most couples in domestic difficulty need education in sex relations—knowledge and understanding. But how are they to get it? Parents are tense around their children when they discuss sex, and the children feel it and become like that themselves. It's a chain reaction, from generation to generation. Even with parents who struggle to shrug off taboos, somehow they will impart the idea that something is "wrong" about sex. Our culture has developed to the point where we blatantly advertise sex from every billboard and movie screen, and yet we seldom present it in an honest, forthright manner. We appear shockingly frank but are not. We teach the facts of anatomy and biology but ignore those of feeling and attitudes.

If parents would only relax, if they would discuss the subject easily and factually and frankly, the way they do other matters of everyday living—this would help. It would help, too, if couples would stop to consider that since God created them and this method of procreation, the use of the sexual act in marriage is altogether wholesome. Exercised by married lovers with mutual considerateness, it becomes a source of comfort, happiness, and contentment.

This was what we tried to impart to Amy and Rex. They listened and seemed to understand. Again, though, how much did they feel, or want to feel, that afternoon as they left my chambers? I said a silent prayer for them, a hope that they would find themselves. Because they were our first couple to sign these sections of the Reconciliation Agreement, and were so likable, we had taken them into our hearts. And since they had two children, there were many reasons why this was a marriage we wanted to save.

Yet the obstacles they were up against seemed overwhelming. They hadn't even had what most couples have—a good start when they were married.

In the months that followed, we received some reports from the counselors. Set forth in the cold phraseology of all such reports, they offered little hope. The most that could be said was that Amy and Rex were still living together. Rex had assumed more responsibilities around the home. He was handling the finances and doing a fair job. Sometimes he offered to take care of the children. But their sexual life was still a matter of frequent dispute, and she still couldn't cast aside completely her ambivalent feelings toward the marriage.

Then one morning early, the clerk informed me that Amy Bulland was outside.

"By herself?" I asked, and the clerk nodded. Immediately, I thought that she had come to seek a dismissal of her petition for a reconciliation.

She had that piquant, sober little expression as she walked toward me. "I was downtown, Judge, and wanted to come in. I shouldn't be taking up your time, but you tried so hard to help Rex and me."

She tossed back her dark hair. "You have so many cases, but Rex and I got to talking last night, and we thought you'd like to know that everything's fine with us now. Oh, we still make a lot of mistakes, but now we try to talk them out, and it makes a big difference."

She laughed. "We're not exactly the ideal couple."

If she could laugh about it, then they were going to be all right.

She hurried on, "Do you know what did it mostly, Judge? It was what you told us about the *will to love*. It wasn't too hard, once we got to thinking about it, because we had been in love in high school. Terribly so."

The will to love. By keeping ever present in your mind the good things about that person, by refusing to listen to those who are forever criticizing and tearing down, you can capture and build up a warmth of feeling toward him. In time you will want to do things for him, to give of yourself to him—and then you'll be on your way to the kind of love that sustains marriage.

chapter seven

Squaring a Triangle

Husband *agrees not to visit, consort with, contact or correspond with* third party.

—RECONCILIATION AGREEMENT

In all outward manifestations but one, the lady on the witness stand was typical of the majority—belligerent, hurt, vindictive, highly emotional, the doeskin of her gloves stretched smooth by clenched hands. The veteran judge in the divorce court quickly noted the distinguishing exception. This woman was plainly fighting back the tears. He interrupted to ask the attorneys if this were not a case which should be referred to the Conciliation Court.

Before the lawyers could speak, the woman blurted out, "How could I take him back after what he and that woman have done? No, he can go his way and the children and I will go ours. We are better off without him."

Her attorney arose quickly. "Your Honor, this man has been living in adultery, and I fear that all the regard my client once held for him is now dead."

"We will not resist the making of any reasonable offer," the husband's lawyer countered. "However, in the papers served upon us, the wife seeks by way of child support and temporary alimony a sum which exceeds the take-home pay of my client."

There was a moment of charged silence during which I

imagine the judge was weighing the tears in the woman's voice and the quick look of hope which flicked across the man's face at the mention of reconciliation, rather than their expressed feelings. At his suggestion the attorneys were permitted to confer, and after the details of a temporary order had been agreed to, both parties were instructed to proceed to the clerk's office of the Conciliation Court.

I cite the case of this couple, whom I shall call Martha and Harry Clark, and the young woman involved, whose name was *not* June, because it illustrates that no matter how great the odds, it is sometimes possible to square a triangle. Like all couples similarly enmeshed, they approached the court with the conviction that infidelity makes reconciliation hopeless, a state of mind which practically dooms the outcome of a case at its inception. Adultery is admittedly a grievance very hard to forgive and therefore the most difficult to reconcile. It is legal grounds for divorce in every state.

And then there is the problem of the third person. As in many cases of this sort, June was not a cheap, tawdry character. Neither were Martha and Harry. All three were basically decent, very real, lovable people. While Harry was the obvious aggressor, none was completely without blame.

When Martha and Harry reported at the clerk's office, each was given an affidavit to fill in, setting forth the basic information pertaining to the family and the causes of the difficulty. Martha marked "infidelity" and "immaturity" on the part of her husband, and "temper" on her part. She also checked intimate relations as one of their difficulties. Harry cited "nagging" on the part of his wife, and on his side "infidelity" and "in recent months, heavy drinking."

When each finished, the clerk set a date when they would

appear before me. Then came the pronouncement which must have given them both pause. "Since Mrs. Clark has named a third person," the clerk continued, "the Court may find it desirable to have this person appear at the hearing so that the judge may talk to her as well."

When he could find his voice, Harry muttered, "I don't think it's necessary to drag the young lady into court."

Martha looked at him defiantly. "It's all right with me—but I certainly don't want to have anything to do with her."

On the appointed day, each of them—including June—arrived by separate means and entered the clerk's office. I can well imagine that with the two women seeing each other for the first time, from opposite corners of the reception room, and the husband not knowing which way to look, the ordeal must have been all that each in the awesome silence of his thoughts had envisaged.

As was customary, the clerk brought Harry and Martha in together to meet me. There remained plenty of evidence that Martha had once been a very beautiful girl—large, expressive eyes and auburn hair—but her clothes had lost the struggle with her figure and she had made no attempt to salvage her really good features with make-up. Harry, on the other hand, was tall and slender and impeccably groomed. From the clerk's report, I knew both were in their mid-thirties and college graduates. Harry had a thriving furniture business.

They avoided each other as though the slightest contact, physical or visual, would touch off a fatal explosion. I attempted to lessen the tension by explaining the concern of the courts over the breakup of the marriage, particularly in view of their three children, two boys of school age and a girl slightly younger. At the mention of the children, Harry controlled his emotion with difficulty.

"Which one of you wishes to speak first?" I asked.

Martha, still vindictive, spoke up. "Let him. It was all his fault."

"Very well," I agreed, and Martha returned to the reception room, where she was given a copy of a typical Reconciliation Agreement. In asking one party to read the document while the other was in conference, it was our hope that he or she would realize that his own problems were not insurmountable, nor was his case unique. In the sobering atmosphere of a court and faced with a formal document, most people take an honest look at themselves.

Harry talked with difficulty at first, groping for words, stumbling over his own embarrassment and guilt. It is not easy for a man to throw open the closets of his mind, to air impartially all the hopes, the triumphs, the guilt, the failures, the generosities, the pettiness—all the mixed emotions which heretofore had never demanded explanation nor expression.

This marriage had been happy for twelve years, he told me, but little by little the two began to take each other for granted.

To compensate for the increasing coolness, Martha found herself showering more and more love on the children and paying less attention to him. She also ceased thinking about her own appearance, and her once attractive figure began to suffer.

It was about this time that Harry met June. He had seen her many times behind the polished mahogany counter at the bank, where she was a junior officer. She was quick, direct, capable, and attractive, and yet possessed of an impersonal reserve which served her and the bank well.

In her earlier years, she had devoted herself to the care of an invalid father. With his passing, she had calmly taken inventory and, not given to self-deception, decided romance had passed her by. She lost no hours in sympathizing with herself and accepted the comforts of business success to fill the well of loneliness within her.

It was at a business party in the holiday season that Harry became acquainted with her. Inhibitions lowered as infectious good cheer mounted. By several lunches later and rides to and from the bank, their mutual hunger for attention ripened into a warm relationship. The soft music and solitude of her apartment and her warm acceptance of his attentions were in marked contrast to the turmoil at home, with the youngsters bickering over TV programs, and the ever-sharpening edge of his wife's voice when she spoke to him. To the pricking of his conscience, he told himself he was doing the girl no harm. She was obviously in need of affection and after all, she did know he was married and that nothing serious could ever come of the affair. He also consoled himself that his wife knew nothing of this and consequently neither she nor the children could be harmed.

As the weeks rolled by, June fell in love with him, hopelessly and completely. Her whole life hung on the few stolen hours a week that they could spend together.

Meantime, Harry, anesthetized by the comforts of the moment, kept pushing back into his subconscious the ever-growing realization of what he meant to this girl, the great injustice to his wife and children.

And then the inevitable happened. Martha found out. At first it came as a deadly traumatic shock; then, with her quick temper, hot, harsh words, dishes, everything flew. It was the end. For her, no explanations on his part were even conceivable, and Harry, after a few feeble attempts, quietly packed a suitcase of bare necessities and took a room at a hotel.

As the months rolled by, the separation left its mark even on the children. Every evening at seven, he would phone to say hello to each in turn. The little girl missed him so much that the end of every phone call found her fighting back the tears. And the boys were having trouble at school. Danny, the younger and most like his mother, came home one day crying, with a broken hand. The fight had started when another boy asked him whether his father had left them for good.

And that was Harry's story. "I still love my wife, Judge," he said. "In spite of everything I've done to the contrary, I do love her. And living away from the children is killing me. But it's too late, Judge. I made a mistake, and nothing can be done about it."

"If your wife would reconcile," I asked, "would you agree to stay away from the young lady under penalty of going to jail?"

He replied unhesitatingly. "I would. I would promise anything within my power, but she'll never forgive me. It's hopeless."

"Let me see what I can do." I handed him a copy of the Reconciliation Agreement to read in the outer office, where, in the silent but charged presence of June, he would have ample time to pore over the document.

As Martha rose at my nod, she and Harry brushed by each other, their eyes averted. In my chambers, sitting on the edge of her chair, she faced me squarely. She was crying. Laying her copy of the agreement on the desk, she said, "So many things apply so directly to our marriage. In reading it over I had the feeling we had already talked to you and you had written it about us. I only wish we had read it together a year or so ago when we began drifting apart. Now, of course, that woman has her hold on him."

She paused, "And anyway we have hurt each other beyond repair."

I gripped the armrests of my chair, then hoisted my lanky six-foot-two for a short tour around the desk. Long years in the law, during which I had been exposed to all kinds of emotion, had failed to immunize me to the effects of tears. The deep hurt and the other woman—these to her were the insurmountable obstacles. I resolved first to salve the wound. Meanwhile I would try to find out a way to explain the adultery—not to justify or excuse but somehow to have her understand. . . .

"I believe that's where you're wrong," I said quietly. "Your husband sat here for three-quarters of an hour, and mostly he talked about what a wonderfully fine and kind person you are, and what a happy life you all had together until, as you say, for some reason you started to drift apart. I believe I can help you put your finger on the reasons why you struck a lull in your marriage, but first let's talk about the other woman.

"To begin with, what happened between your husband and this girl was wrong, very wrong. To you what happened is inexplainable. Try as you might, you cannot imagine yourself entering into such a relationship with some other man. This is largely because with you an intimate union is only conceivable as part of a deep and abiding love that you would feel for that person. And that is as it should be.

"With some men, and to a lesser degree with some women, love and intimacy are not necessarily so interrelated. The relationship with this woman does not mean that your husband stopped loving you. I'm not saying this to mitigate his wrong, but to point out that it is entirely possible for a person to have a sudden infatuation for someone else and even become intimate with her without losing his real love for his marital partner.

"No one goes through life without making mistakes," I continued. "Each is human, and it is human to err. The important thing is that we recognize the mistake, are truly sorry and seek to right the wrong done, and have a firm purpose of amendment. These things your husband has done. It is within your power to forgive him, and after all, how can any of us ask God to forgive our transgressions if we do not forgive those who transgress against us?"

I waited while she thought this over.

"But how could I ever be sure it wouldn't happen again?" she asked finally.

"Your husband has agreed to promise in writing that he will never consort with the lady again under penalty of going to jail. This is how sincere he feels about it. For a man of his standing, the penalty of jail assures you that his promise is not one that has been lightly made."

I then explained that everyone requires a certain amount of attention and love, and some more than others. Chance had thrown her husband and the girl together at a time when the outward manifestations of affection between herself and her husband had hit their lowest level. Gradually, she was brought to realize that this low point was a joint responsibility which she shared with her husband.

"Love is a gift of one's self to another," I explained. "In essence it must be reciprocal. When we cease making sacrifices for one another, when each takes the other for granted, then love lies dormant or may even die, and the situation is ripe for disaster."

By now Martha was ready to admit some of her own shortcomings. She acknowledged how hard the children were taking the separation from their father, and for the first time expressed the wish that they could forget what had happened and start again.

"Let me ask your husband to step in for a moment," I said, and she nodded. As Harry entered, I excused myself. As I left I heard Harry's voice, whispering over and over again, "Thank God, thank God."

June didn't exactly resemble the mental picture I had formed of her from Harry's build-up. She was plainer, not so pretty, and I belatedly realized, older. She was every day as old as Martha. Nevertheless, she was slender and so well groomed that she appeared years younger at first glance. She walked as though propelled by a force she fought but was powerless to resist. I admired her discipline. Although obviously shaken, she spoke calmly, quietly, with words well chosen to indicate her resentment at being subpoenaed. I knew that what she wanted was an argument, so she could bolster her defenses. She was obviously only trying to convince herself. So I was sympathetic—genuinely so—and told her how highly Harry had spoken of her, that he was deeply sorry for having placed her in this position.

Tears came then, and she became the warm, generous, understanding person Harry had been attracted to.

"It's every bit as much my own fault as his," she said. "I was willfully blind, I guess, and it was all wrong. But there's one thing you must believe. Not that it matters except to my pride. I do love him." She added in a whisper as though to herself—or to him, "I always will."

After a moment, she straightened and said, "Now what do we do?"

I explained Harry's agreement not to see her any more. "Would you be willing to help him keep that promise?" I asked.

There were tears in her eyes but with the slow and deliberate way of a person condemned, she said, "Yes," adding, "That's the only way it can be—isn't it?"

I nodded, tried to clear my throat for suitable words, but they wouldn't come.

In a few moments more Harry and June had signed a simple agreement to the effect they would not consort with each other again. A court order was issued requiring each to comply with the agreement under penalty of being held in contempt. With this done, June walked out of the room, leaving behind her the first real love she had ever known—and probably the only one. . . .

My feeling of warmth and satisfaction about the agreement Harry and Martha worked out did not blind me to the problems before them. They did not, from that day forth, live happily together forever afterward, and I would have failed them had I not attempted to prepare them for difficult times ahead. "This," I told them, after they had signed, "is not a release from suffering any more than the physical amputation of an intolerable member means a sudden stoppage of pain. The healing process may be far more painful than the actual operation."

"You are now under the anesthetizing effect of new hopes, firm resolutions—and that's good. The real test will come in the weeks and months that follow, when in the cold clear daylight you put the Agreement into operation."

The Clarks worked it out as I felt they would—not in a week, not in a month, not without scars, not without some additional counseling. At first they made the common mistake of believing that all that was required of them was to forgive and forget. They were rational, intelligent people, they reasoned, still in love with each other, so they would just rip out this page of their past and forget it. But any burden as heavy as infidelity cannot be simply forgotten. The Clarks had to be shown that it was healthy and good to discuss their difficulties with a counselor. Only after each had learned to live with the ugly facts and face them squarely, did the mention of them cease to threaten the reconciliation.

It is not a simple process, this learning, particularly in cases involving infidelity. To begin with, each must be brought to realize the need for an understanding of forces in another person's behavior not present in his own. For instance, Martha had to be convinced that infidelity on the part of a man can take place entirely independent of his love for his wife and children.

She had to understand, too, that the ideal to strive for in marriage is that which combines sex, or lust, and love. Dr. Shostrom has phrased it in this manner: "Another way of viewing adultery, other than legally, is as the experience of lust without warmth and tenderness, even with a marriage partner. Sexual intimacy within marriage which does not combine with it respect and love is a form of adultery in this sense. Such a pattern often is a root cause for the husband to seek affection elsewhere, where warmth and tenderness are also present with sexual expression. Wives such as Martha often come to see that such a situation did exist in their own relationship to their husbands. When this is so, they realize that the unfaithfulness outside of marriage resulted, at least in part, from lack of a union of desire and love within their own marriage. At any rate, this manner of viewing the problem makes it clear that adultery in the legal sense is more often a symptom of a sick marriage rather than a problem in itself."

I am sure Martha knew down deep that Harry loved her and the children, but the thoughts of physical intimacies between her husband and June were so revolting to her that she found it impossible to consider the situation rationally. She had suffered a great emotional jolt, and as was normal and human, indulged in self-pity.

Lest I seem to place undue responsibility on Martha's shoulders, let me add that it is always the victim who must do the bulk of the adjusting. The aggressor is far ahead; the facts are not new to him. He or she has already learned his lesson, and in most cases is willing and eager to renew the marriage. In his repentant thoughts, he has already resumed his niche in the family and girded himself for certain concessions. Nevertheless, Harry also had plenty to learn. There were "those forces" in Martha's behavior not present in his own, such as her own feeling of neglect as they grew apart, and her resultant humiliation.

Together they learned the need for mutual trust and freedom, for excitement and times of quiet, for the contrast and variety necessary to forestall the recurrence of boredom in their marriage. They needed no further warning that when the admiration and attention paid either one by the other becomes tempered by time and indifference, then the neglected one may turn elsewhere for that admiration and attention his normal ego demands.

Eventually, as Martha grasped her own need for emotional stability and was able clearly to assess the situation, the reconciliation process found a firm footing and their family life began again where it had been interrupted.

When we feel it may help, we do not hesitate to hail the third party into Conciliation Court. This procedure serves one of two objectives. Most frequently it proves to the betrayed partner that his or her rival is not a lecherous, cheap, promiscuous home-breaker but an ordinary human being with normal feelings and emotions. The shadowy "other person" thus comes out into the open to become a measuring stick for his or her shortcomings or assets.

Less often, we come across a third member who is up to no good. In this case, nothing can put out the fire faster than to bring the illicit affair to light. Somehow cocktail bar romances suddenly lose their allure. In one case we subpoenaed a mistress at her place of employment. She lost face with the office force when the story leaked out, and disillusionment quickly set in when she faced the wronged wife in court. The wife's appearance belied the false, sympathy-seeking impression the "misunderstood" husband had given his girl friend.

While the law gives us jurisdiction over home-wreckers, as parties whose conduct affects the marriage, we can't compel them to sign the noninterference clauses of the Reconciliation Agreement. But if they consent to do so of their own accord, they automatically become liable for contempt of court if they break their promises.

In a few instances, I have sent offenders to jail. I once caught up with a prosperous husband and his paramour, both of whom had signed the court contract. I can still remember the shock on their faces when I pronounced a sentence of five days. They certainly weren't dressed for jail.

The days were not without occasional humor, even though the situations were tragic. One morning a case came before me in which the wife charged her husband with consorting with another woman. He was a car washer, a big, good-looking fellow in his late twenties and as persuasive as an automobile salesman.

"Judge, your honor," he said, "I give you my word I'll never go back near that gal no more. If my wife will come back home with me and the kids where she belongs, I promise I'll stay home and be a good husband."

His voice dripped with sincerity. Even his wife was showing signs of believing him. So I instructed the clerk to prepare an agreement for them to sign. As the husband thumbed through the various pages, he would vent his enthusiasm with words of praise and approval. Finally, he reached page twelve, the last, and suddenly fell silent.

"Judge, what's . . . what's this here say about jail?" he stuttered.

I explained that if he willfully failed to comply with his promises, he could be brought into court to face a contempt charge.

There was a long pause.

"Well, your honor, I fully intend to keep my promises, just like I said. But," he continued, shaking his head, "you know, Judge, they ain't nobody knows me as well as I know myself. And you know, Judge, I'm an awful weak person. . . ."

The failure to square a triangle may be attributed to many factors, most of which usually boil down to a lack of trust. Like Martha Clark, the wife inevitably and quite understandably asks, "How can I ever trust him again?" And experience would seem to prove it even more difficult for a man to forgive and again trust his wife. Right or wrong, culture places a more severe judgment on the wife who betrays her husband. The mother instinct still clings to a man's concept of a woman, and he holds her largely responsible for the nest.

Strangely enough, the errant husband is apt to see no parallel in his case. As my friend Dr. Shostrom puts it, there is an element of the conqueror in a man. Before he marries, he is the male wooing his mate. With marriage, he has won his objective and feels no longer the necessity to court her. But let a wife break faith, and he finds it next to impossible to forgive her.

I can think of no better example than the case of Lynn and Sid Pendleton. It was a second marriage for both. Sid, then divorced, met Lynn at a party a former college friend gave. There were other guests, but Sid's eyes were taken with his friend's wife, Lynn. In carrying on a mild flirtation, he intended nothing more than a little fun, but Lynn found him a relief from domestic boredom and friction. Eventually, the harmless affair turned into an illicit romance. Sid's friend learned the truth, confronted his wife with it, and a quiet divorce followed.

Sid and Lynn couldn't wait until the California one-year interlocutory period had passed, so they emulated others who wink at the law and crossed the border into Mexico to go through a so-called "proxy wedding." Since both were residents of California and unable to comply with the Mexican law, the "marriage" had no validity whatever. In fact, at least 95 per cent of all marriages of nonresidents performed in Tijuana and other Mexican border cities prove to be illegal. Also, this particular "marriage" was illegal for an additional reason: Lynn was not as yet lawfully divorced.

Six months later, Lynn had a child. After the youngster reached the walking stage, Sid and Lynn resumed the active social life which they so thoroughly enjoyed. Each, however, was very jealous of the other, and any suspicious circumstance always led to a quizzing bee until the early hours of the morning. Consciously or unconsciously, the fact that they had cheated on Lynn's former husband made it difficult for them to trust each other. They were quick with accusations and with indignant denials. Ultimately they parted, and some time later came into the Conciliation Court through a petition filed by Lynn.

I found Sid rough-spoken. "If she'd do it with me when she was married to my best friend, she'd do it with anyone. Not that I'm so holy. I've done plenty of running around. But it's different with a woman."

"How's it different?" I asked. They were both from the same ugly woof. It was one of the few cases where I felt no sympathy.

He shrugged. "Nobody wants his wife to be an easy pickup, does he? She's got only one thing on her mind. I guess I ought to know."

In a marriage devoid of any spirituality, there was nothing that could be done. Sid agreed to support the child, and the "marriage" received a decent burial.

That evening I sat slumped in the groaning old swivel, too beaten down and weary to move my bones. The Sid and Lynn Pendletons who came before me, defiant, mocking, caring not, seemed too much at times.

I was discouraged on another score. The Court's critics were busy. They intimated that the Court was an unjustifiable expense. If couples wanted to divorce, why not let them? That was their business, and good riddance to the lot. The critics talked about statistics, as though human happiness could be measured by figures.

As so often happened when I was downcast, my eyes went to a wood carving on my desk from Oberammergau, a carving of the Madonna. Just the presence of all that was good and pure lifted my heart. My thoughts drifted to Germany.

The tanks were still burning in the streets, the dead were

unburied, and the city was in utter ruin when I was ordered to establish the first military government court in Cologne. I prowled the streets, looking for a building sufficiently intact, and at last found one. With flashlight in one hand and a 0.45 automatic in the other, I traced a wisp of smoke down darkened stairs into the basement. Kicking open a door, I came upon a motley group surrounding a pot in which they were cooking what smelled like old shoes.

My appearance was as startling to them as theirs to me. In good English a gray-haired man identified himself as the headwaiter of the Dom hotel, now bombed out of existence. The others present, he said, had all been employed by the Dom.

The next morning I swore them all in as civilian employees of the United States. The hotel's chief clerk became the clerk of my court. A former professor of languages, an anti-Nazi, became the court interpreter, and later gave me the Madonna carving. The headwaiter proved a most excellent bailiff. Within twenty-four hours we were holding court.

Everything ran smoothly for a few days. Then one morning as I approached through a milling crowd, a haughty little man stopped me and announced that the building had been set aside as the new city hall of Cologne. "This staircase," he said, indicating the grand staircase, "will be used only by persons having business with Der Burgermeister. All others will use the back stairs."

In the sharpest voice I could command, I told the bailiff to inform the gentleman that the court would continue using the grand staircase, and that I would be pleased to allocate to Der Burgermeister any portions of the building that we were not occupying.

Having said as much, I turned on my heel, and my staff

fell into single line behind me in order of rank to follow me up the grand staircase. Der Burgermeister and I never met during the weeks that followed, and I am certain the haughty gentleman who stopped me did not represent his sentiments. I later learned Der Burgermeister's name—Konrad Adenauer . . .

Now, in thinking back, I suddenly squared my shoulders and shook off the despair. I would continue using the grand staircase.

chapter eight

Green Eyes

Each of us will do the other the honor of reposing implicit trust in him, and will so behave as to deserve that loyal trust by never doing anything to violate it.

—RECONCILIATION AGREEMENT

Big Matt told me the story graphically—told it with all the drama and emotion of a natural-born storyteller. He spared no one, least of all himself.

Molly told me the story—with heart and a strange mixture of confusion and gentle understanding.

Officer Donahue filled in the chinks.

This, then, is the way it happened.

Big Matt looked at the clock for the fiftieth time. Ten minutes after 2 A.M. He lit another cigarette but smashed it on the ash tray before drawing a puff. His mouth felt like an old burnt rag. He tilted the half-emptied bottle of beer and swished it around before swallowing. It gave only momentary relief. If anything, the aftertaste was worse.

He had been waiting now for four hours, alternately pacing the floor and sitting in the leather chair by the fireplace. "Could something have happened to her?" he kept asking himself. He should have put his foot down about her taking that job in the first place. And why in the world had he consented to her attending the office party? Molly had said he was welcome to go along. But he hadn't gone for that. He didn't enjoy meeting other people. He didn't like to dance—and watching Molly dancing with others did things to his blood pressure.

It was 2:30. He would give her another five minutes. If she were not back by then... "By all that's holy, I'll bust in there and drag her out by the hair!" The several quarts of beer were beginning to take a firm hold.

Suddenly he stopped fuming. A carload of noisy people had pulled up in front. He watched as Molly got out and started up the walk, followed by a man moving unsteadily. She swung the man around by the arm and shoved him toward the car. He refused to get in without "one l'il goo-nite kiss." Molly kissed his cheek and pushed him in.

Big Matt just stood there while Molly fumbled with her house key at the door. She stopped short as she saw him. His breathing was fast, his large hands were opening and closing. It was his eyes, bloodshot, maniacal, that terrified her.

"Matt," she said quickly, "don't go making anything of what you just saw. That man works at the plant. I can't even tell you his name."

Matt took two steps toward her. Molly backed up. "Please, Matt, don't look at me like that. Matt, you'll only hurt me and then you'll be sorry later."

Matt grabbed her. With a wrench, he tore her evening dress from her, slip and all. She squirmed out of his grasp, ran into the bedroom, slammed the door, and put her shoulder to it.

Matt boomed out, "Open the door, Molly, or by heaven, I'll break it in!"

Not waiting for an answer, he crashed into it with his

shoulder and it burst open, carrying part of the door jamb with it. The blow knocked Molly to the floor stunned. He pulled his belt out of his trousers, doubled it up, and started beating her. Molly bit her lip to keep from screaming, but the noise of the crashing door had already awakened their boy, Pat. Shocked suddenly out of a sound sleep, he stood in the doorway a moment, watching in disbelief. Then screaming, he grabbed for his father's arm and the swinging belt.

"Your mother is an evil woman and I'll give her what she deserves!" Matt swung the boy off the floor. "Get back and keep out of this!" he warned. But the boy hung onto his arm and sank his teeth deep into the straining muscles. Matt let out a yell and made a wild swing to free his arm, throwing the boy from him. The boy's head hit the dresser and he crumpled up in a heap.

"Pat!" Molly cried hysterically and crawled to him. The sight of the child stopped Big Matt, and he dropped to his knees beside his wife and son. Neither heard the siren of the patrol car, summoned by calls from neighbors, and it was thus that Officer Mike Donahue found them. His eye took in the angry red stripes crisscrossing the woman's bare back as she crouched over the boy.

"Pat, Pat. It's Mother, Pat," she kept whispering.

The boy lay very still.

Donahue called out to his partner, rookie officer Muzarka, "Ed, put a radio call through for an ambulance."

Big Matt shoved Donahue roughly aside. Bending over the boy, he started to lift him in his arms.

Donahue and Molly both cried out in protest. Donahue gripped Matt's shoulder and pulled him backward. Thrown off balance, the big man sprawled on his back.

Suddenly Big Matt had something nearly his size that

he could vent his unspent fury on. "Stop me from picking up my own kid, will you? Get out of my way." He bowed his shaggy head and rushed at the officer. It had been a long, hard night, one emergency after another, and Mike Donahue was in no mood to be wrestling drunks. He side-stepped the charging man, slipped his "sap" out of its slit in his trouser leg pocket, and brought it down in a sharp glancing motion on Matt's skull. Matt crash landed into the night stand.

Outside the house the neighborhood was coming alive. By now, lights had gone on half-way up the block. From a distance came the wail of a siren, gradually growing louder, and reaching a crescendo as the ambulance screeched around the corner.

Inside the bedroom, the attendant glanced from the man's form to the child's. Donahue motioned toward the boy. Seconds later, oblivious to all but the boy's silent form on the stretcher, Molly trotted behind its bearers, her bathrobe clutched around her. . . .

The next day, the turnkey rustled Big Matt out of Tank 3, reserved for drunks. Sergeant Malone wanted to see him.

"You remember Officer Donahue," Malone said, indicating a man in uniform.

Big Matt instinctively felt the knot on the back of his head. "What about my boy?"

"The doc thinks he'll be all right," Malone told him. "But a half-inch lower on the temple, and he wouldn't have made it."

Sergeant Malone consulted the make sheet. The record showed no arrests for the past ten years. He continued, "We saw your wife today. She's a fine woman, McGuire, apparently a lot better than you deserve. She refuses to sign a complaint for the beating you gave her. So we're turning you loose—unless Officer Donahue wants to hang a resisting-arrest charge on you."

Donahue bore the big man no malice. A drunk was a drunk to him.

"He was drinking, Sergeant. He didn't intend to do me any harm. . . ."

A few weeks later, Molly and Big Matt came into the Conciliation Court. In the meantime, Molly had returned to her job at the office because she felt certain that the quicker she faced people, the sooner they would quit talking about her and Matt. It had taken courage to face people, both at the office and in the neighborhood. But pride with Molly was a big thing.

Matt, too, had reported back to his job as driver of a cement truck. He couldn't stand another layoff after the big one during the recent strike. In fact, it had been because of the layoff that Molly had gone to work. The "big, easy-payment" loan sold them by the "friendly" loan office to replace their monthly payments on car, furniture, and home had to be met or they would lose all they had acquired.

With Big Matt overpowering a chair in the reception room, Molly and I aimed for the heart of the matter. After the first few nervous, self-conscious false starts, she finally began at the beginning.

That first night when Matt returned home, she told me, she was in bed, lying face down, the only position she could bear. He had wanted to do something to show her how sorry he was, and so he pulled back the sheet and applied soothing ointment with a gentleness unbelievable in such large, rough hands.

"Don't let's try to talk tonight," she said. "The problems we face we won't be able to settle just with words. They're bigger'n us. I don't know the answers. I only know now we can't live as we have been. And I'm not putting the blame all on you."

After a moment, she added, "I'm deathly afraid, Matt, really scared. Not just for me . . . not just for me."

She was thoughtful a moment. "Judge, I've loved and protected him as long as I can remember. And if I was the only one to be considered, I'd go on like I've been doing and take my chances. But we've got Pat to think about. The boy worships his father.

"Before Pat came along I'd just about decided I couldn't stand it any more. He had me so hemmed in and scared that I was terribly self-conscious. I'm a very social person. I love people. I like to do things for them. I like to visit, to listen to music, to have company, to dance and have fun. Matt wants none of these things. He wants to possess me, to dominate me body and soul. I'm his personal property and others may neither look nor touch."

Again there was a silence. Sometimes a counselor can help most by being just a sounding board. I studied her. She wasn't exactly pretty, feature by feature, but she had social charm written all over her. Friendly, vivacious, capable, with merry blue eyes and little weblike lines running out of their corners. They twinkled when she laughed.

"Matt seemed happiest when he had me off balance and ungainly, carrying Pat. The fact I was pregnant and totally dependent on him made him feel secure in some way. After the baby's birth, the boy furnished some diversion and escape. But when he started to kindergarten and I was left home alone, I slipped back into the old captive feeling."

She glanced to see if I understood, and I nodded. "Matt loves the boy, but when he gets angry he punishes him in front of his friends. The boy doesn't mind the punishment, but what breaks his heart is to have the 'fellas' see his father acting that way. He's so proud of him.

"Forgive me for rambling around, but up until now I've fought this battle alone. It's gotten too big for me. I can't lick it and I can't live with it."

"This isn't the first time he's struck you?"

"No . . . he's . . . he's strange. When I've been sick, he's picked me up and cared for me like I was a baby. But when jealousy strikes him, he gets in a blind rage and with his enormous strength I'm the one that gets hurt."

Her eyes took on a faraway look. "One time in a restaurant, a sort of night club, a man came up to our table and said, 'Say, haven't we met before?' You know, the old gag to get acquainted. That's about all he got out. Matt had him by the throat in nothing flat. Three waiters had all they could do to stop Matt from choking him to death. Matt had gotten the notion I must have encouraged the man to make the approach, and he grabbed me by the arm and pulled me out of doors after him. When he got me to the parking lot, he upended me like one would a child, sat himself on the car bumper, and spanked me. I couldn't sit down for a week."

In some instances, Molly herself had fired Big Matt's jealousy. She had a natural flair for having a good time. Unconsciously, she had egged him on with her thoughtless and innocent flippancies with men friends.

Too, the fact that she worked added fuel. She was out in the business world, and to Big Matt, every woman in an office was a prey for some man. And here he constantly employed the device which psychologists call projection. That is, unconsciously he kept imagining how he would behave toward an attractive woman such as Molly if he were shut up in an office with her. Then he would project thoughts into Molly's mind, although in reality they were his thoughts solely.

Molly was given to understand that God had placed this feeling of jealousy in animal and man alike, that jealousy reactions are normal and good to protect the family unit, that they are living proof to a woman that a man loves her. In addition, I explained to Molly that Matt had had a strong feeling of insecurity since childhood, and in all probability, his desire to dominate her and their son had grown out of a compulsion to satisfy that basic hunger to assert himself as a man. Gradually, Molly came to understand how these motivations nurtured a jealousy complex to such an extent that his jealousy became an obsession with him, a kind of psychological sickness, making him hypersensitive to any appearance of interest in people other than himself. She would have to be on guard and at the same time strive to do little things that would give him the reassurance that his complex needed.

"You'll have to handle him as you would a child," I said. "It'll take understanding and patience, but in the end, I think you'll see a change."

With Matt, I tried hard to break down his desire "to possess," which was such a deeply rooted part of his character. He agreed, along with his wife, to spend two hours a week with a marriage counselor.

While jealousy in an abnormal stage had wrecked their marriage, there were other factors, of course, some deeper, some merely contributing. There was Big Matt's overwhelming feeling of insecurity, and their divergent views on social activities and how to handle the boy, Pat. Big Matt would have a hard, long row to hoe. But there was no doubt that the near tragic turn of the last episode had shocked him. I doubted that he would be guilty again of violence against his wife or child.

After spending considerable time with me, the two returned home together, each with a copy of the long Reconciliation Agreement they had signed. In it, we got down to specifics in the matter of the spankings Big Matt gave Molly on occasions. It had been his way of working off his pent-up feelings. He had reacted as an animal might. But now that he thought it over, he was the first to admit that he had "behaved pretty bad."

He willingly agreed to the following clause:

> The husband admits that in the past he has treated spouse like a child and has "punished" such spouse in various ways. He agrees to treat such spouse hereafter as a "better half" and not as a child.

Molly and Matt referred to the agreement frequently. Only a few weeks later, a small incident occurred, and Molly was quick to remind Matt of the near tragic turn of the last event. Matt went to the buffet drawer, used in the family as a catchall for papers of importance. He hauled out his copy of their agreement and read out loud to Molly the paragraph "Forgetting the Past." There they had agreed that they could not attain happiness together unless they made a fresh start. Molly quickly admitted that she had been wrong.

Still later, Molly and Matt were invited to spend an evening with some mutual friends. Matt was quick to cast about for excuses. It was Molly's turn to pull out their agreement and to remind him he had promised they would go out for social activities of one kind or another at least one evening every ten days. Matt grumbled but stayed by his promise.

This may seem rather an arbitrary and wooden approach to human relations. On the other hand, it must be remembered that much discussion of the feelings and perceptions of both Big Matt and Molly went into the formulation of this part of the agreement.

In addition to the counseling agency, I enlisted the aid of their pastor, since both had a religious background. Later, the pastor told me he had explained to Big Matt: "None of us really can possess anything except our own soul. Everything we are given, including the bodies we inhabit on this earth, come from our Creator. Even the land we 'own' existed for eons before we exercised dominion over it and will continue to exist long after our comparatively slight additions to its surface have dwindled away to dust. So it is with our life partners and our children. They don't *belong* to us. They come from God. The time they spend with us is infinitesimal compared with eternity.

"And as for your wife Molly," he continued, "I baptized her when she first came into the world, and have known her ever since. No one ever had a nicer wife. God gave her to you, Matt, in the sacrament of matrimony, to cherish, to protect and to love, and as a helpmate to guide you back to Him. When you strike her in anger you raise your hand against the One who entrusted her to you."

And so, with a big "assist" from the strong forces of religion, Matt and Molly started a new life together. And

Pat, well, no boy ever felt he had more to be proud of than did he—with parents like Big Matt and lovely, lively Molly.

Many others gripped by jealousy followed Big Matt and Molly through the Conciliation Court. Some I remember well. One husband nearing forty confided he had had all the women he wanted before marriage, and every time he saw his wife with another man, he couldn't help but be suspicious. He himself had had affairs in his premarital days with married women. Again, this situation resulted from "projection," as it had in Big Matt's case. He was projecting his own guilt from his own immoral past, which is a most common mechanism in marital difficulty.

Many cases involved other forms of jealousy. One wife well past middle age confessed she was "terribly jealous" of her husband's career as a brilliant advertising executive. She thought of herself as a dull housewife taking care of onerous jobs. He had a wonderful personality, she said, and she thought she had none.

Most of our couples failed to realize that no two people can live exactly on the same level, that each has needs he must satisfy. If a woman wants to become a singer and has a great talent, then surely her husband should realize her hunger to express herself, and help her, even if her glory eventually should overshadow his place in the sun.

From these cases came several "sailing directions," the bonds of a good and strong marriage that I was jotting down and tossing into the bottom desk drawer. By now I had only a scattered few, but I hoped that in time I would have enough to draw a chart showing the way past the shoals. These couples who had come close to failing would unknowingly help others.

One of the most disconcerting cases that came before me, and yet typical, concerned a woman who was not only intensely jealous of her own husband but also of her children.

Their names were Doris and Dan Somerset. They were thirty-four, and the parents of a boy, four, and a daughter, six. She was a thin, quiet, withdrawn, moody person—the kind who would be easily hurt. He, on the other hand, was a big fellow with a smile to equal his size, and extremely sociable. They were about as unlike as two people could be.

As we talked, their troubles slowly took shape. Doris was, in her own eyes, a good wife and mother. She was the first up in the morning and the last to bed. She worked so hard about the house that by night she would be exhausted, too exhausted to go out with Dan or play with the youngsters. She couldn't relax, she said, because she never had time to. This was a type who came frequently into the Conciliation Court, the person who drove himself too hard, who never let up a single minute.

Dan, on the other hand, had plenty of friends and at parties was always joking with the girls who seemed naturally to gravitate to him. Much as Doris resented this behavior, the greater hurt was the way their own children worshipped him. Nights, she told me, Dan would cut up with the youngsters until they were like wild Indians. She would tell him to act his age, but he would laugh it off. When bedtime came, the children would run to him to be hugged and kissed. They seldom went to her unless he reminded them. Every night the knife turned deeper.

To make matters worse, his mother lived next door and was like her son. She never minded her grandchildren tracking mud through the house and always had time to play with them, which Doris didn't. And Doris's house was neat and dustless, and the children were scolded if they disturbed anything.

When we were alone, Dan said, "She comes from a home where no affection was ever shown, and she doesn't like affection. She can't bear to see me kiss and hug the kids, and I think they know it. Anyway, they feel it. She keeps accusing me of trying to take the youngsters away from her—of trying to alienate them. I tell her she's crazy—that I can play with my own children, can't I?"

He hesitated. "I'm not going to have them brought up like her—like hermits. To tell the truth, Judge, I would have left her a long time ago except I feel sorry for her. I think she'd wither away without me and the children—and yet she can't seem to live with us, either."

Among the suggestions I offered Dan, as a preliminary means of relieving the situation, were these: They should move some distance from his mother. The clash of personalities was too great, and naturally Doris would be jealous of another woman whom the children seemed to like better. He should hire household help to ease the physical strain on his wife, if he could afford it, and he said he could. Her complete exhaustion by nightfall destroyed her ability to think and act sensibly.

And even though his efforts would meet with rebuff at the start, he should show Doris all kinds of attentions and affection. Except for the children, he should avoid bestowing any affection on others, no matter how innocent his intentions. And he should encourage the children to do little things for their mother. He should mention occasionally to them what a wonderful mother she is, so that they would notice her more. He should engage in play with the children that she could participate in, such as going on picnics and the like. He should seek to draw her into all their activities, so she wouldn't feel shut out, and hence, jealous.

"You and Doris need to communicate more with each other," I continued. "Perhaps you can get away from the house oftener nights, maybe take an occasional week-end trip, so that she will feel that you love her as well as the children. I believe in time she may become affectionate herself, and if she does, then the children will respond to her, too."

These were only suggestions, since the two were in desperate need of long and thoughtful counseling.

He left my chambers, disturbed and bewildered. It was evident he still thought a divorce was the only solution, despite the fact that they loved each other. Outside in the reception room, he told her matter of factly that I wanted to see her.

She was struggling with herself as she sat before me. Her whole body was trembling, and before many minutes, she was sobbing as I'd never seen a woman cry before. Eventually the tears ran their course, and the heavy breathing subsided. She looked up with a face I will never forget, full of deep hurt, despair, and fear. Her voice which before had been sharp and brittle, was now soft and low.

Quietly, I told her how much her husband and the children loved her—and wanted to love her, if she would only let them. Her problem, I said, was to understand herself thoroughly, to learn why she was so jealous of all people, including even her husband and the children, and consequently felt hostile toward them. Partly, it was a matter of learning how to play with the children—yes, and even learning how to act toward them so that they would feel her love. It was a matter of learning, the same as learning to walk. Somehow she had missed this training and understanding that most of us acquire naturally in our homes in our childhood. It would come hard for her at first, as everything new does.

"I'll die if I lose them," she said so softly I could barely hear. "Dan and the children—they're all I want in this world. When Dan went to the lawyer—about the divorce —I thought I'd never live the night through."

She looked up. "I'm at the end of the road. I'll do anything, Judge, anything."

Excusing myself, I went to the door and asked Dan to come in. He took one look at Doris. He saw the tear-marked, haggard, defeated face, and dropped on his knees by her chair. It was clear he had never seen her cry. His voice was filled with tenderness and love as he pulled her to him. This time there was no resistance.

Quietly, I left the room.

chapter nine

A House Becomes a Home

. . . With children a house becomes a home. The married couple becomes a family. . . .

—RECONCILIATION AGREEMENT

In most homes the birth of a child brings the greatest happiness a couple can know. Out of their love has come a baby girl or boy to teach to walk and talk, to bring up through cowboy days and mud battles and high heels or a jalopy with pipes, to console during teen-age loves, to watch graduate and start to work and marry.

This is the picture as it should be. But it doesn't always turn out that way. Children may be unwanted, often actively resented. Their discipline and rearing may cause dissension. They bring to the divorce courts many couples who fail to understand that a sound and warm relationship between parent and child must be second in importance only to that between husband and wife.

Such was the situation with Jim and Irene Dalton, who sat before me one gloomy January day. They were two sensible, intelligent beings who seemingly could cope with everything except themselves. He was a tall, likable fellow, a little on the homely side, a supervisor with a large drug firm, and she, before her marriage, had been a librarian. Their problem centered around their three-year-old boy, Roddy.

From what they told me, I was able to put the following together in more or less chronological order. This was a case deeply rooted in the past—in Jim Dalton's childhood.

His mother had been a warm, sweet person, generous in her love and attentions for her only child. He recalled vividly that night when she had tiptoed in to tuck him in. He was thinking of his birthday the next Sunday, and she had smiled down at him and whispered, "You'll have the nicest birthday ever—with six candles, and all your little friends. Now it's very late. You'd better be off to sleep, my little man."

He was never to forget that night—because he never saw her again. His stepfather awoke him before dawn to tell him she had died in an automobile accident.

He had a lonesome childhood after that. Relatives took turns rearing him, and while they were good people, none ever succeeded in filling the gap within.

When Jim was twenty-six, he met Irene, who was two years older. He was reading in the library that afternoon when he first noticed her. She came from behind the counter with some books, and put them in a brief case for one of the little girls who was waiting in the children's section. Then Irene knelt beside her, and buttoned her winter coat, and patted her cheek. The little girl threw her arm about the young woman and gave her the hug she had coming. The scene captivated the young man watching them over the top of a book.

In time, Irene took Jim in, too. No one needed loving more, since he was a lonesome soul, and they were blissfully happy that first year of marriage. When she learned she was pregnant, she could scarcely wait for him to return home. She felt like sending a telegram to his office. And when Jim brought them home from the hospital,

Irene and a handsome, eight-pound boy, he was the proudest fellow on earth.

The first six months were rough. The child, Roddy, underwent an operation for a stomach disorder. Irene's time was taken up almost entirely with the baby and the household. Since Jim, her "oldest," was hale and hearty, it was natural that she should devote most of her care to Roddy. The baby came first in her life now, and all plans were adjusted to him.

Try as he could, Jim couldn't conquer his growing feeling that the child was crowding him out of Irene's life. He grew irritable with both Irene and Roddy, and spent more and more time away from home. The situation worsened as Roddy became a toddler with all the possessiveness of an only child and one who has had a long illness.

Roddy himself was quick to sense his father's feelings toward him. And when Jim would order the child around, as though he had the understanding of a ten-year-old, Irene would chide him for it. Jim could take almost anything except criticism from the one he loved, and by the time Irene recognized the growing problem, it had assumed serious proportions.

With Jim home less and less, Irene took her troubles to her former boss at the library, and that wise old spinster suggested she should ask help of the Conciliation Court before her marriage was completely disrupted. The librarian said she would pick up the forms for her to fill out. She didn't tell her that she also had in mind having a word with the judge. As a result, I was well informed about Irene, Jim, and Roddy before I ever met them.

Irene realized the full extent of the problem. "It's all my fault, Judge. Jim needed me—and all the time I talked about nothing but Roddy."

It was evident that the very attraction that had brought them together—her mother love toward the little girl in the library that day—had finally come between them. In the library he had seen himself in the place of the child. He had envisioned Irene lavishing affection on him.

He needed a psychologist to explain that in marriage, the roles should always be that of husband and wife, and never that of mother and son. If a man marries a woman to mother him, a struggle is bound to ensue within himself. While he actively wants the wife to pamper him, he still wants to act as head of the household, to fulfill his male role as an active partner in the marriage. He is bound to resent the intrusion of children, yet if the wife does baby him he is apt to feel she is attempting to dominate him.

Jim agreed with Irene that the two should attend a child guidance clinic with Roddy. A better name for such centers would be parent-and-child clinic, since in so many cases, the parents need more help than the youngster. At the clinic, all three would learn to understand themselves better. Irene would recognize that Jim probably would always need more love and attention than most husbands. Jim might eventually realize that the great tragedy he suffered when he was six had colored his entire life, that he was not at fault, that this was a natural hunger for mother love that would have developed in most individuals who had lived through the same set of circumstances. He would be taught, though, that a wife's love could be as rewarding and satisfying as that of a mother, that he must never misinterpret Irene's attention to Roddy as a turning away from him.

As for Roddy himself, he would be placed in a group therapy class. The clinical psychologist and social workers would study his play behavior when he was with other youngsters, and would evolve a plan whereby Roddy might be brought out of his antagonism toward his father. With Jim's help, Roddy would come to love him.

From the experiences of Jim and Irene Dalton evolved one of the most important clauses in the Reconciliation Agreement:

> The coming of children must not be permitted to disturb the warm relationship between husband and wife. One must not neglect the other.

I wish I could underline those words, especially for couples just marrying. Pregnancy brings such a variety of emotions, ranging from ecstasy to shock, and so often the husband and wife are unconditioned by any advance thinking. They drift or are suddenly propelled into situations that might have been avoided if they had had counseling from their parents or pastor or a trusted confidant.

The facts are sharply at variance with the popular conception that children invariably bring happiness. Children come by chance as well as by choice. Sometimes the wife resents losing her figure and being tied down. The husband may see a child as a threat to financial security or to his good times. With most people, both the wife and husband will change in the normal course of events. When they do not, however, a counselor could be of great help in explaining that many prospective parents experience this feeling of resentment toward the child, but that they eventually will want and love their child. A good counselor will do more; he will seek to elicit their negative feelings, and draw them out, on the theory that an individual comes by positive feelings about any problem or subject only after his negative ones have been examined and discarded.

A baby, the counselor will tell them, calls for a complete readjustment in living habits. But what may seem like a sacrifice in the beginning has a way of evaporating. New pleasures take the place of old ones.

To express this feeling, we wrote into the Agreement:

> God entrusts to the parents a new life, a body and soul. The child is His child and theirs. They become God's agents in the upbringing of the child. And what an awesome responsibility it is. It is estimated that eighty per cent of what a child is, or turns out to be, is attributable to his parents, or to those in whom his upbringing is entrusted.

Resentment may take an even more intense turn than it did with Jim Dalton. There was the case of Jean and Tom Zbysco, who were as unlike as any two individuals possibly could be. Theirs had been an office romance. She was a secretary, tidy, orderly, well-scrubbed and polished, and he, a young engineer so absorbed in his work that he would forget to go out to lunch. He was as serious as she was gay, and found most girls boring. But as she sat across from him, taking his reports in shorthand, he discovered himself admiring her efficiency, her calmness, her unobtrusiveness. He began wondering what it would be like to have a wife who would bring orderliness to his world, to his helter-skelter apartment, a wife who would understand that his work was his whole life and would help him attain the goals he had set for himself in the field of science.

She, too, in her neat little room with the organdy curtains, thought about him. A real nice boy. Polite, good-looking if one were not too particular about details, on the outdoor side with his abundance of unruly black hair. She had never seen him smile, and suddenly she wanted to do something to make him smile.

In the first months of their marriage they were very happy, both working on their jobs and living in her apartment. Then came the afternoon when the doctor told her she was pregnant. She was delighted, but hesitant to inform Tom. At times she felt there was barely enough room in his life for her. So, fearing his reaction, she put off telling him for several months. Any other man would have noticed.

When he found out from one of the girls in the office, he went straight to her cubicle. "You're not pregnant, are you, Jean?"

It sounded more like an accusation than a question, and she burst into tears. For months afterwards, she felt the hurt of his reaction to her pregnancy.

Tom's attitude failed to soften even after the birth of the child—a girl—and he became more and more engrossed in his own affairs. But she was happy, and the long hours when Tom was at the office were blissful as she cared for her daughter.

Tom, though, feared a second pregnancy, and suggested the use of contraceptives. He said children should be planned, and wanted to avoid any future "mistakes." Since she was a devout Catholic, she felt that to agree to his wishes would be to commit a mortal sin. She explained that her religious beliefs would permit her to follow the rhythm system if the reasons for doing so were sufficiently grave. They could avoid pregnancy by refraining from intercourse during those days of the month when she might conceive. He refused to discuss it. He thought it would be safer if they omitted having any sexual intercourse for the time being. He avoided any more contact with her than was necessary. Their love-making, hence, and the normal affection they would have shown each other, dropped to a minimum. As a result, she grew increasingly nervous and became a neurotic with many psychosomatic disorders.

She was short-tempered, and his cool and calculated answers would be met with an emotional scene. One morning at the office, suffering from frustrated rage at his wife, he went to pieces at a staff meeting, slammed his file of calculations down, and stormed out.

It was the first time he had ever permitted his emotions to interfere with his work, and to Tom Zbysco, it was unpardonable. His home life was definitely responsible. He told Jean about it that night in no uncertain terms, and she took the baby and left for her parents' home.

Time accentuated Jean's loneliness for him. She sent him a card on his birthday signed, "With all our love, Melinda and Jean." Touched by her thoughtfulness, and lonesome, too, he knocked on her door the next Sunday. When she opened it and saw him, so many conflicting emotions welled up within her that she burst into a deluge of tears. He was convinced then he had made a horrible mistake in coming. Never again would she be the collected, efficient girl he had married.

When she tearfully told me about the reunion in my office, I went to the window and turned my back to control my own emotions. I had never felt so sorry for anyone.

Though I talked at length with both, they seemed unable to help themselves. He refused all counseling. He told me flatly his goal was the same, success in his field, and he would permit nothing to interfere with that, neither love nor wife nor child. On the other hand, she was willing to sacrifice anything to keep her family intact. She still loved him with a compelling passion. But he was adamant, and when the period of conciliation was over, he obtained a divorce.

I couldn't help thinking that their separation was for the best. Barring a radical change on his part, they never would know happiness. They would have lived in a state of constant frustration and anxieties that would have told on the child. In my own mind, I felt confident Jean would give the girl immeasurably more happiness than the two could have. Though I have cited that a large percentage of delinquent youngsters come from broken homes, yet this is only one side of the picture. Many wonderful boys and girls stand witness to the love and devotion that a mother or father alone has given them. And while we make every effort to reconcile couples, nevertheless we recognize what a mistake we would be making if we forced a child to live in a home stored with hate, extreme cruelty, or gross immorality, or in a constantly frustrating environment where there is an "emotional separation."

A month later, I received a letter from Jean.

My dear Judge,

Please accept these belated thanks for all that you tried to do for Tom, Melinda and me. It just wasn't to be, I guess.

I've decided to return to college to take up some form of social work. Since I can't help the one I love because he won't let me, I'm going to devote the rest of my life to trying to help other people with their troubles. This way I hope to do something useful with my life.

Again, my thanks. You will always occupy a special place in my prayers.

Jean

I was sure that Melinda was in good hands.

While the attitude of couples toward pregnancy and children ruins many marriages, another factor equally as threatening revolves around the question of how a child should be reared. Couple after couple would come into the Conciliation Court and break out wrangling before our counselors and myself. The father was too strict with their boy. The mother was too lax. Their daughter was a problem child, and it was all the father's fault. And so it went. How should parents treat a child? How should they themselves behave before him? How much should they expect of their youngsters? It was an age-old question, of course, this matter of rearing a son or daughter, a question that civilization has been debating since the beginning of the spoken word.

One couple who etched themselves sharply in my memory were the Ed Browns. They were responsible for the incipient stages of that section in the Reconciliation Agreement headed, "Parents' Conduct toward Child."

The second time they returned to my chambers, I summed up the previous conversation. "Your difficulties obviously have centered around your son, David. To you, he is a problem child. Now twelve, he has run away from home twice. He shows no respect, fights with other boys, and generally speaking, is headed toward real trouble. That's the story, isn't it?"

"That's it in a nutshell, Judge," the gaunt-faced man said simply. The equally gaunt-faced woman nodded agreement. They were a grim-looking couple. Material things in life had come the hard way. Ed Brown was now the top finish carpenter for a construction company, and a fine craftsman. One of nine children, left to shift for himself at fourteen, he had difficulty even remembering what childhood was like. Life had been rough for his wife, Margaret, too. She had been reared as an only child in a home with a drunkard for a father. As children, neither had ever known laughter or love. I couldn't help wondering how long it had been since Ed had last kissed his wife.

They were God-fearing rather that God-loving people,

and were bringing Davey up under the theory that fear of punishment was the best deterrent to evil-doing. They expected him to behave with the understanding and maturity of an adult. They made no attempt to comprehend the workings of a childish mind. Neither had patience nor forgiveness. When Davey misbehaved, his wrongdoing was held against him for a long time. And it was easy for him to violate the strict code of rules, since his parents were exacting people who lived by punctuality, neatness, cleanliness, and such virtues. Also, since they themselves were in open conflict most of the time, each blaming the other for this problem child, Davey never knew where he stood. As a result, he hid in a world of his own silence which they termed sullenness.

For a time, the Browns and I talked about this matter of discipline. "I think parents err," I said, "when they tell a child that he is bad. It's not the child but the act. They should say, 'We still love *you*—but what you *did* is wrong. We love you, but not what you did.' "

The night before I had struggled to find a plan which would help these two really get to know their boy. But what plan? Ed Brown couldn't very well take Davey hiking or camping because he wasn't that kind of man. For the same reason, I couldn't suggest that Mrs. Brown ask the neighborhood gang in for Cokes and cookies. She wouldn't fit in the picture, and a troop of boys would sense it and be uneasy. If only Ed Brown played ball or fished or even went to the movies . . .

It was a hard nut to crack, and I couldn't seem to come up with the answer. As I roamed about the house, I stopped by the ping-pong table, remembering how I had been quite the champion until my boy, Mike, grew up and soundly trounced me.

Mike. That set me to thinking. When the war ended and I was separated from the service, I had not seen my own little tribe for more than two years. Mike, our oldest, was just stretching into his teens, and after the long absence we were almost strangers to each other. I felt we had to have a common field of interest, a sport or hobby we could share. The war had driven us out of our little "ranch," consisting of several acres of permanent pasture, a six-box stall barn, two riding horses, and a couple of colts. With hay prices high, and help scarce, Ruth had had to dispose of the livestock and eventually of the property.

So Mike and I didn't have the old setting of former good times to roam around in. Then one day when we were wandering along Balboa Bay, we borrowed a Watson dinghy, a little bathtub of a boat from a friend. The "friend" forgot to explain that a leeboard was a necessary part of its equipment, although providentially she did recall that oars were a good precaution. After a sail down wind, we asked ourselves what was so hard about this. As we started back, we found out, and I finished the sail by ignominiously rowing back with sail still hoisted and fluttering in the breeze. My brother chose that moment to stand on the dock and make a permanent record with a camera of our first "sail."

As Mike and I trudged homeward, hands blistered, tired, sunburned, and ravenous, there was a good feeling between us. It was as if there were no missing years. So that was how we became sailors. With Mike as skipper, my brother and I as crew, we sailed a succession of boats, and acquired a love of the sea and fifty-seven racing trophies during the next five years. But the true gain was not the tarnished cups Ruth is always after me to polish. It was that Mike learned to respect racing rules, to plan ahead, to play hard and square, to take hard knocks, triumphs, and defeats in stride, to be a good loser as well as a good winner, to care properly for property, to work in a team. . . .

The Ed Browns looked at me oddly. I had sat lost in thought for a minute or two. Now I asked if they could remember any incident when they had heard Davey bragging to his friends about either of them. I explained how important it is to a child to be proud of his mother and father. Every boy wants to think his parents the best in the world, and even though he must know they have faults, he doesn't want the world to find them out.

They thought a long time, and then Mrs. Brown recalled a desk that Ed had built for Davey. The boy had been delighted and had brought his friends over to the house to show them the "desk that Dad built for me and with his own hands!"

This was what I had been looking for. Exploring further, I discovered that Davey, like his father, found tools exciting. Perhaps tools might do for them what boating had done for Mike and me.

But Ed Brown quickly gave my enthusiasm a setback. He had tried several times to teach Davey how to use tools, but neither was patient with the other, and the boy had ended by ruining one of his dad's best chisels.

Then an idea struck me and gathered size as it raced through my mind. The problem was, could I sell it to Ed Brown? Would either of them, for that matter, accept it? This was my brainstorm: I suggested that Ed buy his son three tools of his own—hammer, screwdriver, and saw. Next, he was to arrange a pegboard for them back of his workbench. The outline of the tools could be drawn on the pegboard so that the absence of any one from its proper place would be noticed. He could tell Davey that if every Saturday morning the tools were in their proper place, then he would buy him a new one until he had a complete set. Each week he would lay out a simple project for Davey to construct, and tell him how to use the particular tool involved.

After considerable deliberation, Ed, justifiably dubious, agreed to give it a try.

There remained one more aspect of the child's behavior to be explained to the baffled parents, although it should have been clarion clear to both of them. Why, they wondered, did Davey never bring any of his friends home? Obviously they were never comfortable there. It was always, "Don't do this—don't do that."

And suddenly I saw the answer—the "sailboat" for father and son, the lure for Davey's friends, the stopgap for mother, all rolled into one. It was so simple I wondered why I hadn't thought of it before. Ed was no longer dubious and Mrs. Brown was moved to grateful tears.

The idea was a two-story playhouse in the back yard to be built by Ed and Davey. Ed would put in a lath fence to cut off a part of the back yard, and that portion would be set aside as a play area. Davey could dig holes in it, make tunnels, mud baths, anything. He would be required to police the area to keep it reasonably respectable.

The playhouse would be left open on the side which faced the house so that the players could be observed. A fireman's ladder to go up and a pole to slide down would add to the enjoyment. A small flagpole above the second floor would permit pirate flags to be raised, and by leaving all or a part of that story open or with a railing around, it could readily become the bridge of a ship or the top of a fort.

I suggested that Ed defer building the playhouse until Davey had learned enough about tools so that he could really help. Then he could tell his friends, "Dad and I are building this fort!"

Still, nothing that could be told these two within the course of a few hours would send them sailing easily over the gap which lay between them and Davey. Nothing that I could say in such a brief time could explore deeply into causes. But they were honest and well-meaning people, and when I suggested counseling, both agreed to attend a child guidance clinic.

The next time I saw the Browns, I knew even partial means to an end sometimes help. They weren't exactly warm, and never would be since they weren't that way by birth or rearing. They had loosened up considerably, however, and Ed Brown even had a faint glimmer of a proud smile as he said, "The boy's doing all right, Judge."

I felt so good that when I reached home, I got out the pruning shears to work off my exuberance in the yard. I heard Mary racing to her mother, shouting, "Mama, Mama, Daddy's going to give the yard a haircut."

Ruth came hurrying out. I guess there was cause for alarm, since I usually get carried away and give the yard a "butch." And this particular evening I probably would have snipped it bald as an eagle.

chapter ten

A House Divided

We realize that a child is the outgrowth of the love of its parents and just as his conception required their joint act so will each step in his training and development require the love, attention and self sacrifice of each parent.

—RECONCILIATION AGREEMENT

What of those cases that do end ultimately in the divorce courts, where the children are torn from one parent and handed to another?

This, the question of the custody of a child, is the most difficult problem a divorce court judge ever considers. His decision will mold the developing years of a boy or girl. If he errs, he may wreck a life.

An old principle of law, followed widely, holds that a child of tender years should be given to his mother when all other considerations are equal. Of course, "when all other things are equal" covers a wide range, and there can be no hard and fast rules to guide the judge through the myriad gradations of good and evil found in each set of parents. From common experience, we know that no person is wholly good and no person the reverse.

A good judge will take into consideration, too, that most psychologists believe there is a strong development of the masculine and feminine roles in a child between the ages of four and six. The boy needs a father around, and the girl a mother. After six, the child can better accept the parent into whose custody he has been placed, until he reaches high school age. There again, the boy should have a father's help in determining his life's work, and a girl her mother's counsel.

The basic factor in determining custody, however, is this: What is in the best interest of the *child*? The solution should be based not on the father's best interest nor the mother's, but always on where the child would best develop and mature and find the most happiness.

Believe me, many are the carpets in court chambers which show the wear resulting from the long and tortuous walks of judges as they seek the wisdom of Solomon in determining the fate of some boy or girl. Sometimes the facts balance so equally between parents that it is the word of the child uttered to the judge in his chambers which tips the scales.

Such was the case with Elizabeth, aged ten. It began one scorching September day when the presiding judge called me. Every department was loaded, and he had four cases he was trying to place. One was a contested custody case.

"Both counsel have agreed to waive a jury provided I assign the case to a judge with some experience in custody matters. I suggested your department just on the off-chance you might be able to crowd it in, and both were very agreeable. Could you possibly take it?"

There was a moment of silence. Perhaps more than a moment, for the "PJ" felt it necessary to do a little more selling. "They say they will stipulate as to property, with the sole real issue being the custody of one child. They will want you to see the child in chambers. I don't want to mislead you. The custody issue will be bitterly contested."

"I understand," I said. "Send them over."

A fight over child custody! Each side would throw every aspersion and innuendo in the book at the other, attempting to prove unfitness.

The intercom buzzed. "They're all ready for you, Judge," the court clerk said.

"I'll be right out, Jim." I put on my robe and pushed the buzzer to alert the bailiff. Maynor *v.* Maynor was about to begin.

As I entered the courtroom, the bailiff intoned, "All rise, please, in the presence of the flag, emblem of the Constitution, with liberty and justice for all, the Superior Court of the County of Los Angeles, State of California, Department 51, is now in session, the Honorable Louis H. Burke, judge presiding. Be seated, please."

For a self-conscious judge, the pause during this ritual is an awkward one. He knows furtive glances are being cast his way by the participants, wondering what manner of person he is. I found it helpful to utilize these moments to invoke silently God's help to be patient, considerate, and just.

Through witness after witness I pieced together a picture of the marriage. Marian Maynor had been born on the wrong side of the tracks. Her husband, Paul Maynor, had been born so far from the tracks that he and his doting mother hardly knew they existed. And in the same way that she protected Paul from the discomforts of life, Mother Maynor did her best to protect him from girls. None of his affairs ever became serious until he met Marian. And in Marian, Mother Maynor found a worthy foe.

At their first meeting it was clear that no holds would be barred. It would be strictly catch-as-catch-can with

Paul as the prize. But Mother Maynor, trained in the old school, was relatively inexperienced in the hard infighting that Marian had been brought up on. Her introduction came when Marian, over a cigarette, sweetly announced she was going to have a baby—Paul's.

Staggered, Mother Maynor tried cajolery, sarcasm, threats, and finally, bribery, but Marian merely rolled with the punches like a pro.

"What *do* you want?" the gray-haired old lady finally asked.

Marian blew out the smoke thoughtfully. "A wedding," she said. "One in the old tradition."

Mother Maynor suffered from indigestion for a week.

The wedding was a big affair. And no more chic bride ever paraded up the aisle. Mother Maynor paid the price to keep the breath of scandal from scorching her beloved Paul. But she never forgave Marian.

As time went on, Paul's amusement over his wife's boundless energy and drive waned. Marian was not happy until she had maneuvered him into a partnership in a brokerage firm. The birth of Elizabeth diverted her only briefly. She always had an eye on a higher rung on the ladder for her and Paul.

Unaccustomed to the nervous strain of the business world, his health gave way. A nervous breakdown, the specialists called it, complicated by stomach ulcers. While Paul was in the hospital, Marian took it upon herself to protect their interests in the brokerage office. The sharp lines in her face hardened. Eventually she pushed his partners out and took full control.

Although she kept urging Paul to return to the office, he spent more and more of his time with Elizabeth. He had recovered his strength, but he was still sick in spirit.

Finally, Marian could no longer stand the frustration of this never-ending convalescence, and one day a cool little note informed Paul that she had left and taken Elizabeth. Her lawyer would get in touch with his.

A bitter battle ensued. Finally, the only issue which remained was the custody of Elizabeth, whom Paul wanted desperately. And this question rested upon the evidence adduced and on an interview in chambers with the child.

In the several years I had had in the domestic relations court, I had gone through many such interviews. I had seen a whole parade of nail-biting, bed-wetting, nervous, distraught, unhappy children, seated one by one before me. They included youngsters barely above the toddling stage, and youngsters so carefully coached they couldn't wait to recite their piece. Many were being used in the worst sense, used as weapons by fathers and mothers who seemingly cared nothing for the child's feelings, so long as they themselves gained their immediate point.

Elizabeth was brought in by a young woman court reporter and left with me. She was a curious child, totally different from what I had expected. She was far more at ease than I. She settled herself in the big leather chair, her shoes not quite reaching the floor. She smoothed her skirt about her round brown knees, then folded her hands in her lap, her large sober eyes never leaving my face. Interesting eyes they were, brown and deep. On her head, not a hair was out of place, and the ends in two short braids hung down her back.

By way of making conversation, I said, "Do they call you Elizabeth at home?"

"Mother does," she said.

"And your father?" I asked.

"My father calls me Liz."

"Do you know why you are here, Elizabeth?"

"Yes, my father told me. He said I was to see the judge and you would ask me questions and then decide what's to become of me—whether I'd live with my father or my mother. He said whatever you decided I should accept. He said it must be very hard for a judge to know what to do with children like me, where parents don't want to live together any more."

Quietly I explained that under the law the custody of children of tender years—and that would mean children like her—should be given to the mother, unless the mother was morally unfit. I explained that both her parents were fit to have her custody and I was extremely sorry that there seemed to be no way of getting them back together, so that she could live with them both. I said I was sure that each loved her in his and her own way. The sober face nodded agreement.

"Since you are a girl, there is also an added reason why you should spend a great deal of time with your mother. Mothers are able to teach girls a lot of things that fathers know very little about."

Finally, I asked her if she cared to tell me what she thought I should do, before I reached a final decision.

She said very simply and directly, "I'd like to stay with my father."

"Why?"

"Because my father needs me. You see, sir, my mother loves me too, but my mother doesn't need me. When grandmama dies, my father won't have anybody to look after him. My mother can always take care of herself, but my father . . . my father . . ."

The words died out, and a big tear splashed down the front of her starched organdy dress.

I thought of Little Jacob. Here was another child with wisdom and understanding far beyond her years. An only child, brought up in an environment entirely different from that of the little country boy I had known. But like the boy, she had been forced into early maturity by the cares and burdens of adults which had been thrust upon her. It was hard to imagine either child, Jacob or Elizabeth, playing games with the carefree abandon of normal children. This was something their parents and a chain of circumstances had stolen from them.

"Elizabeth," I said, "I believe you're right. Your father needs you and you need him."

But it wasn't the fact that her father needed her that decided me. It was the fact she herself felt his need. The satisfaction that she was doing something for a person she loved would be far more important to her than any relationship she could have with her constantly busy, overambitious mother.

"Will I see my mother?" Elizabeth asked.

"Of course you will. You'll visit her often and divide your vacations with her."

She went on. "When I've been with Daddy, Mother wants to know everything Daddy has been doing, and then when I tell her she gets mad. If I don't say anything, she gets mad too."

I answered, "It will be hard, Elizabeth, but you must try to keep your life with your father and the things that happen with him entirely separate and apart from your life with your mother. Be careful not to carry tales from one household to the other. Do you understand, Elizabeth?"

"Yes, I do." She seemed relieved. "I'll try my best."

Then and there I made a note to include in the Reconciliation Agreement the statement:

We promise not to unload on the child the worries and troubles of adults. He will be a child only once.

As I mounted the bench two hours later, the face of Little Jacob was before my eyes. I began: "I need not say that the determination of the question of custody in a case like this is exceedingly difficult. The child loves each of her parents equally, and obviously each of the parents loves her. Final responsibility to determine what is for her best interests rests with the court. There is no question of unfitness here on the part of either parent. Custody of Elizabeth Maynor is vested in her father, Paul Maynor, with the right of reasonable visitation reserved to the child's mother, Marian Maynor, including but not limited to the right to have the physical custody of the child on alternate week ends, holidays, and one-third of the vacation period."

The young lawyer jumped to his feet to protest with vehemence. "Granting the custody of a little girl of ten to a sick man who has not worked in several years, it's unthinkable—outrageous."

I pictured myself at his age, pleading Little Jacob's cause. I listened patiently, carefully, thinking how to answer. But there was too much to say. It was a matter between Elizabeth and me.

Slowly I said, "Court is adjourned," and as I descended the three short steps from the bench, I took a last glance at the little sober face in the front row and thought I saw the ghost of a smile. Maynor *v.* Maynor was behind me.

chapter eleven

A Stepchild's Surrender

The love of a stepchild can never be forced. In these matters the child must be permitted to do most of the leading. The stepparent's attitude must indicate at all times: interest in the child, patience, warmth....

—RECONCILIATION AGREEMENT

Charles Buckley had a son, John, and no two persons were ever closer. They knew each other's moods and wishes without need of words. John's mother had died when he was three, and Charles had been both father and mother to him. He was now ten, and all boy to outward appearances, but part baby, too, deep down inside.

Ann Nielson had two daughters, Karen and Christine, ages seven and five, and three blonder, more attractive heads it would be difficult to find. Ann had had an unfortunate child marriage to a man much older than herself, and after ten years of domination and unhappiness had sought escape in divorce. Shortly thereafter, he had died in an accident.

Several years later, Charles met Ann, and after a long courtship, they decided to marry. Charles had lived alone with John for so many years that he had nearly forgotten what softness there could be in the touch of a woman's hand, or what warmth her presence could give to the old home on Monterey Road. And here in one package he acquired three women, a whole flood of femininity. The bachelor quarters took on bright new colors. Windows were softened with new curtains and drapes, and the house and grounds came alive. Happiness abounded in the hearts of all—all, that is, but one—Charles's son, John.

John bitterly resented the intrusion of this army of women upon his close relationship with his father. It wasn't that he disliked Ann or Karen or Christine. He had liked them immensely when he had gone to visit them with his dad.

The boy admitted to his father, "Sure, the meals are terrific, and Ann's real good to us. And as for the girls, well, you know, girls are girls. There's just no understanding them. They can't do anything, although they sure try."

Yet he never had been so unhappy. He got into trouble in school, his grades tumbled, and he was lectured from all sides. Worst of all, he and his dad just couldn't talk about things the way they once had.

Not able to stand the pressure at home, where he felt himself out of step, the boy started going with a crowd of fellows down at the corner. Because he generally had money in his pocket, they let him in on some of their own fun, and one night very late Charles Buckley received a phone call.

"Sergeant Malone at the Norwood Station, Mr. Buckley. We've got your son here. I think you'd better come down."

"You must have the wrong Buckley," Charles said at first, until Sergeant Malone convinced him. At the station, bewildered and disbelieving, he was ushered into a room where John sat alone. The boy was defiant, scared, quick to defend the other boys but not really sorry. He had been caught along with three others shoplifting in a drugstore.

He had taken a ball-point pen, though he had two in his desk at home.

He was released to his father but sat sullen and uncommunicative on the way home. Nor did his mood change in the long session that followed. He played the role of a branded criminal, unwanted and utterly alone, and not understanding him, Charles was unable to get through to him, either that night or in the days and weeks that followed.

After a few months of earnest endeavor to rehabilitate John, Charles and Ann had to admit defeat. They placed him in a boarding school for problem children.

Lost without his son, Charles grew increasingly short-tempered with Ann. Somehow without saying it, he made her feel she was at fault, and she resented this feeling. Her temper, too, was quick.

Finally, facing the fact that he was only hurting Ann, he packed a bag and went to live at the club for a week or so, until he could get hold of himself. The week stretched into several months, and at last, desperate, Ann filed a petition in the Conciliation Court. She had gone through one divorce and was determined she never would another.

They both sat across from me, intelligent, kindly, courteous, and very much in love. As we talked, it became obvious that Charles Buckley was suffering from a guilt complex. In marrying Ann, he had failed his son. He loved Ann deeply, but his duty as a father came first. He could see only one solution, divorce. He would be free then to set up a home again for John, and they could return to the happiness they once had known.

Ann believed that such a solution was unfair both to him and to her and her girls. She and Charles had entered into marriage knowing they would have to work out adjustments for all three children. Surely, there must be some way.

Her hand closed over Charles's as she said, "No one could have been better or kinder to my Karen and Christine than Charles. And they were quick to respond with genuine love for him. I thought John would for me, too. I tried my best. I treated him as I did my own children. And the girls, too, wanted to love him. But he felt we were taking his father from him. He just rejected us, Karen, Chris, and me. Why, Judge, when we tried so hard?"

These were the questions that always raced about a man sitting as a counselor, questions that stung and jabbed and demanded an answer, like the persistent ringing of a phone. Here was a family of five, its very existence at stake. An answer might help them bridge the crisis, a right answer. No counselor ever forgot that.

Slowly, I talked along, feeling my way. "The word 'stepchild' has come to mean the forgotten one in our common concept of it. This is because people are likely to treat their own children much better than they do the stepchild."

They listened intently, hungry for anything that might help. "However, there's another situation," I continued, "that may have just as bad an effect on the child—where in our desire to bridge the gap to the stepchildren, we're kinder to them than we are to our own. John may have felt that way—that his father was placing the girls ahead of him."

I turned to Ann. "And you in turn, may have tried too hard. No one likes to have love forced on him, especially a stepchild. Instead of winning him over, a stepparent may drive him even further away if she's too affectionate. He has to come to love her of his own free will."

It took them a few moments to accept this possibility. I continued with another closely related situation. Could it be, I asked, that they were demonstrative before John, that they kissed warmly and said little affectionate things, and otherwise showed their love for each other? And that Charles was attentive to the girls in front of the boy?

They nodded. "That's perfectly normal, of course," I added, "but can't you see what it was doing to John? He had had an exclusive on the love of his father, and then when he saw his father loving a strange woman and two little girls, he began to feel crowded out. It was more than he could assimilate so quickly. If he had had a period of preparation—if the open show of love had come gradually, he might have adjusted to the new situation."

As we continued talking, the Buckleys said they both had done everything possible to discipline John. "John may have resented you deeply when you took him to task," I suggested to Ann. "You meant well—but in his eyes, you were the hated enemy, the woman who had stolen his father."

Most psychologists hold, I pointed out, that as far as possible, the natural parent should discipline the child and give the orders. If the stepmother wishes the child to correct his behavior, she should whenever possible tell the father when the child is absent.

"Another thing," I continued, "every child needs some time alone with his parents. He shouldn't have to share them constantly with the other children. A parent should have little talks with him when no one else is around, when the child can discuss anything he wants, so he will feel he is something special.

"John may have felt a greater need for this than most

children. Suddenly, he was thrust into a home where he was competing with two little girls for your love. He had been something very special, and then overnight, he was only one of three children."

"God knows," Charles said, "I didn't have any idea what was going on in the boy's heart."

"I didn't either," Ann put in. "I should've—but I didn't. I never stopped to reason out how he was thinking."

The crux of so many troubles, I thought. If we could only put ourselves in our child's place, or in our mate's place, then we might gain in understanding. If we could only stop occasionally and say to ourselves, "What would I be thinking, or feeling, if I were my wife? How do the things I say sound to her, and how do the things I do strike her?"

I thought of what Dr. Shostrom was always advocating—empathy, or getting into the frame of reference of another person. This difficult thing—a sincere and genuine effort to think not *for* or *about* the other person, but to think *with* him—might save many of our troubled marriages.

Charles Buckley returned to his club that night to do some heavy thinking. Ann had failed to persuade him that the five of them should try again. He felt somehow he had to rekindle that old warm feeling he had had with his son.

That week end, during a visit with the boy at the boarding school, he suggested they go on a fishing trip.

"You mean all of us? The girls, too?" the boy asked.

"No—just you and me."

The boy's eyes brightened. "Golly," was all he could get out. "Golly." Then doubts beset him. "You really mean it, Dad?"

His father nodded. "I've been thinking we ought to get away more, like we used to. They tell me the fish are running good."

John turned away, and Charles stepped out for a smoke. The boy wouldn't want him to see the tears.

Thus it was that around a campfire a few nights later in the High Sierras, Charles Buckley rambled along while they devoured some trout they had caught that day. He let John know that having a son—his very own son—was something. It was something special to have a girl, too, but it was especially special to have a son to go camping and fishing with, and to yell with at football games, and to help about the yard.

Little by little, they found each other again. And back home, John, reassured of his father's love, gradually surrendered to the three blonde heads around him.

chapter twelve

Pathological Optimist

> ——— *agrees to refrain from gambling or from attending places where gambling is being conducted and particularly from such places as* ———.
>
> —RECONCILIATION AGREEMENT

The day was a warm, bright one in mid-June, the sparkling variety that banishes troubles from the minds of most of us.

But there were plenty of troubles in Department 8, the main domestic relations department, situated in the Plaza Justicia of Los Angeles' Civic Center. Judge Elmer D. Doyle studied the long calendar of "order to show cause" cases, and then let his glance rise to the crowded courtroom. Faces sober and distraught looked back at him, eyes drawn by tension and grief.

He spoke slowly, so that even the most disturbed might understand. "The court wishes to advise all litigants that if they would like to consider the possibilities of a reconciliation, then they may ask that divorce proceedings be suspended and a petition filed with the Conciliation Court next door."

A few weeks before, we had moved the Conciliation Court from the City Hall to the Plaza Justicia, feeling that much more good might be accomplished if it were in closer proximity to Department 8.

The judge waited, and was about to commence the call of the calendar when a woman's strident voice came from far back. "I no want a divorce, Mr. Judge."

She elbowed her way toward the bench, a tall, big-boned woman with striking, pleasant features. "My name, Gina Arena, Judge. I no speak good English. I hear right? You say I no want a divorce, I go to another court?"

And so it was that Mrs. Gina Arena and her husband, Antonio, came before me. He was a well-turned man of about fifty, his jet hair slicked down, his dark suit immaculately pressed, and his shoes polished to a glasslike surface. He was a maitre d'hotel and looked it. He had filed for divorce, charging extreme cruelty, a term often used but without specific meaning, a term that covers a multitude of causes and sometimes sins. They had been married for twenty-seven years.

Their story was this, and they both agreed on the details: she would secrete money until she had accumulated a stake, and then while he worked nights, she would slip off to the gambling parlors. If she lost, she would return home and he would not be the wiser. But if she started to win, her temperature would go up, hours would fly by, and she would gamble the clock around, stopping only occasionally for a few drinks and black coffee. Since the places she frequented never closed, she would keep going until her luck would eventually change for the worse. Remorse then would set in, ending in more drinks and tears. The management would phone her husband. He would come and take her home. She would always promise it would never happen again.

"But for the last time, Judge," I could hear the husband's

excited voice protesting, "I tell you, never again. How you think I feel, Judge, your honor, knowing these wise guys at the joints are giving me the laugh? Me, Antonio Arena, maitre de, a guy who knows his way around. His wife a stumble bum with a crying jag, bawling so that everyone in the joint knows who it is has come to take her home."

He shook his head sadly. "For months, what I do, Judge? I take her home, undress her like baby, and put her to bed. Stay home from work and care for her like nurse. Tell all my friends she has flu. I don't fool them much, but my pride, she's hurt! She's hurt bad. But for the last time, Judge. Someone else dig her out of dirt and wash her up. Not me. I'm through."

Then the woman's tired voice. "Tony, Tony, lissen to me. I been sick, Tony. I no do it no more. I promise, Tony. By the grave of my dear dead mother, God rest her, I promise, Tony, no more . . . no more. . . ."

The words were lost in the heaviest of sobs. Tears came to Antonio's eyes, too, and he looked away.

"Tony," Gina started again, but this time with a restrained voice, "tell me, have I not made you a good wife? Remember when you were waiter in the depresh working maybe one night week, and I work out cleaning and cooking for rich people so we can live? I never kick, I no complain, I always give to you and say what's mine's yours. When doctor say, after little Tony die, I never have other kid, I want die, too, but I no want leave you alone. So I ask God, make me live just for you. You all I got. You go—I no want live no more. Give me other chance, Tony. I promise I stay home. I no gamble. I promise!"

For an hour, the argument went back and forth, and always ended where it started. He was finished.

I felt myself in a state of nervous exhaustion. Obviously,

the woman was a neurotic, would-be mother who needed psychiatric help. In her extreme state of frustration, gambling had become a consuming urge. It was an escape for her. She could lose herself completely and black out her troubled thoughts until she was no longer aware of them.

He needed assistance, too, in understanding the nature of his wife's trouble. With the right counseling, he might realize in time that it was not malice that motivated her, but that she was mentally ill. If she had had tuberculosis, or polio, or a broken leg, he would have understood, but he was like many who fail to recognize mental illness when the person continues to possess the outward appearance of physical health.

When I was alone with him, I pointed out that when people are sick, they go to a doctor, and when a marriage is sick, they should seek the same high level of professional help. It sounded like nonsense to him. He was a practical man. If he could see something, or feel it, or taste it, he could understand it. But he finally agreed.

In the Reconciliation Agreement, Gina promised to quit gambling and to stop frequenting gambling places and bars. This was the kind of promise a psychologist might challenge as being impossible of fulfillment, since her gambling had become a compulsion—that is, an act not subject to willful control. Whatever her intentions, she would have little check on herself until she had undergone psychotherapy and a personality change. Still, the Reconciliation Agreement might restrain her from further gambling until such time as the psychological treatment could take effect.

At my suggestion, Gina Arena agreed to a month's separation. My reasoning was this: her fear of losing her husband forever might do more to keep her out of the casinos than anything else. A separation would intensify her desire to win him back.

This was a solution tailored for Gina and Antonio Arena. With some couples, a separation would have aggravated the situation and perhaps hastened divorce. No matter what the problem, there can be no common solution. Each case calls for individual study, for the simple reason that we are all individuals with our own individual problems.

Before leaving, they chose a counseling service with a staff that included a psychologist, a psychiatrist, a physician, and a social worker. Gina Arena would need all four, I thought, and it would be a rugged road she and her Tony would travel for possibly the next twelve to eighteen months.

They were quiet as they left. It was the quiet of suddenly realizing what they were up against, and of wondering—wondering if they could ever return to those twenty-seven years they had known. I was quiet myself, for the same reason.

Gambling wrecks more homes than most of us realize. The gambler doesn't advertise himself as blatantly as the heavy drinker. Yet the fellow who squanders his week's salary with regularity at the race track or in a poker session is driven by the same sort of compulsion.

Many reasons compel a man or woman to gamble. As with Gina Arena, escape is one of them. Because of pressures in their lives, many seek to withdraw as completely as possible from the world, to build air castles, to fall back into the same kind of daydreams they had as children. For them, gambling becomes a narcotic.

Like so many things in this world, the need for escape is good when not carried to excess. We all need it. Most of us find it in such ways as fishing or gardening week ends, or in novels or television. It provides a change from our routine, but if we are too much wracked by worries, we often seek escapes that will absorb us completely, that will black out all reality. Hence, we may turn to gambling or drinking or sex.

Closely related is the power motive. I remember a physician who was earning $20,000 a year and gambling away twice that. As we talked, it developed that his wife was a brilliant person, far more brilliant than he, and she was not above letting him know it. At home, he was reduced to the irreducible minimum, but at the roulette table he became in his mind a very clever man, debonair, witty, and astute.

But there are other reasons for gambling besides escape and a hunger for importance and power. With many, gambling satisfies a need for excitement and adventure. Strangely, a man works hard for security, for a home and savings in the bank and good health, and yet he longs at times for insecurity. Nature has given us bipolar needs—a need to balance one need against another. After a long rest, we seek activity. When we are hungry, we eat. When we have eaten, nothing in the way of food can tempt us. And it's the same with security. Once we have a certain degree of it, we feel a need to take chances. Some find this need for risk in the stock market, in exploring remote corners of the world, in building a house or redecorating one, in ice skating or skiing, and in a thousand other pursuits where an element of chance plays a part. But when this need becomes compulsive, then the result may be a neurotic gambler.

Compulsive gambling, like any other neurotic activity,

has certain characteristics. First, the person doesn't just "want" to gamble, he is "driven" to it. As one psychiatrist puts it, when we are driven, we are not just acting spontaneously, but rather we are driven with an utter disregard for our best interests. Furthermore, the neurotic gambler's hunger is insatiable. He never feels he has won enough.

One wife helped her husband overcome his compulsion by remembering that when he was young he liked mountain climbing. She interested him in it again, and instead of going to the races Saturdays, they headed for the Sierras. While such a remedy was far too simple for most cases, we did find that substitution of a hobby or sport often helped.

At one time or another, the gambling temptation comes to most of us. My colleague, Dr. Shostrom, explains that it conquers some of us because we fail to realize its power.

"But if we can understand and deal with its power," he said, "we need not fall prey to it. The power of gambling comes because it offers satisfaction of two tremendous drives: the desire for almighty power and the wish for the easy way. These desires are easily seen in dice playing. The gambler *knows* the percentages are against him, but he feels he has a God-like power over the dice. He actually 'commands' the dice, and when he wins, this is proof of his power. He is sometimes referred to as a 'pathological optimist.' "

Dr. Shostrom maintains that the neurotic gambler must first admit his false picture of himself and recognize his human limitations. "He must learn to face life directly and simply. He must learn to trust himself and his abilities to conquer life directly instead of trying to do it in a primitive and magical way."

What happened with Gina Arena? Occasionally, we had reports. The two went back together at the end of the month's separation. She told her counselor that during that month she fought with herself every waking moment. Once she left the house and headed for a gambling place, but at the very door turned away, and most of the night walked the streets. In time, Antonio helped her. He was an intelligent man, and from the psychologist he learned more about his wife than he had in the twenty-seven years of their marriage. At his suggestion, they moved to a suburban home, as far from temptation as possible. He got her interested, too, in a hospital for handicapped children, and she spent two days a week there as a Gray Lady. She didn't have time to get bored!

About a year later, he stopped by. They were going on a visit to Italy, he said, to a little hill town south of Naples where some of her folks lived.

He still didn't think much of psychology. "They all crazy over there," he said, referring to the counseling agency. "Nothing but bosh. Gina and me, we get everything fixed up in spite of them."

He grinned, pumped my hand, and left. Alone, propping my feet on the desk, I grinned, too.

chapter thirteen

Turning the Corner

Alcoholism is now regarded by competent medical authorities as a disease. The old idea that the alcoholic was just a weak-willed or bad person has been displaced by the realization that such a person is sick.

—RECONCILIATION AGREEMENT

The National Committee for the Prevention of Alcoholism asked me a couple of years ago to prepare a paper on the part that alcohol plays in the divorce picture. In preparation I made a study of our files and found that in one hundred cases, ten petitioners admitted the excessive use of alcohol by "self" and ten more said it had been used excessively by "spouse." Thus, in twenty out of one hundred cases, the parties themselves admitted alcohol was a problem in the marriage.

In many other instances, we found the trouble present but not acknowledged by either of the parties. The composite opinion of our staff was that in about 50 per cent of the cases heard, excessive drinking was a major factor in the disruption of the home. We realized, of course, that alcoholism is often a symptom of an underlying personality defect and that in homes where other causes had led to tensions, one of the marriage partners may have turned to heavy drinking as an escape. Such drinking then becomes a contributing factor rather than the principal one.

Many couples who came before us were like Carol and Jim Morrow, good, forthright, sensitive people, very much in love but caught up in a nightmare from which there seemed no awakening. So emotionally disturbed she could scarcely get the words out, Carol told me about the day she decided to seek a divorce, despite her love for Jim and an almost fanatical desire to keep her family intact.

It was a Monday morning, she said, and for the third straight time she got a different result when she added the long column of figures. At last she shoved the adding machine aside. She just had to know or she would never get anything accomplished on her monthly report for the law firm of Burns, Brown, Simmons, and Baker.

She had told herself a hundred times that morning that this time it would be different. Jim would keep his promise. He understood fully the effect his conduct was having upon Nancy, their eight-year-old. Phoning him now would only indicate that she doubted him. She kept telling herself this even as she dialed their home number. At the fourth ring she felt a sinking sensation. Now she must hang on. She must know. Finally there was a click and the phone ceased ringing. A long pause followed, then an unsteady, thick-tongued voice saying, "H'llo."

So bitter was her disappointment that words came hard. "Jim, you stay where you are. I'm coming right home." She added quickly, "Don't you dare leave."

When she turned into the driveway, she saw that his car was gone from the garage. Frantic, she headed for the neighborhood bars. He had had an accident the last time he'd driven while drinking, and the court had threatened him with a jail term.

At last, after checking all his known haunts in vain, she

unburdened herself to Sergeant Jerry Monohan, a friend since high school days.

"I've covered all the bars on Willow Street," she told him, "and I just don't know what to do."

"I'll see if I can find him, Carol," Jerry said. "I'm sorry to hear he's off the wagon. I sort of thought that last time would cure him once and for all."

Back at the office the hours dragged tediously. The story she thought up on the way home failed to convince Nancy. The big brown eyes saw right through her. "Daddy's drinking again, isn't he, Mommy?"

The usual long vigil began. At about two in the morning, Carol heard the child's door open. She called gently, "Nan, is that you?" She heard the rush of small feet down the hall and felt the cold arms flung around her. Tears flowed freely. This was the way it had been for months. A half-hour later, the child succumbed to a troubled sleep. Carol cat-napped the rest of the night.

All the next day passed without word, and shortly after midnight Sergeant Monahan brought Jim home. He had found him at a bar about 5 miles out on the highway. "I left him in the car so Nancy wouldn't see him."

But the child was standing in the hallway, her robe clutched tightly about her throat. "Is Daddy all right?"

Carol answered, "Yes, Nan. Now back to your room." Her voice had a note of hardness. "I'll help you bring him in, Jerry. But it's for the last time. I can't take it."

Jim Morrow sat across the desk from me, a big, robust fellow who fumbled constantly with his fingers. He had been cold sober for a month. The threatened loss of his wife and family had hit him hard.

"You see, Judge," he said, "I'm not an alcoholic. I know

my wife thinks I am and I guess I've acted the part a few times, but I ask you, if I was an alcoholic, could I stay away from it for a whole month?"

From his record, I knew he was only kidding himself. I wondered if I could jolt him out of his complacency. "Jim, I'll tell you what let's do. Here's a list of questions I want you to answer for me, frankly and truthfully. Just call them the way you see them."

He went down the list. The first few questions he checked off quite rapidly. They read:

	Yes	*No*
Do you lose time from work due to drinking?		
Is drinking making your home life unhappy?		
Do you drink because you are shy with other people?		
Is drinking affecting your reputation?		
Have you gotten into financial difficulties as a result of drinking?		

By the time he was down to the eighth question, he had slowed up noticeably. By the twentieth, he was struggling with each answer.

"That's the best I can do with it, Judge," he said.

"The list you've just checked, Jim, is a group of twenty questions used by Johns Hopkins University Hospital, Baltimore, Maryland, to aid them in determining whether a patient is an alcoholic. They believe that if you answer yes to any one question you may be an alcoholic. If you answer yes to any two, then the odds are that you are an alcoholic. If you answered yes to three or more, it stamps you as an alcoholic."

His whole body sagged. He had answered yes to eleven questions.

Slowly, I continued, "As long as you believe you can lick this problem by yourself, no one can do much for you. When you realize you need help, then there's hope for you. At such a time, Alcoholics Anonymous could do wonders for you. But not so long as you keep saying to yourself, 'I can take a drink or leave it alone.' "

The room lay breathless while I gave him a moment for thought. "In your present frame of mind, I can *ask* your wife to take you back, but I must inform her that you will probably fall time and time again. It'll be up to her to make the decision."

"Tell her I'll do anything, anything she wants," he said in desperation as he left the room.

"Mrs. Morrow," I said to her after we were alone, "you're a sensible person, and you're entitled to know exactly what you're facing."

"There's no hope for him, is there?" The words came hard, words drawn from many sleepless nights.

I said, "He needs you badly, more than you'll ever know. The fact is, Carol, your husband is a very sick person."

She was listening attentively, but I couldn't tell how she was taking it. I continued, "You will have to stop lying for him, stop covering up for him, and have Nancy do the same. You'll have to treat him both publicly and privately for exactly what he is, a sick person."

Her face was grave. "Just this change of attitude might have a very beneficial effect upon your husband. In saying this, I don't want you to count on such treatment curing him, for the cure rests almost entirely within his hands." I added, "If we can interest him in joining Alcoholics Anonymous, you should attend, too, in order to learn the role the wife of an alcoholic must play."

She nodded. She was seeing a new horizon and weighing her part in it.

I continued, "The only requirement for membership is an honest desire to stop drinking. It must not be just lip service, as I fear Jim is now giving us. The organization has no dues or fees. It is not allied with any denomination. It is simply a fellowship of men and women who share their experience, strength, and hope with each other, that they may solve their common problem."

Carol had been following my words closely. "I've been so ashamed of Jim," she said. "So ashamed for his sake as well as for Nan's and mine, and I've covered up for him so long."

She paused deep in thought, trying to view Nancy and herself not as Jim's private policemen but as the understanding daughter and wife of a very sick man. "Whenever I've found liquor in the house, I've always poured it down the sink. What do I do now?"

"Just explain to Jim that he needn't hide it any more. Establish a liquor cabinet and let him keep it there. Tell him if he feels compelled to drink, you wish he would do so at home. That way, you won't worry about accidents."

"Poor Jim," she said. "It'll surely be a switch for him, having his wife tell him he can take a drink whenever he wants to."

She mustered a faint smile. The tension was broken.

"He'll continue to hate himself for drinking," I said, "and your kindness and understanding will make the pain even worse. However, it's his battle. Only he can win it, and he has to want to do it, not for your sake or Nancy's or anyone else's, but because *he* wants to do it for his own sake."

We talked further about AA. "When Jim finally drinks to the point where he realizes he can't lick the problem alone, where he has to have help to survive, the AA will suggest that he let someone else guide his life, someone who has the power to help him. He will be told to put his body and soul in the hands of God and to ask His help for the next ten minutes. If he adopts the suggestion, he will have turned the corner. From then on, he will live from one ten-minute period to the next. The past will be unimportant. Only the next ten minutes will count. He will slip occasionally but the slips will be farther apart. He will have the love of his daughter and wife to help sustain him. He will never be truly 'cured.' No alcoholic ever is. But he will be able to live a happy, useful life."

I paused a moment. "One more thought before we have Jim come back. When he has turned the corner and looks back over his past life, he will be filled with self-condemnation. Even though God and his family have forgiven him, he'll find it hard to forgive himself. You will have to remind him often that God attaches but one condition to His forgiveness, that we strive to sin no more."

Jim had sat in the reception room an hour, a long time for a man to think. I'm sure his entire life had swept before him, and he had appraised it as one standing at a distance. It must have been an honest, and hence, brutal appraisal. He had scarcely sat down, he said, when he had read that part of the Reconciliation Agreement regarding drinking, and was willing to sign.

These were the two pertinent paragraphs he promised to abide by:

__Husband__ agrees not to partake of any alcoholic beverages of any description in any cocktail bar, beer parlor, or similar establishment, and further agrees not to enter or remain in any such establishment.

__Husband__ agrees to inquire into the organization Alcoholics Anonymous by going in person to the central office in Los Angeles.

The agreement did not *prohibit* his drinking. This would have been useless in his case.

A few days later he contacted AA, and he and Carol started attending meetings of a unit composed of persons in the same age and economic bracket. He was given the phone number of a member to call at any hour of the day or night when he felt he needed help. No one lectured him. It was confusing to Jim, this change in attitude, and he started thinking. Outwardly, at least, he quit blaming others for his troubles, and considered them of his own making.

Meanwhile, the wives of several active AA members were helping Carol. Little by little, she and Nancy succeeded in their new roles. "Jim is sick, very sick, he needs our help, our understanding, our prayers," Carol would repeat. Before long, the neighbors who used to whisper over the back fence were finding ways in which they, too, could help.

Time passed. Jim lost his job through his many unauthorized leaves of absence. He looked much worse physically. He was thin and worried. He rarely left the house evenings.

One night the man from AA got a phone call. "Bert, this is Jim. You know, Jim Morrow. Please come over. I'm dying, I need help, I can't live any more. Please, Bert, I've been going through hell. There are things crawling on the walls. Carol isn't home. Bert, honest, I'm losing my mind. . . ."

Bert left the dinner party at his home without even waiting to say good-by. He had needed help once himself, and badly.

When he opened the door to Jim's bedroom, the stale smoke of cigarettes and liquor floated out to engulf him. Through the fog, a welcome sight greeted his eyes. Jim had slipped out of bed to his knees and was murmuring, "Please, God, please. . . ."

Jim had turned the corner.

As we went along, we found that for some who drink too much, the problem was one of moderation in drinking. They were not yet alcoholics. But their drinking to excess on occasions threatened their marriages. For them we wrote the following:

> _______ agrees not to partake of any alcoholic beverages except _______ and only in the family domicile, or on social occasions when spouse is present.

We realized that in this matter of moderation we ran counter to the teaching of complete abstinence by many faiths. This whole problem of drinking, of course, is one that mankind has failed to solve, probably because as individuals each of us has strong convictions and these often conflict with those of our neighbor. But frequently the Court could obtain a pledge of moderation when the party would never have agreed to total abstinence. If such a course could rescue a marriage, we felt it was wise to recommend it.

In some instances, however, it was obvious that complete abstinence was the only solution. If a person's record indicated that he could not take a first drink any time or any where without losing control, the Court would suggest that this sentence be included in the Agreement:

> ________ agrees not to partake of any alcoholic beverages of any kind.

In time we discovered that the "pay-day drinker" constituted a major problem. This is the fellow who stops on pay day to take a few drinks to start the week end right, and eventually reaches home late Sunday night, barely in time to sober up and report back on the job Monday morning. Most of the pay check never reaches home. We developed the following paragraph for such cases:

> Husband agrees to authorize and request his employer in writing to mail his pay check to the family address where the parties can jointly arrange for its deposit in the family bank account. . . .

Generally, we referred persons in need of further help to AA, and sometimes in addition to other agencies that cooperated with the courts. Among these were the state clinics. In California, as elsewhere, the State Alcoholic Rehabilitation Commission maintains clinics in most of the larger communities. Aside from providing patients with medical treatment, some of the centers number a psychologist, a psychiatrist, and a clergyman on their staffs. This many-sided team approach has proved exceptionally effective, even with skid row habitués who once were considered virtually hopeless.

Private groups, too, have been active. In some cities, they have taken over entire hotels which serve only alcoholics. In Los Angeles, the Mary-Lind Foundation, known also as the 512 Fellowship, operating three hotels with rooms for 211 guests, offers meals, counseling, group therapy, referrals to physicians and psychiatrists, meditation rooms, social activities, and most important of all, association with others who themselves have struggled with alcoholism.

Most of the Court's alcoholism cases fell into three categories: (1) The drinker like Jim Morrow who begins in a moderate way, the "controlled" imbiber whose desire for liquor slips up on him until it completely overwhelms him, (2) the man or woman who starts in the teens and drinks more with each year, and (3) the individual who turns to liquor as a means of relief from a serious problem.

Many "lone wolves" fall into the second category. They are the ones who lack friends, who don't have anyone they may confide in. Even when they marry, they live much to themselves. Here, lifted verbatim from a court counselor's report, is the case of a lone wolf:

> The husband had been married and divorced once before. He had been an only child whose parents had died and he had been reared by relatives. An attack of polio had left him with a shriveled left arm and a slight limp. The couple had two children.
>
> The wife said she felt bitter about liquor by reason of an alcoholic father, and as a result her husband would leave home to drink, sometimes disappearing for several days. She felt he had an inferiority complex and could not stand any strain at work or at home. She acknowledged she nagged him about it.
>
> The husband said he had never confided in his wife, nor for that matter, ever had had anyone with whom he felt free to share his troubles.
>
> By administering the Johns Hopkins test, counselor in-

dicated to the husband that he was showing signs of approaching alcoholism.

Counselor explained that just as the husband feels he needs to drink to release his tensions, his leaving home to do so builds up tensions in his wife. In talking to the two together, he discovered they could afford to get a baby sitter and go out upon occasion. The wife agreed to relax her views on drinking, and to permit the husband to do his beer drinking at home. He agreed to limit the quantity and both admitted that some continuing counseling would be helpful.

One salient point, common to many cases stemming from acute alcoholism, stands out in this report. The husband, unlike Jim Morrow, was unable to discuss his troubles with his wife or anyone else. Consequently, his road might be rougher than Morrow's. No human being was ever made to live unto himself, to fight all his struggles alone. Most of us, often unconsciously, turn to our wives or husbands for aid, or our parents, or a close friend. If our marriage is happy, our mates should provide this sounding board, since marriage should include full communication with each other.

Suddenly it broke on me that here was one of the "sailing directions" for a good marriage that I was collecting, and I had almost forgotten to jot it down. *No human being was ever made to live unto himself*, I wrote on a memo sheet, tossed it in the bottom desk drawer, and toed the drawer shut.

My associate, Dr. Shostrom, pointed out one day that the motives for alcoholism are complex and there are no simple reasons for this sickness.

"Certain patterns, however, seem clear," he said. "Many alcoholics have a strong craving for loving maternal care.

They are like a child who has not matured. The child wants his mother to love him for himself, no matter how he behaves. The alcoholic hungers for this type of mother love. But most of us give him father love. 'I will love you only if you do not drink—if you live up to my expectations.'

"In many alcoholics," Dr. Shostrom continued, "there is also a very strong aggressive need, often repressed (unintentionally forgotten) or suppressed (intentionally forgotten). Alcohol does a lot for both needs. It allows the alcoholic to act as aggressive as he feels without feeling responsible. It permits him to be dependent and childlike, also without having to recognize this need.

"The treatment of alcoholics is often difficult because alcohol is so available and so attractive as an easy solution to life's problems. Alcoholics cannot admit that they have strong dependency and aggressive needs. Also, many alcoholics refuse to accept the fact that total abstinence is the best solution. Specialists in this field may use certain drugs to reduce the craving. But this often is not enough. Psychotherapy, combined with techniques of support, such as Alcoholics Anonymous, is usually the most successful."

Individuals who drink to escape the memory of some early catastrophe are among the most tragic cases. These are the people who normally never would have drunk at all, the ones about whom the neighbors say, "She's such a sweet person. How in the world *could* she?"

That was what the friends of Debbie Patterson must have said. She was old far beyond her thirty years. But it was not entirely liquor that had aged her. The cause was rooted in the distant past, when she was Debbie Owens and dating Bill Patterson.

They had met on a blind date and had been instantly attracted to each other. He was just getting started as a salesman for a wholesale hardware company, and she was a secretary with an airplane parts concern a couple blocks away. He had no close family; and she, only a father who was domineering and tyrannical. So she and Bill became inseparable. He drove her to work mornings, called for her evenings, and took her to movies and dances.

She told her story with the greatest reluctance, beginning with the evening they entered what looked like a store building, and pushed through a door on the second floor. The letters on the door read: "Dr. Norris Spolling—Industrial Accident Cases." They walked into a cheerless, once-white reception room. A blowzy, fortyish woman with hat and coat on sat at a small desk.

"Hi, I'm Min, the Doc's nurse. Guess you're the two the Doc's expecting. I won't ask your names—but for the same reason I'll ask for the money."

The combination of office and "nurse" was almost too much for Debbie. She pulled her coat closer and turned to Bill. He was anxious to get it over with, though his hands shook as he handed the buxom, part-time blonde $300 in bills. They heard a door in the back open and close.

"That's the Doc now," the blonde said. "Come on, sweetheart, the Doc doesn't like to be kept waiting."

When Debbie hesitated, the nurse took her arm and half pushed her into the room, saying to Bill, "If we need your help, we'll holler." Bill touched her hand, and Debbie wanted to grab and hold it, but didn't.

The office contained only a surgical table. "Here's a robe to put on."

"You mean I'm to undress right here?"

The nurse laughed. "There ain't no other place unless you'd druther do it where your boy friend is."

"Maybe I'd better talk to the doctor first," Debbie said. "I—I don't feel very well. Would you call Dr. Spolling?"

"Dr. Spolling? Oh, Doc Spolling's just here days. The other Doc, he don't like us to give out his name. Touchy about it, he is. But you just lie down here. Me and him will have you fixed up in no time."

A gruff voice called out from the back. "If you're ready, fix the lights." Min turned the big light on over the table. Debbie was aware of a figure in a short white coat walking in. In the reception room outside, Bill heard her crying, and the Doc saying, "Keep her quiet. How do you expect me to work?" Shortly afterwards, Min called him in to help hold Debbie down while the doctor administered an anesthetic.

After the doctor finished and was gone, Bill waited an hour before they could arouse Debbie. "What'll I do if she needs a doctor?" he asked.

"Just call her regular one. But for hell's sake, don't try and contact this doc. He's got nothing more to do with it."

Peritonitis set in, and by the end of the week, Debbie lay dangerously ill in the county hospital. A young intern diagnosed her trouble, and in due time a district attorney's investigator and one from the state medical board called to take a statement. They wanted to know why she had had the abortion, and it was difficult explaining about her father, how she had feared him since she could remember, and loved him, too; how he would have beaten her if he'd found out, how she wanted only one thing at the time, to rid herself of her pregnancy so her father would never know. Bill had readily agreed. He wanted to save some money before marrying. His folks, he said, had begun life with nothing, and suffered many hardships.

Her father, of course, knew the truth now. He visited her only once at the hospital to inform her he never wanted to see her again.

Bill came every morning and evening, and they planned their marriage for the time when she was well again, but it was a long and painful year before the worst of the ill effects were over. Their marriage brought her her first happiness in a long time, but it was dimmed by the knowledge, imparted to her when she left the hospital, that she never would be able to have a child. She realized how much better it would have been if they had slipped away when she discovered she was pregnant, and been married, and had their baby.

An ambitious, driving fellow, Bill forged his way to the top of the wholesale hardware company. As he climbed each rung on the ladder, his self-esteem grew, and he became more voluble and more of an extrovert. On the other hand, Debbie withdrew more and more. Life meant nothing, she was accomplishing nothing, and the thought gnawed at her that she could never have a child. Once she suggested they adopt a little girl, but Bill was dead set against it. "I'm not having any other man's kid," he said.

It was several years after her marriage before she took her first drink. After that, she was never a day without the bolstering effect alcohol gave her.

The situation worsened month by month. Bill went to the stores in the neighborhood and begged, and then threatened, them not to sell her liquor. He got rid of the second car at the time of her first drunk-driving arrest. He took every step he could to help her in a purely mechanistic way. But he never thought to consult their doctor or pastor or to seek psychiatric treatment. It never occurred to him that unconsciously she still carried the guilt of her pregnancy and the abortion.

Finally, he sold their house and moved to a suburb where she would be a mile from the nearest store. Still he would return home to find her in a half stupor. Each week she had a new place to hide the bottles—in the washing machine, bathroom, water tank, stove, shrubbery, incinerator, furnace. Her ingenuity was boundless. It was equally good for obtaining a supply. He would miss a table radio, his cuff links, a camera, pieces of silverware. They went one by one to door-to-door salesmen, milkmen, bill collectors, anyone she could wheedle into getting her the "wine tonic" she said her doctor had prescribed and which her cruel husband refused to buy.

Finally, he brought home a housekeeper. At this point, Debbie gave up completely. Seeing the other woman moving competently about doing the household chores made her sense her own inadequacies all the more.

One day she talked a tradesman into driving her to the city. She entered the nearest bar, painfully sober. Once accustomed to the dim light, she noticed a man seated at a nearby table with his head in his arms.

She ordered a drink, "Straight and double," and sat looking at it for the longest time. A sudden, deep sob shifted her attention from the drink to the man at the table. He wasn't blissfully drunk as she had imagined. He was crying. Going to the table, she gently placed her hand on the man's shoulder. "Is there anything I can do?"

That was the way it started. It ended a week later when the police found them in his apartment, both dead drunk. She was never to remember what happened that week. It was as lost as though she had never lived it.

The doctors advised a sanitarium, and Bill placed her in one. A month later, the man called at the sanitarium and said he was her brother. When the nurse had gone, Debbie said, "How could you come here after all the trouble you've caused me?" She started to cry, but subsided when he offered her the flask. They slipped out to his car and sat for a time talking. He depended on her, he said. Would she help him?

Debbie thought to herself, "He is the only person on earth whom I can do anything for. . . ."

When the police picked them up again, it was the end for Bill, who filed suit for divorce. A few days later, she was committed to a state institution for ninety days as a chronic alcoholic.

They came in together, the quiet girl afraid to speak, and the father stern and unbending. It was he, he explained, who insisted, after Debbie's release from the state institution, that she file a petition in the Conciliation Court. Bill had ruined his daughter, and now Bill could take care of her. She was a sinful woman and he wanted no part of her. I let him talk, since it gave me an opportunity to study the girl who sat looking at her hands in her lap.

As soon as her father left, she looked up at me, made a brave start, and then said, "It's no use, Judge. Bill's given up on me—and I don't blame him."

"Tell me about Bill," I said.

When she had finished, she sat very still, the pinched face colorless behind the lipstick and make-up. Once there had been tears, but now even those afforded no relief. She had lost all confidence in herself and could think of no reason for living.

She had one parting request. Would I tell Bill how sorry

she was that she had brought him into court? Then she smiled wanly and left.

That noon I ate without knowing what I was eating, and then walked the hot pavement. People milled past me but I didn't see them. Someone said hello and I answered by rote. Lights changed at crossings, and I went with the crowd. If I could find something, some one word that would reawaken a memory in her husband, that would call up a touch of the love he had had for her, if I could make him see that she was a sick person, perhaps picture the life together they might share when she was well again. One thing I must not mention—her premarital pregnancy and abortion. Bill might think he was being pushed into a corner.

Within seconds after he walked in, I knew he wasn't the man she had described. She had told me about a memory—and the memory was dead. Bill was confident, sure of himself, determined—and cold.

Scarcely had I begun when he interrupted. "Judge, I'm always for putting the cards on the table."

I nodded, and he continued, "She was O.K. when I married her and I guess no guy could've loved anybody more. But let's face it. She's a lush and a tramp. I've done everything I could for her, and it's no dice. You can ask her friends, the neighbors, anybody. She isn't going to change—and I'm not going through life living with a drunk."

I felt the anger rising. "Surely you realize you have to assume some responsibility. . . ." Before the words were out, I wanted to call them back.

He smiled. "You mean the abortion?" "Well, let me tell you, it was as much her idea as mine—and to put it bluntly, she got pregnant the same way." He shrugged. "That all happened years ago. What's that got to do with it now?"

"It's got a lot to do with it," I said firmly. "She's been carrying the guilt with her all these years. . . ."

"Maybe so. But nobody can expect me to stay with her when she runs away with a barfly."

"If both of you would get some counseling. . . ."

"She's sick—not me."

Nothing I could say would change him, and he walked out on me shortly afterwards. When he had gone, I laid my head on my arms, sick at my stomach. I had felt so confident I could see a road back for them, a tortuous one but a road nonetheless. Maybe if I had taken another approach. . . .

Ten days later, when Debbie received notice of the court hearing on the divorce action, she fell apart again and was recommitted to the hospital. Her father told me about it, and it was all I could do to be civil to him.

Debbie's fate now rested with God, and I asked Him to take over.

chapter fourteen

In the Image and Likeness

As individuals, men and women have been endowed by God with an equality in dignity and potential....

—RECONCILIATION AGREEMENT

My father was a big, rugged Irishman with a tremendous zest for living. A land surveyor in Western Canada in his early years, he became active in government and politics. He was the most generous person I have ever known, and quick to shoulder the burdens of all who came his way. We agreed, my brother and I, that he was the best father in the whole wide world.

Only in one way did he ever distress me. He possessed a difficult temper. Although we were quite young when he died, I can still remember how mother and we would tiptoe around the house when he was angry about something, and how in my childhood memories of him, I was always trying to justify or excuse this one great weakness. He was my ideal, and I didn't want to believe he had any faults. But the memory of his temper preyed on me, and I was worried as only a child can be.

Then one Sunday years later I heard a sermon that helped me understand him. The pastor said, "A bad temper often contributes to unrest in a home. If the members of the family hope to minimize its effects, they must first understand its nature. Generally speaking, you are born with a good or bad temper. It is something like the color of your skin, or hair, or eyes, or an aptitude for music. It's not your fault that you are color blind, or have no ear for music, or suffer a short temper."

Now I understood. My father had been born with his bad temper. He had been a handicapped person. He should have had our understanding and help in coping with it.

I was thinking about this as the clerk ushered in the Rineharts, the last couple on the calendar for the day. They were an interesting pair, a strange study in contrasts. Rudy Rinehart was a medical laboratory technician, engaged in an exacting occupation which took its daily toll of physical and nervous energy. He was extremely jittery, shifting constantly in the chair.

She was one of those sweet, almost angelic women. She was very calm—probably maddeningly so at times to this man who was as jumpy as a "souped-up" car. The records showed they had a girl of five, a boy nine; that they had been separated only three weeks; and that he had taken a room in a cheap hotel. He had filed the petition for conciliation.

As their story unfolded piecemeal, it developed that she had a tendency to unload the trials of her day on her husband at dinner each night when he was exhausted. He simply sat until he reached the point of combustion, and then exploded, often over some very trivial matter.

To complicate matters, her mother lived next door and had the unfortunate custom of running in whenever the notion struck her. Sometimes this happened when Rudy Rinehart was blowing his top, as he worded it.

Now, angry words between a husband and wife always assume undue proportions when they are overheard by an in-law. The result was that he would leave home, head for the nearest bar, and drink until stupor dulled the pains in his ulcerated stomach and his soul. He would then stagger home, open the garage door, and sleep in the back seat of the car. He was no alcoholic, however, and never drank except after giving vent to his fierce temper.

When alone with me, his wife said, "I don't want you to get the idea he isn't a good man, Judge. But how can the Court expect me to put up with someone who flies into a rage on the slightest excuse? What kind of an example is that for our little boy and girl?"

She was so dead set against reconciliation that I could see little hope. On the other hand, he was anxious to return home. "I've been doing a lot of thinking, Judge, and I talked to our minister about this and believe I can lick it. I don't know what gets into me. She gets to harping on something, and I see red and blow up."

In talking with her, I attempted to explain the nature of temper. "Your husband's a handicapped person, Mrs. Rinehart. That doesn't excuse him from doing his best to control his temper, but the others in the family have a grave responsibility, too." If her husband were blind, I said, she wouldn't place furniture where he might stumble over it. The same should be true with his temper. She should do everything possible to avoid irritating him.

The finger of blame had never been pointed at her before. Both she and her mother had been self-righteous about the situation. It was all Rudy's fault.

We talked along easily. I pointed out that each of us has to learn to cope with temper in some fashion. We can seek to modify it, but we cannot basically change it. Instead, we should try, perhaps through counseling, to help her husband understand his feelings—that is, to understand why he gets angry. If he knows why, he may be able to exert some control. And if she understands the basic causes, then she may avoid saying or doing the things that act as a trigger in setting him off.

"On the other hand, there's a limit to what therapy can do. Your husband is in his forties. And a person is like a plastic ball. When you're young, you are more soft and pliable. But as you get older, the bounce wears out of the ball. We all have to accept a certain amount of crystallization. At his age, it may prove more difficult for him to modify his temper than if he were younger."

It seemed I was offering her little hope, except the hope of understanding, and this she grasped quickly. But the profanity he had used on her was hard to forgive. She refused to resume living with him but agreed he might come in for dinner. "It'll be good for the children," she said.

Since dinnertime seemed the zero hour for them, I suggested they avoid discussing any unpleasant subject. Only a couple of weeks before, we had drawn up a section concerning mealtimes, since so many couples take this occasion to iron out their differences. As any physician could tell them, it is the worst possible time. Almost invariably, both are tired from the day and need a surcease from problems. The nourishment of food will strengthen them and give them a far better chance for talking out their difficulties later in the evening, perhaps after they have had an hour or so of rest. Parts of this section, I read to the Rineharts:

> Mealtimes should be times of great peace and calmness.... Some people with a background of religious training have found that the pausing of the family at the start of each meal for the invoking of God's blessing serves as a great deterrent to discord....

Since they were devout people, both agreed to ask God's blessing before dinner. But they still refused to sign the Agreement. They promised, though, to return in three weeks.

Long after they were gone, I sat lost in thought. Even with all our research studies, man knows so little about himself, not nearly as much as he does about molecules. He knows so little about such basic personality traits as temper, the extent to which they are hereditary, and the degree to which they may be influenced by training. If we grow up around parents, for example, who burst into rages, we become "infected" and tend to solve our own dilemmas the same way. Thus a small boy at play will burst into an uncontrolled paroxysm of rage, using the same words he heard his father shout at the breakfast table that morning. Even though we may be born with a temper, therefore, we may by training bring it partly under control.

While the room grew dim, I thought of a close friend of years past, a man with uncontrollable anger, who one day drew himself up short and told himself that with God's help he was going to conquer his temper. He did considerable praying about it, he told me later, and with God's help and his own will power he did seem to master it. He became one of the most even-dispositioned individuals I have ever known. So there may be exceptions to the accepted notion that a man may modify his temper only to a certain extent.

I thought, too, of a young woman who had sat before me only the day before. With some pride, she acknowledged that she often screamed at her husband and sometimes threw things. Unhappily for him, she was a ceramic artist. As a creative individual, she explained, she had "temperament," and she considered it the inalienable right of creative people to indulge in outbursts. She was a "primitive," she told me, giving vent to any fancy that struck her. She had been indulged in this notion by her parents and expected her husband to do likewise. If he really loved her, wouldn't he accept these outbursts as the natural expressions of a creative soul?

Well, she almost stopped me, to be frank. I was sure her husband wouldn't go for the handicapped routine. She was handicapped, certainly, but not in the usual sense. She exemplified a type, not too common, that indulges in anger as something to be enjoyed. She would never seek to modify her temper. When I suggested counseling, she felt highly insulted. I thought of suggesting to her husband that he, too, go "primitive" and turn her over his knee, but a close appraisal of him indicated that he'd muff the job. My father had stopped my promising career of self-induced "tantrums" in one short lesson in this way.

The Rineharts returned three weeks later, as comfortable with each other as two old shoes. They admitted they had had one violent quarrel. They were both a little proud that it hadn't taken place at dinner. Both wanted to sign copies of the Reconciliation Agreement.

One quarrel in three weeks, I told them, was a good start. "We all have to blow our tops once in a while—and then kiss and make up."

I added a thought that had been recurring more and more, "A seemingly happy family is not always a happy one. Sometimes we have to be unhappy to find happiness. It's a lot better to battle over something that's troubling us than to sulk over it. And the making up often brings us closer together than we've ever been. This business of forgiving and being forgiven can help a marriage grow."

Temper may, of course, take a far more violent turn than it did with the Rineharts. In numerous divorce actions, the wife would charge that her husband beat her. As a divorce court judge, I was sickened as I heard these accounts. How could anyone treat another human being so cruelly, especially one they had once professed to love?

In the Conciliation Court, we termed these cases "Offenses against Human Dignity." Dignity of human beings is what Jesus taught and what mankind has lived by and for ever since. It is the heart of all therapy, the heart of all sound thinking. It is the respect we have for another individual, our ability to see that person as having God-likeness in him.

This dignity—the dignity of the girl he married, the mother of his four children—had been forgotten completely by a husky fellow who came before the Court one day. Their story was this: Their first five years of marriage had run along smoothly. Then he formed the habit of going out nights with his friends and drinking heavily. By way of retaliation, she went to dances and parties with her girl friends, and also drank, though not to excess. The situation was fraught with charges and recriminations. She would nag him when he returned home late nights, and when he could take no more, he would slap her or knock her to the floor. Once he beat and kicked her so severely that she was in bed for three weeks with internal injuries.

The husband aggravated the situation by accusing her of having relations with men she met at the dances. She retaliated with snide remarks about his first wife, who had died.

The counselor's report to the Court read:

> The husband and wife agreed they had allowed their interest in one another to lag. They agreed to a trial reconciliation. The husband said upon reviewing the Reconcilia-

tion Agreement that if that is the way a husband is supposed to act, he could see where he had fallen down in many ways. He wanted a chance to see if he could do better. The wife acknowledged that she nagged at him constantly. She said that her bringing up of his relations with his first wife might well stem from a feeling of jealousy and a need for continuing assurance from him that she was far superior to the first wife.

They signed an agreement which contained a clause about fighting and another about nagging.

In this case the husband had mistreated his wife without giving the matter any thought, either before he beat her or afterwards. As in the home he had come from, it was merely something a man did to keep a woman in line. Now, for the first time he thought about his actions. The Reconciliation Agreement had touched a spark of decency inside him, and in his simple way he was inspired to become more of a man.

It was the wife who created the difficulty. She walked in two weeks later, announced that her husband had become everything she had hoped and prayed for, but that now she didn't want him. She didn't think she loved him. In this case, the counselor was able to persuade her to wait a few more weeks. After all, one couldn't shrug off the mistreatment of years in two weeks' time. When we checked a year later they were still together. Counseling had been effective.

Occasionally we would encounter marriages where it was clearly evident the parties should separate. This was apart from any religious or moral aspects about the indissolubility of the marriage in the eyes of God. It simply happened that the proper ends of marriage could not be attained, as, for example, when the husband inflicted extreme physical suffering upon his wife and children, or persisted in immoral practices that tended to degrade the members of his family or contribute to their delinquency.

Such cases could be readily distinguished from those isolated instances of physical cruelty to the spouse or children. Human beings seem quite resilient and can survive blows struck in anger or intoxication or during moments of extreme jealousy. Very often marriages which have been so threatened can be restored, especially when there is remorse, and forgiveness is sought, and there is a firm purpose to amend one's ways. To counsel separation in such instances would be to court serious and lasting trauma to the wife and children.

But there are other cases, like that of the Bowies. Melvin Bowie had repeatedly abused his wife, Nellie. He had ripped off her clothes in public, spat on her, called her unmentionable names, and blackened her eyes. He had treated the children in the same way, beating them and sometimes their little friends. His word, right or wrong, was law around the house. He was insanely jealous of his wife, and accused both her and their eldest daughter of immoral acts, sometimes in the presence of the smaller children. By the time the family came to the attention of the Conciliation Court, the eldest boy was in Juvenile Hall and the daughter had run away from home and was living, without her father's knowledge, with an aunt.

The Court believed a legal separation was clearly indicated, and issued an order to restrain the husband from molesting either his wife or children. With the husband out of the home, the wife subsequently gathered her brood about her again. The children, though, still bore the effects of his treatment, and we advised the mother that it would take a great deal of love and understanding on her part, tempered with firmness, to enable them to weather their rough start in life.

Once again it was impressed on us that not all marriages can be reclaimed, nor should they be.

In this category of offenses against human dignity, we found some cases in which no blow was ever struck and no temper ever flared. Rather, it was the wearing down by one mate of the other by means of cutting remarks, profane language, the bearing of grudges, and the silent treatment. These methods of belittling the other were as damaging to health and mental welfare as any physical beating.

An attorney, Victor Blassingame, dropped by the clerk's office one afternoon late to ask for an affidavit and petition. He said he wanted to show them to his wife, since he was very much concerned about their marriage of twelve years.

The next morning early, he was back. He said his wife was extremely suspicious of the documents. He asked if one of our counselors would phone her and explain the functions of the Conciliation Court.

Not quite knowing what he might be walking into, the counselor called her. Surprisingly, she was friendly and listened attentively. Then she said her husband had placed the forms before her and demanded that she sign them. She refused, and a furious quarrel ensued. He made his usual cutting remarks, called her names, and then refused to converse the rest of the evening. When the counselor explained that the Conciliation Court forced no party to sign or promise anything, she said she would come in with her husband. She added that she would be open-minded and, for the sake of their two children, hoped something could be done.

When they arrived, Vic Blassingame brought in a list of complaints. She constantly ridiculed him to the children.

She wouldn't permit him to smoke in the living room or sit in an armchair that didn't have doilies. She was always too tired to take part in sexual relations and frequently stayed up until late hours to avoid intercourse.

On her part, Mrs. Blassingame recited several grievances. Her husband, she said, was self-centered, selfish, and immature. Everything had to go his way or not at all. Her suggestions, she said, seemed to constitute a threat to his superiority. As for their sexual relations, she acknowledged they were totally unsatisfactory. She said he knew nothing about the mental and emotional attitude of a woman to sex, that he never prepared her for the act or gave her time to become adjusted to the idea, and that he was crude to the point that he hurt her physically.

Most damaging of all in her eyes was his constant berating of her. "He is always hunting something to say that will cut me to the quick. He barely gets in the door when he begins, and I'm simply a nervous wreck. I can't sleep, and I scarcely eat. And it's telling on the children. They're old enough to know what's going on, and they take it to bed with them."

She said all this calmly, attempting to approach the problem with logic. He reacted, though, with unbridled emotion and at one point, grew furious.

With the two together, the counselor pointed out their differences, and how they needed help to reconcile these divergent points. He suggested they try a counseling agency, preferably one with a team of workers, since he felt they needed both medical and psychological or psychiatric assistance. He pointed out that even if the treatments failed to save their marriage, they would benefit through a better understanding of each other and of their relationship to the children. Finally, they left after signing a Reconciliation Agreement in which they agreed to certain strict rules of conduct, including those bearing on the "silent treatment," holding grudges, and sarcastic or belittling remarks. In the report, the counselor wrote:

> The husband is an individual with strong feelings of insecurity and inadequacy, reflected by his constant need to prove to himself that he is the head of the house.
>
> The wife, an intelligent woman, is refusing more and more to submit completely to her husband, and when he tries to dominate her, she becomes hostile and aloof. The more hostile and aloof she becomes, the more insecure he feels, and consequently the reaction turns into a vicious circle.
>
> They are not meeting each other's needs and are unable to obtain the gratifications required. Both are very discouraged and ready to admit defeat. Both can see that the relationship between each and the children is bad, reflecting in itself the instability of the marriage.

It was their mutual love for their children plus their willingness to admit defeat that ultimately saved their marriage. They worshipped their two youngsters and were willing to go to any ends to protect them. Eight months later, after undergoing psychological treatment twice a week, they were fully reconciled. Their marriage probably would never be much more than a patch job, but they seemingly had found a working basis for living together.

A few days later I received this note scrawled in the penciled handwriting of a nine-year-old:

> Dear sir:
> I thank you for getting my dad
> and mom back together.
>
> Truly yours,
> Bobbie

P.S.

Bobbie told us he would like to thank the judge. We said he could by letter. We knew you would like to know.

V.B.

Those few words said more to me than any supreme court affirmance.

chapter fifteen

In-Laws are People

Generally speaking, the home of the modern family is not designed for the constant presence of an outsider or third person. The lengthy intrusion of such a person into the home life of a family cannot occur without real danger. Such presence has a direct bearing upon the relationship of husband and wife.

—RECONCILIATION AGREEMENT

Millions of couples these days are asking themselves what they should do about mothers and fathers who are in their sixties or seventies. Should they ask them to come and live with them? Or should they get them a house or apartment nearby? Or suggest they go to a home for retired people? Because our life span has increased so greatly, this has become one of the most disturbing problems of our age.

Jane and Ted Walsh wandered into this situation without giving thought to what the future might bring. It began with Jane calling long distance from New York. "It's about Mother, Ted. She's taking it very hard. She's going to find it so depressing to go back to the farmhouse where she and Dad spent so many happy years. I just can't bear to leave her alone."

The pause was significant. "Ted, would it be all right to bring her home for a little while?"

And so it was arranged. Ted remembered Mrs. Graham briefly, a fine, old farm woman accustomed to a hard life.

Her hands were cracked and calloused, her hair was white and her back stooped, and he remembered she always wore an old knit sweater that had seen better days. If they could make life easier for her, he wanted to do it.

She herself, though, wasn't at all happy about leaving the farm where she had spent most of her life. She feared she would be a burden. But Jane was firm as well as persuasive.

From the beginning, Mrs. Graham loved the nine-year-old twins, named Peter and Paula after the saints. The resemblance ended there. Paula was a tomboy, and what mischief she couldn't think up, Peter already had. Before long Mother Graham was chasing after them with sweaters they had forgotten and generally riding herd on them. They complained sometimes to their parents. It bothered Jane and Ted, too, that she was "repressing" them.

At five every morning, when her day on the farm had commenced, Mother Graham would start stirring. Little by little she took over the preparation of breakfast. Ted, who was happy with coffee and toast, found ham and eggs set before him, three eggs, because "two never seemed like a man's meal." He would leave for the office fighting the effects of biscuits, honey, a bowl of mush, and a chunk of homemade coffee cake, all of which went with the ham and eggs. Jane, too, was disturbed over the arrangement. With two women in the kitchen, she could never put her hands on what she wanted.

In the evening when the twins had gone to bed, the three would sit around the big fireplace. It was awkward to talk because Mrs. Graham was a little hard of hearing. And she did love to reminisce. Since Ted had technical material to review nights, he often would read, though he felt guilty about it. Jane would try to read, too, but in the end she would get some sewing to do while her mother rambled.

Then there was the matter of drafts. In the old farmhouse, one was always accustomed to them and dressed for them. In Ted's insulated house, there were none. So Jane's mother provided some by opening windows at opposite ends of a room to "fetch me a breath of air." Ted couldn't stand drafts. He would sneeze once or twice, and Jane would close the windows, leaving her mother to swelter in her old wool sweater.

So went the battle without words. More and more, the whole family grew edgy as the tensions drew as taut as a violin string. They snapped inside Ted one day. Thinking Mrs. Graham out of hearing distance, he let loose, and before Jane could stop him, her mother heard every bitter word. She went to her room to pack. Jane told Ted off, and Ted came right back. It was their first quarrel within earshot of her mother, and the acid words took on double their sting in the knowledge of both that a third party had overheard them.

Ted packed, too, and left for the club. By giving their quarrel that much importance, he angered Jane all the more. When he finally phoned her, she unloaded an accumulation of harsh words she had been storing up. After a month, he filed in the Conciliation Court.

The case came up before Counselor Meyer "Mike" Elkin. As he talked, they saw readily that their marriage had not failed because of any shortcomings on the part of either. It had encountered squalls only because, out of their kindness and generosity, they had introduced a third person into their home. Through no fault, either, on Mrs. Graham's part, she had completely disrupted their lives.

"I don't know what we can do," Jane said. "Mother's strength has failed so much since Dad died. I don't think she's well enough to live by herself."

Mike Elkin had a suggestion. Would it be possible to build her a small apartment on the back of their lot? Perhaps adding to the garage? Ted leaped at the idea. "I'll talk to her about it," he said. "She used to like me a lot, and if I tell her how sorry I am and how I didn't mean what I said —well, it's worth a try."

The Counselor smiled to himself as he watched his suggestion take hold. A good man-and-wife team, they became so engrossed in a possible solution that when they left he knew it was with the understanding that Ted would move back home, although nothing had been said about it.

Several months later, Mike Elkin brought up their case for staff discussion in our weekly conference. Ted had dropped by to tell him how well the plan had worked out. They had converted the garage into a bedroom, the laundry into a bathroom, and had built a kitchen and sitting room adjoining. Jane had furnished it with antique furniture and hooked rugs. Mrs. Graham had made the curtains herself. In the mornings, she would rise with the sun, by nine in the evening she would be in bed. She would come to the main house whenever she wished and visit, and whenever she tired of the youngsters, she would withdraw to the quiet of her apartment.

Mike Elkin drew attention to several points common to many such cases. In the first place, Jane's mother had preferred to remain on the farm. Perhaps she would have been happier there, surrounded by her friends of many years. At least, Jane should have let her try it. In many instances, surprisingly, it is the children who pressure their parents into living with them. They feel the old folks may be lonely, or selfishly, they want them in their homes, to help with the children and prepare meals.

In Jane's and Ted's case, they meant well, but they were

not given to thinking a situation out to its eventual end. Jane was moved by the emotion of the moment. Once Mrs. Graham had come to live with them, and the problems arose, Jane should have taken her aside for a heart-to-heart talk. It might have hurt her mother's feelings for a day or two, but it would have remedied a situation fraught with irritation. Or she might have used the technique of kidding her mother. Good-natured humor can accomplish wonders. I've heard daughters say, "Oh, Mom, come off it. I know you. I remember grandmother telling me you were the best tree skinner in town when you were a little girl."

But most of all, Mrs. Graham probably should not have come to live with them in the first place. In general, a basic rule is that no third person should ever move in on a family, no matter how close the relationship may be. Marriage means establishing a new life, a new home, and the partners must be as free as possible from outside influence. A couple should be willing to make almost any sacrifice to maintain a separate establishment for their parents. Even if the wife should have to work, she will be rewarded far more than she will ever know.

Nor should parents up in their years be exiled. They must be kept near the stream of life, near their loved ones. A mother and father living close to a son or daughter, but preferably not too close, may run over several times during the week. They will enjoy their grandchildren far more than if the youngsters are underfoot all the time. And the children will enjoy them more.

Some of our couples solved their situations in interesting ways. One couldn't afford a separate establishment for the husband's father, so they pitched in one week end and cut a door from his room to the yard, so that he could come and go as he pleased. That one door relieved a lot of traffic, as well as friction in the family.

Trouble developed with another couple over the wife's father. He wanted to find a job, but because of his age, his daughter and son-in-law refused to let him. He grew irritable and became a point of contention between them. Many of the complaints could have been eliminated if they had permitted him to take a light job.

As Dr. Shostrom points out, one of the main problems of elderly people is that they feel futile and useless. They go through a period much like the adolescent does, and they need to prove their worth and value again. They will interfere in many ways to show that they are not old and should not be overlooked.

Some of our petitioners were forced to place their parents in homes maintained by church, fraternal, union, or other groups. In some instances, the parents preferred this, but when they didn't, the couples were wracked by guilt. In one case, the wife had five children and simply didn't possess the strength to care for her infirm parents. She went through purgatory during the time they were being settled. Her parents, though, were surprised to find themselves happy in their new surroundings. The home was more luxurious than any they had ever known, and they developed friendships with people their own age.

It doesn't always work out that pleasantly. In another case, the wife refused even to consider reconciliation. Her husband had suggested a home for her parents, and under pressure she acquiesced. Her parents found themselves miserable, and she wanted them back even if it meant losing her husband. In this instance, it did. He felt her parents intruded on their lives.

While I strongly believe that the admission of third persons into a family may prove hazardous, I must admit I know many homes in which elderly people live with their children in a most peaceful and happy association. These are usually families of great love and understanding, and equally important, made up of individuals who regardless of age adjust easily to new situations. Or they may be thinking people who by sitting down and mapping out their problem, work out an arrangement that reduces strain to a minimum.

Often, however, the family budget decides the matter. Few sons or daughters can finance the care of an aged mother or father who is ill or extremely infirm, and so the care devolves on them. They may want it that way regardless of their financial position, because of their bond of love. And many sons-in-law and daughters-in-law would have it no other way. Rightly, they recognize what society would call an obligation but which they do out of the love of their hearts. In instances such as these, the husband and wife may grow in understanding and discover they have been drawn closer through adversity than they were before.

So there are notable exceptions to this thought about third persons in a home. . . .

When I first went to the Conciliation Court, I took with me the common concept that interference by in-laws constitutes one of the most prolific sources of marital discord. In-law jokes have been such an important segment of the comedian's inventory for so long that we have been unduly and unconsciously influenced by them. Everyone knows the classroom definition of "mixed feelings": "when one sees his mother-in-law going over a cliff in his new Cadillac."

During long days spent in counseling, however, and listening to hundreds of persons blame the failure of their marriage on an in-law, I discovered that most of the complaints were unjustified. The disgruntled husband or wife too often used the in-law as a scapegoat to cover up his or her shortcomings. In-laws outside the home seldom interfere as much as some of us think.

In one case, the wife and husband had invited her mother to stay with them. She had scarcely arrived when troubles between the couple reached the point at which the wife filed a petition in the Conciliation Court. When the hearing came up, the husband placed the blame for their difficulties on his mother-in-law. He said she interfered constantly. The wife pointed out that her mother had lived with them only six weeks. As the conference progressed, the counselor discovered that their basic problem was one of sex. The wife regarded the sexual act as an indignity being performed on her. He considered her "frigid." Because of this lack of sex satisfaction, both had become tense and irritable, yet the husband continued to blame the mother-in-law.

Some in-laws, of course, do attempt to run their children's lives. They will dictate what kind of a house to buy and where, how they should spend their money, where to shop, how they should bring up the children, even what they should eat. They become hypercritical, often simply because their children's way is not their way of handling matters.

Sometimes they fail to realize they are interfering. In one case, the son's mother kept asking her daughter-in-law when she was going to have a baby. Since they were barely getting by, the wife wanted to wait a couple of years. "I was brought up in a poor neighborhood," the girl told the counselor. "I saw kids die because their folks couldn't buy them medicine. I want my baby to have a chance."

When the counselor talked with the mother-in-law, however, she was sincerely shocked to think she had created an issue. "I guess I talked about it more than I knew. I thought they should be starting a family while they were young—but I can see it was none of my business."

When parents interfere, the couple may hesitate to mention it. In the final analysis, it's better to have a few hurt feelings than a broken marriage. The couple should take this attitude: "This is our marriage, and we want to live it the way we want. It may not be the best way, but it's our way, and gives us the most happiness. We want you to help us by listening and understanding when we come to you, but we must make the decisions ourselves."

Most often we would find a mother or father taking sides in an argument between a husband and wife. In such instances, the counselor would suggest to the parents: If the daughter comes over to tell how unreasonable her husband was being about a problem, the mother should say, "Why don't you and your husband drop by tonight, and let's talk about it?" In this way, the husband could present his side without feeling his wife's entire family was barreling down on him, and the mother could listen and perhaps make a suggestion or two, not as advice but merely as a thought for the two of them to consider. And she might be surprised at how some of her thoughts would take root.

A father who had just watched his daughter leave on her honeymoon said something one day that has always stayed with me. "It's rough being a parent, because being a parent is to work yourself right out of a job. We bring them into the world, and care for them one hundred per cent. As they grow older, we loosen the reins a little, and then more and more with each year. By the time they marry, we've finished the job."

As I would hear a case, that thought would recur to me: *A parent is a person who works most of his life to work himself out of a job.*

Differences in previous standards of living of bride and groom often present a major hurdle. This is particularly true when the in-laws, out of an abundance of love, lavish gifts on the young couple which tend to destroy their independence. Michael Riley married into such a family, and working out their problems contributed much to our Reconciliation Agreement.

Michael met Polly Randall aboard a train bound from San Francisco for Los Angeles. She boarded at Palo Alto, complete with mink and evening gown and a score of alcoholic well-wishers, and was listing badly to port when Mike came to her aid. With a laugh, she discovered her friends had not put her bags aboard. She was without tickets, purse, or baggage.

Mike made her explanations to the conductor for her, and even brought her an extra pair of his pajamas and a spare toothbrush. She thought he was wonderful with that thatch of red hair.

In the dining car the next morning, she headed straight for his table. "I've been looking for you," she said, the lovely green eyes surveying him candidly. "I'm so glad you're from Stanford. It takes some of the embarrassment away. Would you stake me to a cup of coffee?"

Covertly, he withdrew a $5 bill from his wallet and handed it to her. He didn't tell her that left only two lonely ones.

A few days later, in the law office where he was employed as a clerk, he received a note from Mrs. Robert Craig Randall, thanking him for his assistance to her daughter. He whistled. So green-eyes was Polly Randall, daughter of Robert Craig Randall, former trustee of the local bar association. He saw Polly occasionally that year while he studied for the bar examination; and when he got the results, informing him he was in the 43 per cent, they celebrated together. A year later, after she returned from Europe, he found himself engaged.

He was making only $300 a month at the time—a sum that seemed fabulous after the $150 he had received as a clerk. He explained to the Randalls that he would feel much more comfortable with a simple wedding, and they agreed. The wedding invitations were therefore limited to personal friends of the family, which included a reception for 500. What the Randalls considered modest and what seemed modest to him were two very distinct things.

He and Polly picked out an apartment for $85 a month unfurnished. But one day Polly and her mother proudly took him out to see their "find." It only cost $165 a month. Polly said, "It'll save us money in the long run because it's completely furnished, including TV and access to the swimming pool."

Polly explained, "The swimming pool will save us at least $500 for a beach summer rental and the TV will save theater costs. Besides the apartment has a garbage disposal unit which will do away with a garbage pickup charge."

She was so completely happy over having saved him all this money, that he restrained himself from exploding these myths.

Out of his meager savings Mike had earmarked $200 for a washing machine, but the $200 went for a spindly-legged antique desk which Polly bought for his "take home" work in the evenings. Polly explained that her mother just insisted she bring the washing over to their home. Mike made a rapid mental calculation that this would mean a 40-mile round trip for each bag of laundry.

In many ways they were well suited. Polly never failed to amuse him, and being subject to moods he needed her. He was as happy as she when he learned she was pregnant.

As soon as they heard the news, the Randalls sent them a few gifts: A perambulator that had its own instrument panel and gear shift, the down payment on "the cutest little ranch" of an acre and a half in San Fernando Valley, and the down payment on a five-passenger car. As a result, Mike's and Polly's living costs climbed far beyond his monthly income. He began walking a tightrope with bankruptcy on all sides.

The arrangement, finally, by the Randalls to pay for Polly's confinement was the last straw. Now they were buying his child! When Mike got home that night, he exploded to Polly, and when he finished, the green eyes were filled with tears. It was the first time he had ever seen her cry, and he burst out of the house blaming himself, the Randalls, and the whole world.

He walked and walked, and when he finally returned home he found the house dark. Almost frantic, he called the Randalls. Mr. Randall answered the phone, and unloaded on Mike a list of adjectives, including "ungrateful, inconsiderate, inhuman, thoughtless, brutal, penny-pinching, miserly, heartless. . . ."

For the first five minutes, he went along with all the adjectives; then the injustice of it struck him, and when he finally got a word in, it was to tell Mr. Randall to "go plumb to hell!"

He sold their interest in the San Fernando "ranch" and the new car, and pawned most of the useless wedding presents. He sent Mr. Randall a polite letter and a check for

$3,450. Then he heaved a sigh of relief. He again owned his own soul.

He wrote Polly a little note. He was terribly sorry he had hurt her feelings. He loved her, and please, would she come back? Her first reaction was a sigh of relief, but by the time her mother and father got through interpreting the note, her deep unhappiness returned. So Mr. Randall filed a divorce complaint in behalf of his daughter, and sought a temporary order to restrain Mike from "annoying, molesting, or threatening" her. It also asked temporary custody of the unborn child upon birth. In the blanks left for inserting the amount of temporary support sought for mother and child, the single word "nothing" was typed in.

Michael Riley was one mad Irishman when the formal documents were served upon him. However, instead of countering with an answer, he filed a petition in the Conciliation Court. He named the Randalls as respondents as well as Polly.

At the hearing, each had his say.

Polly: "How could my husband speak so unkindly of my parents after all they have done for us?"

Mike: "Her parents just took over my wife, my car, my apartment—everything."

Mr. Randall: "Why should this young upstart deny us the right to provide our daughter with some of the comforts of life?"

Mrs. Randall: "We have helped the children some, but we have never meddled in their affairs. Why should we be drawn into this?" She fitted a story I once heard about a woman who shook hands with the preacher after the service and remarked, "Wonderful sermon. Everything you said applies to someone I know."

Each felt sure he or she was right. None was trying to see the situation from the other's vantage point.

Eventually, with good will all around, patience, forbearance, and a good deal of listening, we were able to set Mike's house in pretty good order. In the process the Randalls had to learn a hard and rather deep psychological lesson: No one likes to have too much done for him, even if it is done with good intentions and out of love. Love is sometimes best expressed by *not* doing things for our children. The child learning to walk must be allowed freedom to fall.

Three months after their reconciliation I received a phone call. "Judge Burke, this is Polly—Polly Riley, housewife and *mother*. Yes, Judge, mother! A fine baby boy. Seven-and-a-half pounds with *red* hair and *green* eyes. Handsomest lad you've ever seen! Everything is fine. Mike and I are happy, and we are grateful for all your help. And, I almost forgot, Dad and Mother are the proudest grandparents who ever lived. And you know what? Mike named the baby *Robert Craig* Riley. Isn't that scr-r-umptious?"

It was sometime later before I could even get in a word. Polly was herself again.

chapter sixteen

Innocents Abroad

> *. . . The more inoffensive and "innocent" the third person, the more dangerous is the possibility of attachments being formed which may result in jealousy and misunderstanding, if not worse.*
>
> —RECONCILIATION AGREEMENT

It was Friday evening. Another day, another week. A most discouraging week. Pulling open the bottom desk drawer, I shuffled through the "sailing directions" I had gathered, those elements that strengthen the bond of love in marriage. They were beginning to take shape. One of these days I must get at them, sort them out, and see what positives had come from the hundreds of cases I had heard since I tossed in the first idea.

As I glanced at the docket for Monday morning, I saw the Cory matter was set for 9:30. Fumbling through the stack of cases in the current box on the desk, I found the file, flipped up the cover, and read swiftly:

CASE HISTORY—C C 26320—CORY, Oct. 18, 1955.

Mrs. Virginia Cory, petitioner, filed for conciliation Oct. 11, 1955, stating her husband, Vincent Cory, had filed divorce complaint Oct. 3, 1955.

Mr. and Mrs. Cory were married April 3, 1950, and separated March 4, 1955. This is a first marriage for both parties.

They have one child, Valerie, aged three, who is with Mrs. Cory.

Conciliation Counselor Elkin interviewed Mr. and Mrs. Cory to interpret the Court's function as well as the impartial role of the counselor.

CONFERENCE WITH PETITIONER:

Mrs. Virginia Cory is an attractive, auburn-haired woman of average height and slender build, aged 28. She was well-groomed and tastefully dressed. She appeared anxious, tense, unhappy and nearly desperate in her desire to keep her marriage intact.

The Corys were purchasing a new home at the time of their separation. Her husband and his younger brother are "batching" in the house since she and the baby left. She is residing with her parents. The younger brother, Robert, aged 23, has lived with the Corys for the past year since his discharge from the Air Force.

Mrs. Cory said she loved her husband very dearly. She described him as a very solid person, a hard worker who is highly regarded at the electric company where he is employed as a foreman of a crew of linemen. The nature of his work takes him out of town for several days or even a week at a time. She said she had enjoyed having his brother in the home because she had always been nervous and restless when left alone.

She said her husband had become extremely critical of her, and she would respond in uncontrollable tears, which only served to infuriate him. She said they argued incessantly.

When asked what in her opinion contributed most to the discord, she said it was just a multitude of little things. When pressed for details, she appeared hard put to relate them.

She said that during the three months preceding their separation, her husband had been sleeping on the couch in the baby's room. She said he was no longer affectionate and resisted her efforts at intimacy. Prior to this time, however, they had had a mutually satisfactory marital relationship.

CONFERENCE WITH RESPONDENT:

Mr. Cory is an active-looking young man of 30, very rugged in appearance, approximately six feet tall. He had a friendly manner toward the counselor, but somehow gave the counselor the feeling he had a serious problem he felt unable to share with anyone.

He acknowledged the tension between him and his wife. He said that during the last few months, the least thing would bring them to the boiling point. He held himself partly responsible. Since his promotion to foreman, he had taken on extra duties, and felt he had been neglecting his wife and family. Like his wife, he seemed unable to come up with any specific reasons for their discord.

CONFERENCE WITH PETITIONER AND RESPONDENT:

The couple were then given the opportunity of discussing their problems jointly with the counselor.... Both were receptive to a trial reconciliation....

Counselor had some misgivings ... since they had failed to bring to light any basic causes for their troubles. Counselor felt that they themselves might not be fully aware of them.

Reconciliation Agreement signed by both parties.

Court order signed by Judge Louis H. Burke. Reconciliation effected.

Counselor Elkin

A subsequent entry in the file read:

Nov. 15, 1955. Mr. Vincent Cory telephoned Counselor Elkin to advise their reconciliation attempt had failed. Hearing was scheduled for 9:30 A.M., Nov. 22.

As I closed the file, I sat a moment lost in thought. I was completely baffled. Then I rose, determined to put the case out of mind until Monday morning. On the way out of the room, I stopped to straighten the racing yacht picture on the wall. It was always listing to port.

That Saturday we had a big regatta scheduled at Balboa Bay, and sixteen sloops, including our "Paloma," showed up at the starting line for what developed into a blustering, gusty three-race series. The boats were beating up the coast in the second race, hugging the shore and leaving it for a short tack out only when the breaker line was too ominously close to permit any other course. The Corys sailed with me in my thoughts that stormy day.

These were the difficult cases—where trouble lies too deep to be discussed with the counselor. Perhaps, as he suggested, they didn't know what it was themselves. But what could it be? A judge had to be a detective in this kind of work, hunting for a clue, a bit of evidence.

The water was swishing along the deck, hurtling spray into the cockpit. I had the tiller and was sailing from the low side where I could keep my eye on the jib. The two crew members were out flat on the weather rail applying their weight to help the fighting, plunging boat keep heads up against the 20-knot wind. I settled back on a long port tack. . . .

The husband's work takes him out of town for long periods. But that couldn't be it or she would have said something. He's critical. That means nothing. Many mates are critical. Still, if she is overly sensitive . . .

"Starboard tack!" came a hail, and dangerously close. Automatically I shouted, "Coming about!" and not a moment too soon. A right-of-way boat, tacking out from the coast, was pounding through the white cap of a big swell.

A sheaf of green water clobbered Lane Guthrie, one of my crew, as he slithered up on the new weather side, not having had sufficient warning to clamber back into the cockpit. The look on his drenched face first reproached me, then froze in a grin when he saw the two boats fighting neck and neck, now on the same tack and only a few scant feet apart. Big Paul McClary had put his whole 230 pounds into getting that jib in, 'til the sheet was singing tight.

This is what punishes a man, not knowing what the problem is, feeling time running out. She's affectionate but he pushes her away. He moved out of the bedroom to avoid intimacy. Why would a man do that? He's apparently normal....

Riding each big swell and through the white caps, I pointed the boat higher and higher. By now our speed had picked up. Keeping her close on the wind and given a break or two, we could possibly ride the other boat off.

The dates in the petition! Two dates that were almost the same. Why hadn't I thought of them before? A man had to sift every word. That could be it. It just might be....

It was Monday morning, and the Corys were sitting outside. I talked with Mrs. Cory first. "We tried awfully hard, Judge, but it was just no go. Vince says something that cuts me, and then I say something, and the first we know we're in it deep. I don't know—it just seems there's something inside him that makes him want to hurt me. Only I guess that's crazy, because I know he loves me."

"I'm sorry, too, Mrs. Cory," I said slowly, "because

you're both fine people, and it seems such a shame when you're both still very much in love. . . ."

I let the thought hang a second, then added, "By the way, is your husband's brother still living with you?"

The question surprised her. "Why, yes, he is."

"The reason I ask," I continued, "is that sometimes third persons unknowingly create difficulties. . . ."

She interrupted. "Oh, no, Judge. He's never caused us any trouble. No, he hasn't anything to do with this. He's as broken up about it as we are."

She explained that her husband, Vince, and his brother were orphans, and Vince, being seven years older than Robert, had looked after him since he was a baby. "He's been more than an older brother," she said. "He's been like a father to him—and I've tried to be like an older sister. Bob's been sort of lost since he came out of the Air Corps, and Vince and I have been trying to help him snap out of it."

"How have you been trying to help him, Mrs. Cory?"

"Oh, I encourage him to get out more. I take him with me on my errands. And he comes to me with his problems and troubles."

"What problems, for instance?"

She thought a long moment. "Well, things like he couldn't find a job and didn't know how to sell himself."

She launched into a long discussion of his difficulties, ending with one night a couple of months ago when he knocked on her bedroom door as she was falling asleep. "He was all wrought up and wanted to talk with somebody. He came in and sat on the bed a couple of hours. Vince was on a field trip at the time, and Bob just had to unload on someone."

"Did you tell your husband, Mrs. Cory?"

"Why, yes, of course. Now, wait a minute, Judge, there's never been anything wrong going on between Bob and me."

I nodded. "I'm sure there hasn't been, Mrs. Cory. But what did your husband say when you told him?"

She was puzzled. "I can't remember that he said anything."

"One more question, Mrs. Cory. Did you ever show any affection toward Bob? I mean, in the way an older sister would?"

She fidgeted nervously. "I'd always kiss Vince when he left for work mornings, and sometimes Bob would say, 'What about me?' Vince and I'd laugh, and I'd say, 'Come here, you big baby,' and kiss him on the cheek. He was so starved for someone to make a fuss over him."

She added, "I know it sounds bad, letting him come into my bedroom. But I never thought of him except as Vince's kid brother, and he never thought of me. . . ."

She trailed off, realizing she was becoming bogged down in a situation difficult to explain to an outsider.

"I understand," I said, and I did.

The old swivel groaned as I leaned back. Carefully I studied her, and liked what I saw, a refreshing girl so naïve in her innocence that she seemed ethereal, even in these old dark chambers.

"Has it ever occurred to you," I began slowly, "that Vince would show his jealousy in unmistakable ways if the man were someone outside of his own home, but that he wouldn't want to admit his jealousy even to himself and much less to you in the case of his brother?"

I paused, letting the thought take hold. "So he repressed this emotion. But it kept building up inside him. He kept seeing his brother sitting on the bed beside you. He knew nothing had happened, but deep down even this slight an intimacy was too much for him. Consciously, he would never hurt you, but unconsciously, he wanted to strike back. He said things to hurt you, not meaning them, and perhaps even unaware of what he was doing."

She was as rigid as something inanimate. "If I thought for a moment that was a part of our problem . . ."

"May I suggest," I cautioned her, "that you don't discuss this with your husband. It would be better if he never knew, because if he did he would feel he couldn't explain to you how he felt, and he might change in his relationship to his brother."

"But what do I do? I can't ask Bob to get out of the house."

"No, but your husband can suggest he get a room somewhere. But first, I'm going to suggest to your husband that you go away for a short vacation, just the two of you."

She was a different woman as she left the room. It was wonderful, I thought, what hope can do for a woman.

As I have mentioned, two dates had rung a bell far back in my mind as we were racing. The start of their unhappiness, as set forth in the case history, had coincided with the date the younger brother had come to live with them. Even without that clue, however, I would have explored the possibility as a result of having handled case after case in which the very presence in a home of a brother, sister, cousin, aunt, or even friend had disturbed the normal, peaceful routine of a household.

In one case, the wife's younger sister came to live with them and ran around the house scantily clad when the husband was home. The wife admonished her and eventually accused the younger sister of making a play for her husband. In our conference, it developed that the girl "got a kick out of burning up her older sister." The girl said, "Him? What would I want with him? He's an old man." The husband was twenty-eight, the sister, eighteen.

In another case, an aunt moved in on a couple who lived in a tiny cottage that had walls so thin a breath could be heard. The husband and wife lost their easy way with each other, knowing every word they said was being overheard, even in the privacy of their bedroom. The husband's patience ran out eventually, and he filed for divorce. In this instance, we failed. The wife refused to ask her aunt to leave.

Occasionally, the third-person situation assumed a more brutal aspect. One wife feared, and apparently with reason, that her husband's uncle would attack her. The uncle had openly propositioned her once. When she told her husband about her apprehensions, he thought she was "imagining things." He trusted his uncle implicitly.

Mr. Cory had his jaw well set when he walked in. "We're wasting time, Judge," he said. "Ginny and I've been all over this, and we always get the same answer. We're not suited for each other."

For five minutes, I did the most persuasive speaking of my lifetime. I said I felt they loved each other very deeply, and that a love like theirs came not too often in this world. "People fall into certain habits and patterns around a house," I said. "Sometimes when they get away from home, they see things differently. Why don't you two take a vacation for a week, all by yourselves? If you can't find anyone to leave your little girl with, Mrs. Burke and I will look after her." I didn't know what my wife would think about the sudden appearance of a strange three-year-old. But she has risen to similar situations numerous times and has long since ceased to be daunted.

He looked at me in amazement. "You'd do that?" he asked. He shook his head. "My folks could look after her."

He continued then, "Well, I guess Ginny and I could give it another whirl. But I'm telling you now it won't work."

"I want to suggest one thing more," I said. "When you return, I want your wife to stay with friends until you come back here for another conference."

"Well, if the trip works out pretty good . . . ?"

"No, not even then."

He was completely mystified. "Okay," he said.

Three weeks later the Corys came into my office together. Their free and easy manner answered my question before the words ever formed.

"It was just like a honeymoon," she said, her eyes glowing. Then she reminded me. "I want to get home, Judge—and you said . . ."

"I remember." I turned to Vince Cory. "I've a suggestion to offer, Mr. Cory. It's about your brother. Sometimes the very presence of a third person in a home . . ."

By now, after explaining my theory so often, the words fell naturally into place. "If the third person is of an antagonistic nature, it's easy to see how he disrupts the peace and harmony of a home. But when he's a normal, likeable fellow like your brother, it's not so readily apparent."

Vince Cory shot his wife a little glance, and she nodded in agreement with me. He seemed relieved. "I know you're right, Judge." He turned to his wife. "We could tell him with Valerie growing up, we need his room. . . ."

After that, I don't think they knew I was around. They walked on a cloud on the way out, a little personal cloud all their own.

A week later, the morning mail brought a letter from Vince Cory:

Dec. 15, 1955

Dear Judge Burke:

I just wanted to drop you a line to tell you how deeply grateful I am. Bob has gotten a nice room in the south part of the city and Ginny and I and our little girl are tremendously happy to be home together again.

I have a confession to make.... When Robert came to live with us, I encouraged Virginia to make him feel at home. One day when Bob and I were out driving, he sort of opened up and told me how much her attentions meant to him.

I told myself it was all innocent, but from that moment on, I caught myself fighting against wanting to spy on my brother and my wife....

I feel sure that you knew nothing of all this but now that I have gotten it off my chest, I am beginning to feel better about it. I will always be grateful to you.

Sincerely,
Vincent Cory

I put on my topcoat that night and prepared to brave a raw wind slapping the world outside. Entering the elevator, the words came back: *I feel sure that you knew nothing of all this.*

I chuckled out loud. George, the operator, looked at me quizzically. I squelched the laugh. As I stepped out, he was shaking his head. His face expressed the words, "They better be getting him out of that department. He's gettin' punchy."

chapter seventeen

A Penny Saved

Within ten days from date, the parties agree to work out a family budget....

—RECONCILIATION AGREEMENT

The usual quiet of my ancient, book-lined chambers was so charged with anger and rancor that I felt my own blood pounding.

The girl screamed, "He never gave me a dime I could call my own. I haven't got anything I didn't have when I married him."

The fellow, big-muscled and broad-shouldered, turned to me. "She doesn't know how to handle money, Judge. . . ."

"How do you know?" the girl snapped. She was a slender blonde with green eyes and pouting lips. "You never gave me . . ."

The man turned on her. "Shut up, baby, while I explain this to the judge." His eyes swung back to me. "She tried to ruin me. She opened charge accounts at half a dozen stores and hauled home nearly a thousand dollars' worth of junk. One thousand bucks' worth, Judge. I was a week getting them to take it back."

"I had to get clothes some way," the girl shouted.

"Just a minute," I said firmly. "You're here to attempt . . ."

The fellow cut me off. "I'm not. I've been dragged in here by her."

The girl said, "It's not my idea—and you damn well know it."

"Sit down," I said, raising my voice to make myself heard. "This is a court, even though I'm not in robes and on the bench. I expect the respect due any court, and I can hold you in contempt if I don't get it."

This startled them into silence. I continued, "I don't think you're ready to discuss this matter calmly and logically. I'm postponing this hearing until 2 P.M. tomorrow. You are ordered to return at that time."

They started to rise. "From what I see here," I said, indicating the papers they had filled out, "your only trouble is money. You're both young—only twenty—and you've got two children. Many people find themselves in the same kind of a financial jam as you're in—but they work it out. For those two children of yours, I think you should at least give the problem some thought."

As I nodded in dismissal, the girl hurried out ahead of her husband as though fearful he might say something. Despite the scene they had just staged, they were not bad youngsters, but extremely immature.

Their names were Leona and Perry McDonald. They had quit high school at seventeen to marry. Both wanted a divorce, but the girl, at the urging of her mother, had filed for conciliation and was merely going through the motions. Only the day before, the mother had come to my chambers. According to her, both were still in love but too angry to admit it. "They always got along fine until they got into this mix-up over money."

As the couple left my chambers, the clerk came in to

hand me a case history. "Sounded like a stormy session," he commented.

"Their trouble's money," I remarked.

"Isn't that everyone's?" he asked, grinning.

It was most everyone's, but not to the extent it was the McDonalds'. The records showed that Perry McDonald worked at a service station, earning an average take-home pay of $75 a week. They had weekly payments of $45. That left them $30 a week for food, rent, utilities, and incidentals.

That night I took their file home. While guns roared and horses' hooves pounded in the next room as Patrick watched television, I struggled through the facts. Certain ones stood out:

> Petitioner said her husband cashes his pay check on his way home, that he gives her two dollars a day for expenses, and that he becomes angry whenever she mentions money matters....
>
> Both say they cannot continue their married life, that their constant quarrels over finances are ruining their health....

A few minutes later, when Wyatt Earp got too noisy, I fled upstairs, and there my wife found me pacing back and forth. "What do you say to youngsters like these?" I asked her.

She smiled. "I can remember—if you can't—when we spent $20 for an armchair, and didn't eat for a week."

I laughed then and threw off the feeling that this couple needed a good lecture. When we first try something, whether it's balancing a budget or playing tennis, we're going to make mistakes. We all do, even the smartest. And some of us, as my father would put it, don't have much of a head for figures.

But what to do, how to approach them—that was the question. "It won't help just to talk with them," I said, and added, "The last time I tried that I sounded like Benjamin Franklin. 'A penny saved is a penny earned.' "

I went outdoors for a walk. "Talking won't do any good," I repeated aloud to myself. A passing boxer dog looked at me strangely, and doubled his pace. But a night walk can do wonders. My thoughts began to crystallize, and a plan came to mind, so ridiculously simple that I wondered why I hadn't thought of it before. Until 2 A.M., I sat at my desk scribbling and erasing. But when I finally did get to bed, I slept soundly.

Leona McDonald's billowing skirts filled the big armchair when she sat down alone with me the next day. She was composed outwardly, though I suspect far from it inwardly.

"I'm sorry, Judge, about yesterday," she said.

"We all get excited at times."

For a long time we talked, and the talking did her good. She explained their financial troubles in detail. They had bought everything on time payments, their furniture, appliances, television, hi-fi set, and car. They had succeeded in juggling these payments by stalling first one creditor and then another.

"I was so mad I could've hit him one night," she said. "He brought home a hi-fi set. I told him if he could buy that, he could just get us a better apartment. We've been living in a dump, Judge, and I don't think that's right."

I asked, "Why did you open the charge accounts, Mrs.

McDonald, when you knew you had too many payments already?"

She hesitated, her lips trembling. "I was mad, Judge. I just wanted to get even with Perry."

This was an old story. One mate or the other will go on a spending spree to express the hostility he feels.

When I was alone with her husband, I began, "Money is like everything else in marriage, Mr. McDonald. It belongs to both of you, no matter which one earns it, and both of you should have a say about how it is spent."

As we talked I gradually explained the plan I had formulated the night before. He listened intently, and almost visibly the old antagonisms began to drop away.

I called his wife back in. "You have several factors to consider," I said to both. "First, I believe you still love each other and are only waiting for the other one to take the first step. Second, you have two babies you don't want to see grow up in a broken home. Third, you aren't going to solve anything financially by getting a divorce. Strictly from a money point of view, you can't afford a divorce."

I turned to her. "From a $75-a-week pay check, Mrs. McDonald, you can't hope to get much alimony. The court would order your husband to pay you $7.50 to $10 a week for the support of each child and possibly $15 a week alimony until the children are old enough for you to go to work. In other words, Mr. McDonald, you're going to be maintaining two households, not one."

That stopped them. They hadn't thought far enough ahead to realize that if you cut an apple in two, you end up with only two half apples.

I outlined the plan I had worked out to the McDonalds. They listened with obvious misgivings.

"I don't know," he began in a surly tone. "I don't like the sound of it."

"You don't like the sound of it, Mr. McDonald," I put in, "because you can't spend your pay check the way you have been spending it."

She broke in. "Perry, don't you think . . . ?" She glanced at him hopefully. "He's right, Perry. We owe something to the children, and it isn't going to help any . . . and . . . it isn't as if I didn't love you, Perry."

At that he smiled suddenly, as though that smile had been waiting for the right word. . . .

The plan, which, in principle, was to become a part of the Reconciliation Agreement, was this:

1. The parties acknowledged that a substantial part of their difficulty had resulted from opening charge accounts and purchasing on credit far beyond their financial means. They agreed to exert every effort to arrange for a pooling of their payments and obligations in order to reduce the monthly total required for such purpose. [With the McDonalds, we estimated they could reduce their weekly payments from $45 to $35, thus leaving them $40 out of his $75 salary.]
2. Perry McDonald agreed to a clause in the Reconciliation Agreement by which he promised to give Leona McDonald $20 a week for "the necessary food and clothing for the family."
3. Both agreed, within 10 days, to work out a family budget. They promised they would place money regularly in an envelope for each main budget item.
4. Leona McDonald agreed that her husband should be "the treasurer of the family partnership" and should apply the funds in accord with their budget. "Any remaining balance shall be applied by said party only as agreed upon by husband and wife."

On his part, Perry McDonald promised to keep simple but accurate accounts in a book that "shall be available for inspection by the other party and by the court upon demand."

To help them in drawing up a budget, I submitted a draft of one I had spent considerable time on the night before. This suggested budget provided $110 monthly for food; $70, rent; $15, utilities; $9, insurance; $20, clothing; $25 installment payments on automobile, etc.; $15, automobile maintenance; $5, other transportation; $10, medical and dental; $10, husband's pocket money; $10, wife's pin money; and $26, miscellaneous, such as for church, savings, and entertainment.

After they had signed, he turned to his wife. "Why didn't you say what you just did before we came in here, baby? We could've avoided all this if you'd said it."

She laughed softly. "You big, big baboon. . . ."

A different approach was needed when the money troubles comprised only the surface problem. People spend money riotously for many reasons. Some to "fight back" at injustices, real or imagined. Some because of a feeling of insecurity. Some because of the sense of power it gives them. And some simply because they desire beautiful things far beyond their means.

Often a partner who consistently spends beyond the other's income is unconsciously attempting to communicate hostility over an entirely unrelated issue and honestly does not know the real reason for the spending. Other times, as in the case of Mrs. McDonald, the spender is quite aware of the motive.

Financial troubles do not always spring from a *lack* of money. Strangely enough, in our present culture money seems to be a hush-hush area, and it requires discipline to keep it an "open" subject, even within a family. The secretive husband who never lets his wife know how much he earns and furtively doles money out to her dollar by dollar for household necessities is driving a wedge into their understanding of each other which will push them far apart emotionally. The wife who secretly hoards her money is, of course, giving rise to the same problem.

Take the case of the Samuelsons, a middle-aged couple, married eighteen years, with a daughter in boarding school. At the time of their marriage, each had a good sum in the bank which each continued to handle separately. Then, a year before they separated, they completed plans for a new home. The building was well underway when they began bickering over how they were to participate in the financing.

Shortly before, Mrs. Samuelson had undergone a hysterectomy, and they had suspended marital relations. Because of her illness, she felt a great sense of insecurity. As a result, she put off contributing her share to the new home. She told her husband she would no longer be able to work, and if he left her, she didn't want to be involved financially. This was the first suggestion of a possible separation, and his imagination went to work. He thought she planned to divorce him and take half his money through California's community property law. A few days later, he lost his head and struck her.

Our discussion, in capsule form, went as follows:

Gene Samuelson: "I'd been drinking a little heavily when I hit her, but I haven't had a drop since. I really love her, Judge. But I feel she is selfish. She's very secretive—always has been. She never tells me anything about her money or property. I've always told her about my things.

She tends to call her things hers and our things hers, too."

After an hour of counseling, he told me: "I haven't been as considerate of her as I should have been. I know it was probably the first time in her life she was ever frightened. As you point out, it was the time she needed me the most, and I moved her into a separate bedroom. It was for her own comfort, and to remove temptation on my part, but I can see where she probably felt I was casting her off. I can see, too, how financing the new home must have worried her at a time like that. It was the first time we'd ever tackled anything big together."

Mrs. Samuelson had this to say: "My husband accuses me of being secretive about my money. Well, I don't even know how much he makes or where he spends it. I've always paid my own doctor bills and bought my own clothes as well as my daughter's. He's pushed me aside. I've wondered sometimes—it seems unnatural that our relations should cease and he shouldn't be attracted to someone else—some other woman. . . . The doctor did say it wouldn't be harmful to me to resume normal relations, but since he struck me and there's been all this talk about money, I haven't told him."

During my conference with them together, I pointed out that the California law on community property was a very wise statute. I said: "The law provides that all money, earnings and property acquired after marriage become the joint funds of both the husband and wife, and it contemplates that such funds should be jointly administered.

"When you two married, your joint earnings should have gone into a common account. Had you done so, you probably would have accumulated enough to acquire your new home out of funds earned since marriage. You would have built up a sense of oneness in this field, thinking and speaking of 'our' money, just as you think of your child as 'ours' and not 'my' child. These mental reservations tend to build up feelings of selfishness, of division, of two people living together for the sharing of only parts of their lives.

"Once and for all, let's bury the problem of finances. You, Mrs. Samuelson, have saved $10,000, which admittedly has come from your earnings. This is clearly community funds. It happens to be the amount needed to pay off the loan on your home. When your husband sold the war bonds to make the down payment on the lot and start the building, this was a liquidation, too, of earnings since marriage, and belonged to the two of you even though carried in his name.

"I understand the doctor has indicated there is no reason why normal marital relations shouldn't be engaged in. May I urge that you postpone any resumption until you have been living together for some time and until your feelings for one another bring this about naturally."

They left the court together, determined to work out a reconciliation. She blamed their troubles on the mental attitude she had developed as a result of her illness and operation. But that was only a part truth. Their problem had begun eighteen years before when they entered into a marriage that was only half a marriage.

The Court recognized that every home needs a financial safety valve. Each budget should make provision for occasional irrationality. Fromme suggests this idea:

> We cannot afford to take so hard-bitten a view of human nature as to sneer at every case of self-indulgence. A man is not necessarily weak for finally succumbing and getting himself the fishing rod he wanted for years. Nor is he ir-

> responsible for spending somewhat more than he can afford on his wife's birthday present. The point, as one philosopher put it, is that 'it is not wisdom to be only wise'.... Good living consists in establishing the kind of balance which leaves room for the expression of these impulses within, of course, the limits of reason.

Sometimes the conflict over money cannot be settled, and it becomes a matter of one person's accepting the *status quo* and attempting to hold the marriage together on whatever foundation there is.

This irreconcilable difference shows up most clearly with the "plungers." They are the individuals who risk their money in the hope of big returns. They are the ones who become the financiers of our country, the inventors, the creators. But they also are the ones who walk the streets, looking for jobs. Their number proved far greater than I had ever conceived before I went with the Conciliation Court. Their schemes may involve anywhere from a few hundred dollars, which may be a fortune to their families, up into the many thousands.

In the latter category was George Hallmark. By twenty-five, he had made his first "strike." By thirty, he was in bankruptcy. But he had bounce, and within five years he was back on top in a different line of business. His wife, Grace, had no desire to share in the million dollars George had promised they would have by the time he was forty-five. She wanted only enough of the world's goods for comfort and to educate the children. When he bounced back, therefore, she begged him to profit by previous experience and set aside a sufficient sum to guarantee their security.

He didn't listen to her, and his next speculation failed.

At forty, he was working in an aircraft plant for wages. The youngsters took odd jobs to help out, and Grace looked after the neighbors' children.

Then one day George saw an opportunity to start a small parts plant, and mortgaged their home. Within three years, he was employing 100 people. Not satisfied, he took over a bankrupt company and neglected the profitable parts factory. This was more than Grace could stand, and she filed for separate maintenance. Her attorney got a restraining order so George could not mortgage the parts plant or otherwise encumber it. George rebelled. What kind of a wife was she that she wanted to seize control of her own husband's business?

When Grace Hallmark came before me, she proved a very striking, dark-haired woman, endowed with charm and poise. She had gone along with her husband for years, she explained, though his constant drive had worried her and the children. He was, after all, pushing forty-five. One more failure and he might not bounce back.

By the standards of most people, they had everything—a home, four wonderful children, mutual respect and love, and no vices of any kind. He was earning $25,000 a year from the parts plant. But he was confident the new enterprise would pay him $50,000. He couldn't become a millionaire on $25,000 a year. That was his philosophy, according to his wife. Obviously, he was possessed with a neurotic compulsion to conquer. Seemingly, over and over, he had to prove to himself that he could do the impossible.

When he sat down with me, I saw a large, bulky man, aggressive and hard-driving. He spoke the same way he lived, forthright and to the point. Hammering his words, he talked about the challenge of tackling ventures that others couldn't lick.

"I've invested a lot of time and money in this new deal," he said. "Are the courts going to force me to the wall now, with the help of my wife?"

He was difficult to counsel. Men who are a success in their own eyes usually are. Step by cautious step, however, I explained that there must be compromises in a marriage. The individual who hasn't learned to compromise, to give a little of his freedom of thought and action, to be considerate of the other, doesn't make a good marital partner. And the compromising, I added emphatically, cannot be all one-sided.

The idea got across, and because both were sensible people, we succeeded in working out a compromise: He agreed that his wife and the children were entitled to security, and that morally and under the California community property law, Grace owned one-half of their acquisitions since marriage. Since he had no right to gamble with her half, he would deposit one-half the net earnings from the parts factory in trust for the family's future and the children's education.

On her part, Grace agreed he could do as he pleased with his half, and she would interpose no objections to any speculations he might undertake.

In my long talk with her, she had agreed that it was unrealistic and unreasonable to assume that a man of forty-four could be changed abruptly into another individual. The last thing she said was: "I wouldn't want to change George. He's always been so good to me and the children. He's a fine man, even though I don't understand him and what he's trying to prove by killing himself. But I wouldn't change him—because in the process I might change all the wonderful things about him, too."

chapter eighteen

Working Wife

Where the wife works on the outside, then the husband must share to a larger extent in the work of the home....

—RECONCILIATION AGREEMENT

Just how much right does a husband have to dictate whether his wife should work?

That was the question Pam Cochran asked herself—and her answer took her straight to the Conciliation Court. Her husband, Roy, had told her in no uncertain terms that he wanted a divorce. He was a slender, personable, twenty-nine-year-old junior executive with a chain drug firm. She was twenty-four and had abundant personal charm. She possessed the well-groomed look of exactly what she was, a highly competent private secretary.

If the Cochrans had stopped to think about it, they would have seen that they were the victims of the most radical and sudden shift in home living patterns that has taken place in all history. Up until three decades ago, few women worked outside the home. Today, 21 million draw weekly pay checks. This number includes 12,700,000 wives, or roughly 60 per cent of all women working, an increase of 15 per cent since World War II.

As a result of this upheaval, the historic role of the male as head of the household has been shaken. In millions of homes today, the husband and wife share equally in the making of decisions as well as the actual physical care of the children and the household. In many other homes, the woman has become the head of the household through the power of her earnings as a working wife, and the husband has lost his masculine superiority.

This sharp change in living patterns has brought with it an emotional turmoil that earlier generations never knew. Most couples have taken it in stride, working out their new problems with goodhearted comradeship. With others, though, the change has affected the entire structure of their marriage.

Pam and Roy Cochran were in the latter group. Their surface trouble was simply that she wanted desperately to work, and he was dead set against it. When they came before me, they were both quiet mannered, but beneath the pleasant facade, each was consumed with a resentment for the other that burned out any hopes I had that these two could be brought together again. While it was rougher on my nervous system to listen to individuals who shouted at each other, sometimes I wondered if they weren't better able to find themselves in their tirade of words than these couples who hid their true thoughts and feelings.

After Pam and Roy Cochran were gone, I sat talking into a recording machine for half an hour or better, noting the high points of what they had said. Although they talked separately with me, in dictating I tried to piece their arguments together in their own way of speaking, since the expressions a person uses may tell more than the exact words themselves. This is what my secretary transcribed:

ROY: She knew how I felt about her working when we were married. She was a secretary in our office. That's where I met her.

PAM: That's right. He did tell me how he felt, and I said I'd give this housewife business a whirl. I did try it for a year. We'd thought we'd have a baby by then but we didn't, and I got bored sitting around waiting for Pete to learn to talk. That's our parakeet. So I got up my courage and told Roy I was going back to work, and he got awful mad.

ROY: It hit me like a truck. I figured she didn't love me or she wouldn't want to go back to work. I began noticing then she wasn't nearly as affectionate as she had been.

PAM: He was the one who wasn't affectionate. Every time I got romantic, he'd give me the cold treatment. That was one reason I took the job. Things just weren't going good at home, and I couldn't sit around all day thinking about them, and listening to that blasted parakeet.

ROY: Another thing, Judge, I don't want to feel I'm in competition with my own wife. No man does. Here she was bringing home almost as much money as I was. Sometimes I think she just took the job to show me up. I like to feel I'm the man of the house, like my father was.

PAM: Well, I want to feel I'm the woman of the house, that I've got a part in it, too. Honest, I wasn't trying to show him up. And I never did anything with my money without talking it over with him. I know I've hurt his male ego, but I can't understand why.

ROY: Our home's like a boarding house. Half the time she's not there when I get back nights. We don't need the money. So why should she work?

PAM: Roy can't understand that it's not just the money.

It's doing something that you've got a talent for, and taking pride in your work, and having the boss tell you what a fine job you're doing. It's lots of other things besides the money.

ROY: Sometimes we'd go a week without marital relations because she was too exhausted.

PAM: I've been too tired sometimes, but I told Roy if he would let me know a little in advance, I'd see that I wasn't too tired. I thought everything was fine in that line, and then one day he moved to the athletic club.

ROY: I just got fed up not knowing whether I had a wife or not. She's a wonderful girl, and she's got everything, but I guess I want a girl who hasn't got everything.

PAM: Really, he's a sweet guy. But he always has to prove he's very much the man. He never seems to relax and take things easy. I think maybe it's the way he was brought up. His mother died when he was small, and his father left him with an aunt. He liked the aunt but felt his father had deserted him. Then his father married again and came for him. He didn't like his stepmother and still couldn't forgive his father. Then to top everything off, he fell in love with a girl just out of finishing school. She was playing the field for the best prize she could land and for a time, it was Roy. Then one morning he woke up and read she had eloped with someone else. I felt so sorry for him that I tried to make it up to him around the office, and the first I knew we wound up one night on a date.

ROY: When you get right down to it, I want an old-fashioned home with children.

PAM: Roy doesn't know it but I'm pregnant now. I'm not going to tell him. He'd feel he had to come back to me out of duty. If he comes back, he's got to love me for myself.

That was their story. As with so many cases involving working wives, many other factors besides the fact that Pam had a job contributed to their unhappiness. In this instance, it was Roy Cochran's feeling of inadequacy, an insecurity that stemmed from his childhood, perhaps even an unconscious resentment of women. On her part, Pam had made little effort to understand him.

As best as I could, I pointed out that society today was constituted differently from that of his father's day, and that it was generally acceptable now for women to work outside the home. His wife, I said, had a compulsion to be doing something she felt was worthwhile. She had an education she wanted to use. She was bored with sitting around an apartment, just as he would be if the roles were reversed. She had no intention of hurting his ego or thwarting his desire to assert himself as a man.

When I was alone with her, I tried to persuade her to tell her husband she was pregnant. She refused, and since she had given me the information in confidence, I respected it.

They were a difficult pair to counsel. She was willing to consider a reconciliation, but he balked. Eventually I convinced them they should consult a counseling agency.

The counselors found that Roy Cochran's feelings of inadequacy caused him to expect an inordinate amount of mothering and reassurance from his wife, which she could not always give him when she worked. They found Pam immature. She was accustomed to being the center of attention and was unprepared for the give-and-take relationships of marriage. Moreover, she had developed an intense resentment toward her husband, feeling that he was unreasonable and selfish. The counselors attempted to release this resentment and to develop in her an understanding of her husband's needs. If she would recognize his achievements, cater a little to his male ego, he might change in his attitude toward her working.

By two months later, we still didn't know where we stood with the case of the Cochrans. They still hadn't reconciled.

The Rennsalears posed a different problem. They were in their late thirties and had two teen-age boys who shifted for themselves, roaming the streets. She prepared dinner for the boys and her husband but left home before her husband returned from his work. Mornings, her husband got breakfast and left before she was awake. Actually, they seldom saw each other. Although she quit work at midnight, she always stopped for a few beers with friends before returning around 2 A.M. When her husband remonstrated, she told him he could move out if he didn't like the setup, that she was making plenty of money and could do as she pleased. As for finances, she contributed as much as her husband to the support of the home. He made the payments on the house, furniture, and car. She took care of the food bills. Whenever other expenses came up, they fought bitterly over who was to pay them. They even went their separate ways on vacations.

Their marital relations were virtually by appointment. Since their hours were different, they slept in separate rooms to avoid disturbing each other. Whenever he suggested intimacy, she would bargain with him. "If I'm nice to you, will you vacuum the house Saturday?"

He felt he was buying her as he would a prostitute. He admitted he felt such revulsion that he often took her in such a raw, brutal way that she was bound to hate him.

Still he loved her in a manner of speaking and wanted to effect a reconciliation. When she received the Court's order-to-appear letter, she read it to the boys and tore it up. Although as judge, I could have forced her to appear, I hesitated to do so. The husband, too, recognized that a citation would anger her to the point where she wouldn't even listen. I thought a separation was clearly indicated since their marriage had wasted away until it was no more than an arrangement.

Among other cases that contained common problems were these:

In the beginning, the husband very grudgingly had agreed to his wife's working. Then when she became pregnant and wanted to quit, he objected just as strongly. He had become accustomed to the added income. They reconciled when he realized that his wife, as a partner in the home, should have the final say as to when she should quit her job. At this time we drew up a clause in the Reconciliation Agreement which set forth the premise that the wife's income should be spent on capital investments, such as new furniture, a down payment on a home, or savings for the future, so that if she did leave her job the family budget would not suffer. Several cases came before the Court in which the two had pooled their income for general expenses, thus raising their living standard by buying a better home and perhaps two cars instead of one. Then when the wife quit her work, they had to sell their home or move into a less expensive apartment. Such situations were fraught with recriminations.

Another husband, like the one discussed in the chapter about jealousy, felt the knife turn inside him every time he thought of his wife associating with other men in the plant where she was employed. He considered she was fair game for every man she met. Certainly, a husband must expect his wife to meet the challenge of interest on the part of other men, just as he must meet the challenge of interest by other women. If the couple's love and relationship are strong, and particularly if their consciences have been kept alert by the strong forces of religion, neither will succumb to the pull of such sex attraction.

Another couple who came before the Court were only nineteen. She was working to put her husband through college. Since it was her money supporting them, she assumed the role of head of the household in none-too-diplomatic fashion. He couldn't take his wife's constant orders any more than she could have taken his. They promised to attempt a reconciliation, but two months later, they asked for release from their agreement, and divorce followed.

From experience gathered in the handling of many cases, the Court counselors reached this conclusion about wives working: The husband and wife should decide mutually on their goals. The wife with children shouldn't be working just for the sake of working, especially if she doesn't feel a compelling need to, as Pam Cochran did. If economic necessity requires it to attain a certain objective, then they should determine how much money they will need, and work toward that goal. Upon reaching it, the wife should leave her job. While I recognize that many mothers have to work and have done heroic jobs of running home, children, and a job, still I firmly believe the traditional home should be encouraged. If at all possible, a mother should spend her time and energy with her husband, her children, and her home.

Unfortunately, those mothers who must work discover that society is inclined to place the blame on them for everything unwholesome that happens in their family. If a child becomes delinquent, does poorly in school, or makes any kind of mistake, people invariably hold the working mother accountable when often the cause would have been beyond her control even if she had stayed home.

While children often suffer from lack of supervision, interest, love, and attention when both parents work away from home, still many employed mothers have well-adjusted children. Although they may not spend as much "supervisory time" with their children, working mothers can devote "time alone" with them each evening. Even small amounts of time spent in this way are equal to hours spent when the children are simply "underfoot." Quality of time, not quantity of time, spent seems most important.

We never forgot the Cochrans. Every time I saw their name on our list, I wondered about them. The agency reported they had dropped out after five months of counseling. We wrote them but never had an answer.

Then one morning months later, I slit open one of those envelopes so tiny you wonder how they ever get through the mail. Inside was an announcement of a baby born to Mr. and Mrs. Roy Cochran. The enclosed snapshot showed a very proud mother and a very proud father leaning over a crib.

chapter nineteen

Faith

We acknowledge that religion can become a very important factor in the preservation of our home . . . and that the daily recitation of a family prayer would aid us in keeping uppermost in our minds our responsibilities to God, to our children and to each other.

—RECONCILIATION AGREEMENT

A glance at the clock on my desk told me we had been in conference for more than two hours. The two seated before me were both in their late twenties. They were well-dressed, well-educated members of the white-collar class.

Compared to the average run of marital difficulties, theirs seemed trivial. A lot of little things had gone wrong, resulting in deeply wounded feelings on both sides. False pride had erected a high wall between them, and neither would give an inch.

In desperation, I wondered how I could bring them to their senses. I could see them growing restless, and knew I could hold them only briefly.

These were the minutes that counted, minutes that might change the course of two lives if I could find the right thought. It would have to be more than the mere logic of words. It would have to be a thought that would jar them to their very core.

As the silence lay heavy, I thumbed through the file,

searching for a clue. Then my eyes picked up a sentence that indicated they were churchgoers. Something nudged me, and from my own past came a memory.

"I want to tell you about something that happened to me when I was a young lawyer," I said.

They looked at me strangely. "I hadn't been practicing long when I was called to the deathbed of a widow who had had a hard life. Her daughter had run away from home and never been heard of, and her son was mentally deficient. She ran the farm almost alone, but nothing she did ever turned out right."

Dusk was growing deeper, and I reached over to switch on the desk lamp. "She had a sister, a widow, too, but with four strong boys, and everything that family touched turned out well."

Though it had been twenty-five years, the scene came back with the sharp clarity of impressions gained when young. "When I arrived at the farmhouse, I was admitted by the son, now a full-grown man and a sight to send the shivers up one's back.

"I heard the feeble voice of the stricken woman call from the darkness of a bedroom. I fumbled my way in, stumbled over a chair, and listened while she told me what she wished done after her death to provide care for her son.

"I asked for the names and addresses of her relatives, and she gave them to me, cursing each one as she did. They were the black curses which one associates with the dark ages.

"I was terribly shocked. I knew her sister and nephews had never done her any harm, and here she was on her deathbed. . . .

"She had been active in a church, and on my way home, I stopped by to talk with her pastor, thinking he would want to visit her. He thanked me, and added, "But I must say I'm deeply shocked, my son. Not at the curses of this poor old woman—but at you.

"The pastor's keen, blue eyes seemed to bore straight through me, and what they saw they didn't like. I recoiled as if from a slap in the face."

To the two listening intently to the story, I said, "I've never forgotten what he told me. 'My son,' he said, 'I fear you have been guilty of a most grievous sin. You have judged another human being. You have said to yourself that if this poor old lady dies with these curses on her lips, her soul will be lost forever. You should know that it is only for God to judge. He alone knows the trials and tribulations she has had to bear. He will forgive her much because she has merited much, under burdens which would have broken the backs of most people. He gave her few talents, therefore she will be accountable for but a few. It is the person who has been given much in the way of talents and gifts, including the gift of faith, on whom the burden of responsibility will be heavy."

They both looked at me searchingly. They were beginning to stir under the little old priest's words, recalled from such a long time ago.

"Now let's get back to you two," I said. "Each of you was given many talents; intelligence, a nice appearance, good personality, and the gift of faith. Much is expected of you."

I paused and then continued, "You will want God to be charitable in His judgment of you, but how can He be when you are so uncharitable to each other?"

Neither said a word. It was one of the longest moments of my life. Then suddenly the thought told on both of them, at almost the identical second. They turned to each other, and her eyes filled with tears. He put his hand gently on hers in a touch which said more than a thousand words.

Eventually we went through the steps of working out a Reconciliation Agreement, and when they left I was deep in thought. Those two had needed a new channel of communication to each other and had found it through God. Couldn't other couples reach each other through this same channel, if it were pointed out to them? And what better way to suggest it than through a family prayer, one written out so they might study it—a prayer by which a couple could jointly ask God's forgiveness and, in doing so, communicate forgiveness to the other. We could include such a prayer, one common to all faiths, in the Reconciliation Agreement which each would read while waiting in the reception room.

But what would others think, my colleagues on the bench included, if religion were to be injected into the work of the Court? Might they not ask if this weren't a violation of the doctrine of separation of church and state? The possible criticism gave me pause, but only momentarily. Surely everyone is agreed that this doctrine was never intended as a weapon to separate man from his religion. On the contrary, ours is a religious people and our nation was founded upon a firm belief in God. Remove the concept of our dependence upon God from our form of government and it would collapse.

No, I assured myself that evening, the doctrine of separation means that there shall be no official state religion, that no one form of faith shall be preferred over any other, that every man shall be free to worship God in his own way.

So that night, safely ensconced in the warmth of my home, I set about writing a family prayer that might serve as a guidepost for those whose faith in each other had been shaken but whose faith in God remained steadfast.

While I drafted and redrafted the prayer, numerous petitioners came before the Court whose marriages had been threatened by conflicts over religion.

There was the case of the disbeliever. He was an outspoken, chip-on-the-shoulder man who constantly ridiculed his wife's faith in God and her church activities. His attitude dared me to discuss religion. After talking in generalities, I picked up a small metal paperweight in the shape of a saddle and rapped it on my desk. "To all intents and purposes this is a piece of solid metal," I began. "Yet such is not the case. Actually, it is composed of minute particles whirling around each other in perfect order. If we could make an instrument small enough, we could stick it through that piece of 'solid' metal without touching anything."

His reaction was a noncommittal shrug. I continued, "These minute particles whirl in such a perfect plan that if they should collide we would have an atomic explosion. And because scientists recognize and understand this plan by which tiny particles move, they can predict the order and movements of our entire universe—the moon, the stars, our earth—for many years to come.

"To argue that this perfect order is the result of chance is to deny science and ordinary common sense. And the existence of a plan presupposes a Master Planner—God."

He smiled. "I've heard that argument before, Judge, and I'm not buying it."

I had anticipated that reaction, but it was a thought I wanted to drop. He might get to mulling it over, and even if he never found faith he might grow more tolerant of his wife's beliefs.

Yet how to reach him? I wanted to point out that his wife was interested in his own eternity as well as hers, that he was interested only in his little segment of space and time on earth, that she wanted to believe in and plan for their future for all time.

But to one who didn't believe in God, eternity would have no meaning. For the next few minutes I sat quietly while he talked, seeking to call up something that would touch him.

The idea was slow in coming. I began cautiously. "From our experiences here, we've found it's important that a husband should never interfere in the thoughts and work of his wife or seek to dominate them. What she wants to think and do is vital to her, just as the husband's opinions and beliefs are to him. He has no right to force his beliefs on her."

He was listening, critically to be sure, but at least he was thinking. "Let's look at it this way. What would happen if she gave up her faith and went along with you? She would be troubled constantly and would be a most unsatisfactory wife. She would carry a great sense of guilt. She would never know any true happiness—because her faith directs her way of life, a way I feel certain you cannot change without destroying her."

When I put the matter entirely on a personal basis—pointing out that he would be wrecking a human being's life, as well as dispelling any chance of their happiness together—he finally agreed to keep his own negative thoughts on religion to himself. They signed a Reconciliation Agreement by which he promised to respect her right to her own religious beliefs and agreed that she could continue her church work.

Then there were the cases of interfaith marriages. In one, the girl was Catholic and the boy Protestant. Because of parental objections to their being married in the church of the other, they eloped and were wed by a justice of the peace. Neither had been deeply religious. But upon the death of their first baby, both had turned to God for help. In time, they had fallen into bitter quarrels over which church they should attend. Their parents, in-laws, and friends had lined up on opposite sides, to aggravate the situation.

This problem of interfaith marriages, whether the parties are Catholic, Protestant, or Jewish, develops often into a serious one, and more frequently than not into one that defies reconciliation. Marriage poses enough problems without deliberately adding this one. Couples may differ over many subjects, but a uniformity of thinking on basic matters of faith which bind the individual in conscience seems all-important.

So I would never encourage people of substantially different religions to fall in love or marry. I would do my utmost to discourage them, because the obstacles ahead of them are most difficult and require considerable understanding and compassion. If they persisted in their desires, then I would counsel them to acquire a knowledge of what each religion requires of its members in advance of the marriage, so that a full agreement and understanding may be had and painful heartaches avoided. I know of several instances in which such knowledge, carefully considered, has deterred couples from marrying.

In this case, I told the Catholic girl and the Protestant boy, "You both believe in God. That much you have in common, although the requirements of your respective faiths are substantially different. And since you are intelligent people, you must realize that you should not interfere with each other in the right to worship as each of you wishes or feels bound in conscience to do. In fact, you should support each other in doing those things which you know his or her church asks of its members. You should start by straightening out your marriage itself."

They left promising to live up to this "right to worship" principle. They still had many problems ahead of them. In time, the matter of birth control might become an issue, and the faith in which to rear their children. Given love and understanding, though, they might find their way.

One case, a triangle one, was solved by faith alone. The wife and husband were in their mid-twenties. He had had an affair with her closest friend, and her friend's betrayal of her added to the normal hurt she would have suffered. "Besides, Judge," she said, "this isn't the first time. He's had affairs with three other women since we've been married. He's always sorry and promises me he'll never do it again—but I can't believe him any more."

Their problem seemed hopeless. He was willing to accede to anything, but she was adamant. "I'd never know a moment's peace. Every time he left the house I'd suspect him."

The same old question posed itself. What in the world to do? They had two children, a boy four and a girl five, sitting in the reception room at that very minute. The couple themselves seemed ideally suited except for this recurring transgression on his part. Even if I persuaded her to give him another chance, I had the feeling that there would be a fifth woman and that I would only be postponing the time of reckoning.

As we talked, I discovered they both were deeply religious. Yes, the husband, too, in spite of his adultery. So instead of asking them to sign a Reconciliation Agreement, which would be only another promise to him, I asked if they would do this: Would they talk with their pastor, as they had with me, and seek spiritual guidance?

In asking this, I knew their pastor probably would give them effective marital counseling as well as help them spiritually. Virtually every faith has recognized by now its duty to train its clergy in counseling on home relationships. Most of the Catholic, Protestant, and Jewish schools of theology stress courses in such subjects.

She shook her head. "He'd promise our pastor, but that's all it would be. Just another promise."

"But have you ever taken God into your talks?" She shook her head, and I added, "He would be part of it this time, and your husband would know it."

She assented. Their pastor told me later that they came to him that same day, and both laid bare their souls. He took them from the study into the church where they might feel God's presence more. He didn't ask for any course of action. Before he knew it, the husband was asking forgiveness as he fell to his knees in prayer, and the wife was giving of her forgiveness.

I've always had the feeling there never was a fifth woman.

Though this case was solved by faith, another was wrecked by one partner's interpretation of faith.

The wife constantly flaunted her own goodness in her husband's face. Her religion was the bustling, demonstrative kind. She never talked with anyone five minutes without establishing herself as a prospective angel. In her own eyes, her husband would never get past Gabriel. Finally, the husband could take it no longer and filed for divorce.

When the case was referred to us, the wife proceeded to tell me what a pagan her mate was. It developed that his worst sin was oversleeping Sunday mornings. If he had the proper Christian spirit, she said, he would bound out at the first ring of the alarm.

She was hurt and then angry when I suggested that people give evidence of their faith in different ways and to differing degrees. So I was going to stick up for the sluggard, was I?

Once more, I suggested they seek assistance from their pastor. "I know how to live like a Christian without anybody telling me," she said defiantly.

Her husband laughed. "She's already had a long talk with him, Judge. I don't know what he told her. She'd never tell me."

She was a tragic, pathetic figure as she left my chambers. She was wrecking her life needlessly on her mistaken righteousness. She needed to know and understand that there can be no true faith without a sense of humility.

Late one evening, as I was scribbling away on the prayer I couldn't seem to word just right, the bailiff announced that a young couple wanted to see me. It was unusual for "customers" to ask for the judge at this hour, and I anticipated some grave emergency and steeled myself to withstand the onslaught of still more disturbed emotions.

As they stepped hesitatingly by the bailiff, I received a pleasant surprise. They were two young people, bubbling with happiness and reflecting sparkle and star dust.

The young fellow said, "You don't remember me, Judge, but I heard you speak at a meeting a year ago on marriage. I'm Tom Carroll and this is my fiancée, Mary Lormer. I've told Mary about your work, and we even read a copy of the Reconciliation Agreement, and we're going to live by it."

He hesitated. "We want to ask you to marry us."

"Why, you honor me," I said, and hesitated, wondering how I could tell them so they wouldn't be hurt.

"It's this way," I continued slowly, "I do have the power

as a judge to marry people, but I've never done that. I know many judges do, and I'm not criticizing them. It's just that I feel all marriages should be performed by some minister of God, so that there will be a fourth party to every marriage contract—God Himself."

Tom nodded. "Mary believes in God—but as for me, well, sir, I'm of a scientific bent, and I've always figured the Bible just didn't measure up with the true facts which modern scientific knowledge has proved. Don't misunderstand me. I can see the benefits that come from living in accordance with religious principles. It's—it's just that I don't believe."

Her hand searched his in a consoling little gesture.

"Sit down, please," I said, and proceeded to tell them about the late Dr. Robert A. Millikan of the California Institute of Technology, one of the foremost scientists of this century. From my desk, I took an old clipping that I had treasured, and read: "Dr. Millikan summed up his philosophy thus: 'Science cannot do anything truly useful until it knows what is good for mankind. Religion provides the broad directive. . . .' "

When I finished, I said, "You can see that Dr. Millikan saw no denial of the existence of God in the revelations of science but, on the contrary, ever-increasing evidence that all existence cannot be the result of an accident but required a plan."

After fumbling around in a desk drawer, I brought forth a copy of *Human Destiny* by the noted French scientist, Lecomte du Noüy. Handing the book to Tom, I said, "I want you to read this book. It approaches the question of the existence of God from the purely scientific basis."

Tom nodded. "I've always wanted to believe. To tell the truth, I've always envied those who do."

"Now to get back to the idea of being married in the church," I continued. "In addition to making God a party to the contract and invoking His blessings, there are many other considerations.

"In the first place, the pastor will usually ask the couple in for several conferences to review the rights, duties, and obligations of the contract they are entering into. He helps prepare them for marriage.

"Then secondly, he will take a personal interest in them, and after marriage, if they feel they need help, they will have someone to whom to turn.

"Also, he will encourage them to attend religious services so that they will keep before themselves at all times the true goal of marriage. He will introduce them, moreover, to people their own ages, and they can join organizations of young married people and form new friends in wholesome surroundings."

Mary broke in. She said there was a small community church in the area where they had bought a home. She asked Tom if he would go with her to see the pastor. Well, between the two of us, Tom was trapped. He took it with a laugh and said yes.

After they were gone, I thought about the difference between couples approaching marriage from a purely materialistic point of view and those who enter into it as a spiritual experience. A recent survey disclosed that the three factors most common to happily married couples were: (1) they have an active religious affiliation, (2) they have children, and (3) they own their home or are saving to buy one.

And the greatest of these is faith.

"Walk with God," I had told Tom and Mary. I had tried to do that in my own life, and while I had faltered and tripped from time to time, many memories came back of what that striving had meant to me in times of sickness, danger, despair, indecision, and joy.

In times of sickness: As a youngster, I had had a little more than my share. My mother used to say, "Offer it up to God, all your pain. It will be so much easier." From then on I did, following the custom to this day, of offering every morning all my works, joys, prayers, and sufferings for His intentions.

In times of great danger: It was during World War II, and we were pinned down next to a brick wall under heavy bombardment. We could hear the shells exploding closer and closer, and the debris cascading down in the street. The man next to me was cursing softly because he couldn't smoke. He seemed horribly alone, waiting for the shell whose whine we would never hear. But those of us who prayed were not alone.

In times of blackest despair: Many years ago when a former law partner and I were walking to court, we passed a young Mexican woman heavy with child. She seemed inexpressibly worn and tired. My friend said, "You know, Louis, my mother taught me that whenever I see a woman in her condition, I should say a little prayer that all may go well for her and the child. My mother said I would be building up a treasure house of prayer that would attend my loved one someday through the ordeal of birth."

I never forgot, and I've continued the practice to this day —in crowded elevators, street cars, on sidewalks. The day came then when I sat in a delivery room while one of our youngsters made a belated appearance. When the child arrived, I watched petrified with fear as its tiny body gradually turned blue. The doctor called to the nurse for oxygen, and I helped her wheel up the tank. All the while, I resorted to silent, frantic prayer. Finally, the child gave a weak whimper, and little by little the rosy tint drove out the blue. Every little prayer I had ever offered for countless mothers trudging along was repaid a thousandfold.

In times of indecision: While presiding in the master calendar criminal court, I passed sentence daily on from twenty to thirty individuals in felony cases. Many times I found myself faced with decisions that were all but impossible to make. One day a young man about thirty stood before me, with clear blue eyes, sandy hair, and a sad, thoughtful, expressive face, but one without hope. His record showed he had spent ten years—one-third of his life—in jails and prisons from New York to California. An orphan, he had committed many crimes but never one of violence. The probation report showed that he didn't have a single friend. He was absolutely and completely alone. Attached to the report was a letter he had asked the officer to hand me. It was the story of his life. It was factual and honest and pulled no punches, and showed a lot of insight. He had shouldered a secret burden all his life. He feared others. He could stand jail but not ridicule. So for that reason, he had formed no attachments. Now, for the burglary of a store building for bread-and-butter money, he faced another prison term, and with his record, it could be long. What could a judge do for a person like that? In his letter, he wrote, "What is there in life for me? I am nothing. I can be nothing."

As softly as the loud-speaker in the criminal courtroom would permit, I tried to answer his question when he was brought before me. I told him that all of us are made to the image and likeness of God, and that we are placed here on earth for a definite purpose. We are given certain burdens, just as he had been given his. Some of us have been dealt with more generously than others, but none is given more of a burden than can be borne. We are held accountable only for what has been given us.

"You need faith to give your life purpose and meaning," I said. "You'll find many people anxious to help you, if you will but let them. Your probation officer and the chaplain are among these. And in turn there are many more unfortunate than you whom you can help."

The blue eyes were dimmed. "Yes, sir, I'll—I'll try, sir."

I sentenced him to a short term in the county jail and three years on probation. The last I heard, the probation officer had gotten him a job as an apprentice mechanic in a garage and he was doing well.

And in times of greatest joy: "Walk with God" meant much to the two of us that day twenty-four years ago in San Jose, California, in a historic old church when a much beloved friend and priest married us, and invoked the blessings of God, that thenceforth we would be one in the eyes of God and of each other, for better, for worse, in sickness, in health, until death do us part.

When I had done the best I could with the prayer, I sent a copy with some trepidation to a committee named by the board of supervisors for church and community cooperation. The committee included leading clergymen from the Protestant, Jewish, and Catholic faiths.

They didn't keep me waiting long, and their comments were all favorable. And to my knowledge, though the prayer has been reprinted widely, no opposition has ever been expressed.

This then is the prayer as it appears in the Reconciliation Agreement:

O God, we acknowledge our dependence upon Thee and invoke Thy blessings upon our home.

Teach us how to live in accordance with Thy commandments, that we may know real peace of mind in this life and merit eternal happiness with Thee.

Help us to discharge our responsibilities for the souls of the little ones Thou hast entrusted to our care.

Restrain us, O Lord, from every thoughtless, impatient or malicious word uttered, or deed done, to one another.

Forgive us our transgressions and teach us in turn how to be forgiving, charitable, and patient with one another.

What a comfort it is to know that Thou art ever present, ever kindly and attentive; that through prayer we may gain from Thee the strength and courage so necessary to the keeping of our solemn pledges to Thee and to each other.

Lastly, bless our home and the members of our family, O Lord; guard and protect us from all harm and evil. Amen.

chapter twenty

Saddle Horn

The aid of the Court having been requested to effect a reconciliation, or an amicable settlement of the controversy ... the parties hereby agree, each with the other and with the Court, as follows....

—RECONCILIATION AGREEMENT

The August I encountered the Colonel was a hot one. A friend, showing me around his little ranch, introduced me to the spirited young gelding. The friend knew of my fondness for horses, a love acquired one summer when I worked in Arizona on a ranch called Bull Basin, high in the clear air of the San Francisco Mountains near Flagstaff. So the friend invited me to ride Colonel.

It was with considerable reluctance that I mounted the English postage-stamp saddle. Particularly I decried the absence of the Western saddle's horn, a good mooring, come a sudden squall. For several hundred yards up the country lane, we got along famously although the stirrups were miles short for my long legs. Without warning, a chicken rustling in the weeds livened things up. Colonel wheeled a full half of the compass. I was a quarter of a turn behind, grasping futilely for the horn that wasn't there. The horse wheeled again like an uncoiling spring. I met him half way. One foot lost its stirrup and he chose that moment to buck. I shot over his head, did a jackknife with a half twist, as a diver would describe it, and landed hard on the flat of my back. From that moment on, I couldn't stay away from Colonel. There was a thing or two I wanted to prove to that horse—and to myself. So I wound up buying him, and the ranch, too.

All the time I was writing the Reconciliation Agreement, I felt I was on that hornless saddle. It was a challenge, just as Colonel had been. And then came the day, 50,000 words later and more redrafts than I can remember, when the Agreement was sent to the mimeographer. We had drawn from deep in the emotions and lives of hundreds to write what we considered a blueprint for marriage, a blueprint for that rickety bridge I had long ago wanted to build. By now it covered most of the basic and surface causes for divorce. We hoped, though, that it was more than a negative document, that it set forth in simple, clear fashion the philosophy that a man or woman must live by in marriage, that it had heart and faith and held forth hope as well as pointing up the down-to-earth, everyday practicalities that a couple must abide by if they were to find happiness.

A few mornings later, the clerk brought in the mimeographed copies. As I scanned them, I felt at last I had a good old Western saddle horn to grab for. Once again I went over in my mind the advantages of such an agreement: It would lend dignity and weight to promises made, and help couples remember those promises. It was a document to study at home and refer to if doubts arose. It was a channel of communication for those who were unable to reach each other. It would serve to reeducate couples about their fundamental responsibilities to God and to each other. It would start some couples to thinking seriously about themselves, reappraising their feelings as well as their intellectual approach to their problems. And we hoped that for many about to marry, or in their first years of marriage, it might prove a map setting forth the danger zones as well as the guideposts for the trails they were to take.

As I mentioned, the Court succeeded with 43 per cent of the cases heard during the first two years. That brings up the question, What happened in the other 57 per cent? Why did we fail? Where did we go astray?

To answer those questions, we analyzed the instances in which we had slipped. In doing so, memories kept surging up, memories of faces gaunt and tearful and pleading, and other faces sullen and rebellious and defiant. No matter what we had done, we never could have reconciled some of these couples. But with others, perhaps our approach had been wrong, perhaps we had missed saying that one right word which would have loosened a stream of consciousness in their minds. In this work, words carry such impact, or better stated, ideas do. Nights when the darkness would close in, I would say to myself, "Now if I'd only said so-and-so to them, or if I'd left something else unsaid. . . ."

In studying hundreds of cases, we found these the principle causes for failure:

1. Either one party or both parties came into the Court with closed minds, determined to reject all suggestions. They had decided definitely to separate or divorce. They were going through the process for a variety of reasons. Perhaps to please a close relative or friend. Perhaps to ease their own conscience, so they might say later, "I really did try—but it just didn't work out."

2. The parties wanted to reconcile ostensibly but refused counseling. These were the ones who said that no one was going to tell them how to run their lives. "I can think as

straight as the next fellow," a man told me one day, and another said, "I'm not going to be pushed around by any of those do-gooders."

3. The basic cause was too deeply rooted. From time to time we had to prod ourselves into remembering that not everyone can be reached by counseling, even though they may sincerely and perhaps desperately want a reconciliation. They simply cannot dig out the trouble and hold it up for study, no matter how skilled the psychologist or psychiatrist who is treating them. Just as medicine doesn't know all the answers, so we haven't charted the mind and the way a man or woman thinks and feels.

4. The effort exerted by the couples themselves was insufficient. The parties wanted to stay together but not if it were going to interfere too much with their pleasures or living pattern. In many instances of this type, the parties simply didn't want to put themselves out enough to change old habits. Sometimes I think most of us must have a little cat blood. We detest change of any kind, and marriage demands change, or call it adaptability, from the moment the rite is read.

So, as we discovered in time, the Reconciliation Agreement had definite limitations in its effectiveness. But we liked to think that even in those cases in which we had failed, we helped the parties better to understand themselves and their relationship with their children, so that after their separation or divorce they could act as rational human beings with their children.

Our success in 43 per cent of all cases indicated that virtually everyone thinking of separation or divorce should take steps to determine whether the reconciliation process will benefit them. I would go even further and say that those who are not contemplating separation at all but who are experiencing marital discord should take advantage of the various reconciliation processes that most communities provide, if not directly by a conciliation court then through a family service agency.

More and more attorneys view reconciliation as a desirable legal service. Many look upon themselves as guides for families going through troubled times rather than seeing themselves as paid captains of fighting teams, pitted in emotional combat in the legal arena. In one North Dakota district, lawyers have been helpful in reconciling 50 per cent of the couples coming to them. One attorney has established a 90 per cent record. They have done this notwithstanding a loss to themselves in the way of divorce fees.

With any new process or thought, critics bring up many questions. Most often they have asked just how effective can a promise be? Are we asking too much of some parties when we expect them to live up to the Agreement? Can a man change his habits and pattern of living simply by *willing* to do so?

To me, these questions were more or less theoretical, since I had sat on the bench and watched petitioners and respondents in hundreds of cases *will* to change their ways and *will* to live up to their promises. Many have *willed* to love.

To reassure myself, I asked Dr. Shostrom to study this matter of *willing* in the light of the latest psychological thinking. His findings pointed up that the *will to promise* or *will to change* depends on the change itself that must be undertaken. He broke the changes the Court most often suggested into three basic types: (1) those changes that can be made successfully by resolution alone, (2) those that require an alteration of "perception," which we will explain shortly, and which may be attained by combining the study and signing of the Reconciliation Agreement with counseling by the Court staff, and (3) personality changes that may be effected only through psychotherapy.

Now, for the changes in "perception." This is what Dr. Shostrom had to say: "By perception, psychologists mean the person's unique way of looking at something or someone. It is as though each of us wore a psychologically tinted pair of glasses, each with our own prescription. Our perceptions are determined in large part by the way we feel.

"To love someone involves our perceptions toward that person. Love in marriage involves a decision and a promise to commit one's life to that of another person. Yet we know that sometimes the act of willing or promising to love forever is not enough in marriage, even though two persons make this promise in all good faith.

"Therefore, it requires that we examine the importance of perceptions and feelings in marital love. In a marriage we do not love our partner in the same way as brother or sister. Our partner is a unique, different person whom we have some very specific feelings for. We perceive or 'see' this person as a uniquely lovable person.

"When a couple has difficulty in marriage, their perception of each other has not kept up with changes constantly occurring in each, or their original perceptions of each other have become distorted. To will change by resolution at this time does not change perception.

"Now it seems to me that the reconciliation process *does* change perception. The reconciliation contract is a result of much personal interaction and perceptual investigation by the couple involved. The experience of coming to court, the meeting of a judge or counselor, of having to work through all the unique elements of a personalized contract for two human beings—certainly this is an experience which can create a great deal of feeling and perceptual change. Sometimes counseling is required, which tackles the problem of perceptual change in a more intense way. Finally, psychotherapy may be required in those cases where the feelings and perceptions are so distorted that long-term help is needed before they can change."

Dr. Shostrom drew a continuum to illustrate this matter of changes. It looked like this:

Type of change	WILL CHANGES		PERCEPTION CHANGES		PERSONALITY CHANGES
Primary emphasis	Intellect		Feelings		
Method	Resolution	Marital contract	Marital contract	Counseling	Psychotherapy

"So you can see," he continued, "that a man or woman can resolve to make some changes by *will* alone with the support of the marital contract. He can even effect more drastic changes, those that we call 'perception' changes, through the influence of the marital contract plus counseling along lines that will alter his feelings as well as what he thinks. But once we get to the far right, to the point where there must be a personality change, then the party must undergo a series of treatments, through psychotherapy."

To illustrate his point further, he sketched out another diagram. Here it is:

Situation A

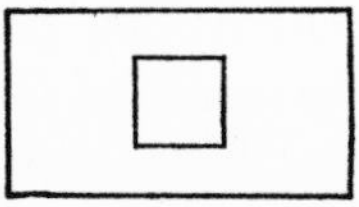

Situation B

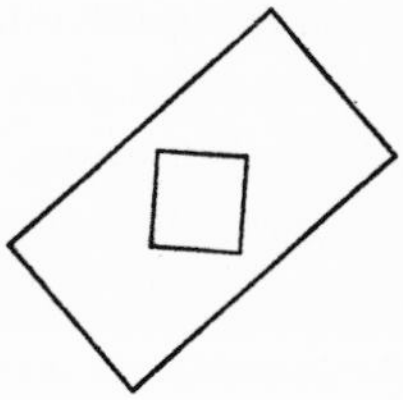

He explained: "In situation A it will be noticed that the 'frame of reference,' or outer frame, causes the reader to 'see' the figure inside as a square. Then when the outer figure is manipulated about, as in Situation B, the inner figure is easily seen as a diamond. The inner figure has not changed at all, just the frame of reference in which it is seen.

"Thus it is in marriage problems. By 'willing' hard we can see the inner figure in Situation A as a diamond, without changing the outer frame of reference. But it requires effort. So many marital differences can be handled by an earnest desire and effort to change.

"However, the danger is like that of trying very hard to be a gentleman. If you force yourself to think about it too much, insincerity creeps in and personal integrity moves out. How much easier it is to see the inner figure in Situation B as a diamond once the frame of reference has changed. Likewise, the jealous husband doesn't have to 'try' so hard to see his wife as not unfaithful if he has changed his feelings and perceptions about her. It comes naturally."

To summarize then, an act of will, a decision, a promise often will bring about the change that is needed. But other times, it will not. Even within the same person, he may *will* to make certain changes easily, but other changes will come about only as his perceptions change. In either case, the conciliation process should prove effective. Only in those instances where the trouble is deeply rooted and a personality change is required must the Court suggest psychotherapy of a prolonged nature.

chapter twenty-one

The Marco Polos

We realize that love deepens because it has survived a crisis in which it might have perished.

—RECONCILIATION AGREEMENT

In a little more than a decade, we have witnessed migrations of our people on a scale unparalleled in history, and some of the most cataclysmic changes in living patterns that any nation has ever gone through.

In the five years following World War II, 40 millions moved to new homes, often hundreds of miles distant, and the trek has continued to this day. Five million farm people alone left their land for the lure of big-pay jobs in the cities. The migrations spawned new communities, some mushrooming overnight from vacant land to teeming cities of 100,000 or more.

This mass movement shook the old roots of many, and sometimes rotted the roots completely. As the crowds settled in new communities, some forgot what was expected of them. They felt carefree, sometimes utterly irresponsible in their new surroundings. They felt they could do as they pleased, and inevitably this attitude permeated their marriages.

Some were so young when the migrations began that they never knew what old ties were like. As a boy living in a small California town, I was well rooted in a community where the neighbors knew me, and my parish priest, and my friends who lived close by. Others like me wanted to live right because we wanted the approval of these people we liked and loved. Ours was a tightly knit family and community with definite morals and standards.

The great majority of the transplanted ones continued living as they always had, but from the remaining group came couples to the Court by the scores, and for these, the Reconciliation Agreement became a plan by which they could live, a substitute for the old roots they had left behind. There was the wife in a trailer court caught up in adultery. "I didn't care who knew," she said. "I didn't know them, and they didn't know me." A husband turned to liquor because he had no friends except the boys down at the tavern. An eighteen-year-old bride, newly arrived in the city, wanted a divorce because she had nothing to do during the day and was bored.

Other causes shook the roots, too. As the economy rose, so did many incomes. New wealth brought about a change in social positions. Sometimes couples changed friends, and not always for the best. Almost invariably they changed neighbors as they bought bigger and more expensive homes. With extra money in their pockets, a few drank more and played more than before. The drinking and the playing colored everything they did, including the way they lived at home. There was the husband who frankly wanted to trade in his wife because she couldn't meet his new social standards. He needed a better-groomed and smarter woman to help him entertain the clients he brought home. In another case, a wife was ashamed of her husband. While she had climbed to a salary of $1,000 a month, he was still at his original job.

Millions found themselves not only with extra money

but also with extra time. For many, the week end began Friday evening and ended Monday morning. Employers, anxious to keep hard-to-get workers happy, gave them longer vacations. So the entire pattern of entertainment and recreation shifted drastically, almost year by year. More persons went to Europe and other far-off places, more trekked into the mountains for fishing and hunting, more paid high prices for football games and stage shows and night clubs. Sometimes this new pattern of fun tore at the home roots. One wife complained her husband never stayed home. He spent four nights a week at night clubs with customers, he said, although she had her doubts and apparently with good reason. Another husband informed the court counselor that his wife refused to go anywhere with him. They could afford a trip around the world but she wanted to stay home. Another couple ended up in the Court as a result of their constant squabbles over where to go and what to do week ends. They admitted their parents never had had any such wonderful choice.

The method of buying and selling changed, too. As discussed previously, a young couple could buy anything with little and sometimes no down payment. Some bought recklessly without ever figuring up their monthly payments. Then when the day of reckoning arrived, they blamed each other, and many drifted, angry or tearful, into the Conciliation Court.

Customs also underwent radical alterations. One perplexed pastor who wrote me put it this way, "In this town the men are drinking heavier and the women dressing lighter than ever before, and the orphanage is packed." The number of alcoholics, despite the advent of new and more effective techniques of treatment, swelled. In some quarters, a certain degree of nudity became fashionable, and in the movies and on the stage it was accepted on a broader scale than before.

Yet despite the flux in customs, manners, and ideas, the divorce rate fell by one-half during the decade, and there were 7 million more marriages on the books at the end of the ten-year period than at the beginning. So, as can be readily seen, the problems mentioned here refer to the comparatively small percentage affected adversely by the changing times.

On the asset side was the fact that many husbands and wives not only worked together but had far more time and money to play together. In this new partnership, the old historic concepts of division of work between husband and wife disappeared to an extent. Wives understood their husbands' businesses better because they themselves worked or had worked at some time or other, and the husbands learned firsthand all about home management and the care of children.

Closely associated with this was the new role that the technological age had brought women, as we discussed in another chapter. Many now had two jobs instead of one—one inside the home and one outside. Even if they didn't work for pay, they worked, and sometimes harder, in community projects that ranged from promoting better schools, to ringing door bells for the Red Cross, to helping handicapped children. But with this newly found independence and these new interests came many problems. A wife took too much interest in outside activities, one husband said, and neglected the children. In another case, the husband complained that his wife wasn't the homemaker his mother had been. In still another, the appointments and activities of the husband and wife conflicted to such an extent that their marriage was threatened. And so on.

Most couples, though, never forgot that despite all the changes, the migrations, the new customs, the extra income and extra time for fun, the very core of their lives centered about their marriage. Faith and religion often provided meaning and direction.

For some of the others, in our own area, the Reconciliation Agreement provided a new look at the old roots—roots that we all need until such time as the science fictionists change us into something other than men and women.

chapter twenty-two

Into the Eye of the Wind

Mutual interest, support and love are as necessary for happiness as food and drink.

—RECONCILIATION AGREEMENT

One windy, winterish night, I pulled the groaning bottom drawer of my old scarred desk open and scooped out the rag-ends of paper on which I had been scribbling my "sailing directions." They were jotted down in my big scrawling handwriting on all kinds of odd bits I had had at hand at the time a thought struck me, which was usually after winding up a case.

By now, 2,000 couples had come and gone through our court, at least a fourth of whom had been seated in these gloomy, old chambers. Strangely, most of them I remembered, perhaps because their problems and their emotions had been a part of me. For most of these couples, there had been no perfect sailing weather in sight, no stiff breezes to blow them along in the full sun with the lulling lap of the waters. Theirs was a faltering course that had to be set nearly dead ahead into the wind.

I had been a long time in accumulating the sailing directions that now cluttered the top of my desk. They were not mine. They had come from the very hearts and souls of couples. As I mulled through them, many seemed to take on voice in the dull quiet. They spoke from faces I recognized. Some voices stumbled and quivered, and others were strong and confident.

This was a moment I had long waited for, a moment toward which I had set my course for two years. Part of my excitement was due to the thought that I might come up with a few directions that might help couples who needed only buoys marking the course.

As I studied the scraps of paper, I found myself surprised at how many I tossed aside. They were so obvious that any sailing man would know them without having them set down. We all say things we don't mean, act in anger, do thoughtless things we regret. Such mistakes, though, are understood by our loved ones if the bond of affection is right.

The bond of affection. That was the very core of marriage, its pulsing heart. So whatever navigational directions I came up with must tend to strengthen it. Accordingly, I culled them out until I had only the basic ones, the ones needed by all of us to sail as high into the wind as we possibly can.

A couple who lived by all these directions would have a perfect marriage, sailing a straight course into the very eye of the wind, and obviously there is no such state, just as such a course would be impossible. We all must tack back and forth in our progress toward the true objective. We achieve happiness for ourselves and others by seeking to reach perfection, though we know we can never attain it. In other words, marital happiness is a process, not an end.

These then are some of the basic navigational rules for a normal marriage as a couple might seek to live them, the sailing directions from that bottom drawer, developed with the help of our counselors out of thousands of cases:

The couple possess a deep and abiding love, and care for it as something very precious.

Some persons are demonstrative in their love, others are not. But in a good marriage, both partners know that love is there, and experience its warm and comforting feeling every day of the world. Both treasure their love as the most precious thing they possess. They think about it often, when they awaken mornings or in those last minutes before falling asleep. If there's something wrong, they seek to put it right before another day ends.

Both nurture it in various ways. They keep it alive with gentleness and kindness, with thoughtfulness in little ways as well as in the big matters, with laughter, with talking things out, with an occasional "date" together, a dinner or a show, with the very act of working and playing together, of developing a closeness, a oneness.

They never permit their love to become routine. They realize a love that has become as commonplace as mowing the yard or drying the dishes may drift eventually into a barren land peopled by two strangers. They look upon marriage as "the life-long miracle, the self-begetting wonder, daily fresh."

They remember, in periods of depression when they feel their love slipping, that a person may recapture love by *willing* to do so . . . *by keeping ever present in mind the good things about a person . . . by doing things for him . . . by giving one's self to him.*

They grow in their love with the years.

Their love is born in the romanticism of the whirlwind days before their marriage. Then one morning they awaken to discover that the other is not so glamorous or exciting or wondrous as the hero or heroine they had pictured in their own work of fiction. They accept the transition for what it is, a facing up to reality. They don't pick up their toys and run away. They will always treasure the memories of the romantic days, but they have the common sense to know that life cannot be lived on a high peak of adventure, that most of it must be lived in a more prosaic but none the less exciting world.

As the months pass, they discover other traits in the one they idealized, good traits they never dreamed existed. They adjust to the faults, realizing that they themselves have shortcomings, that this is human nature.

So their bond grows into a more mature and lasting love. It develops into a love of understanding, and sacrifice, and a healthy relationship that satisfies each other's needs, and a sharing of interests and a closeness they never knew before. It is a love that can meet tough problems and solve them, that grows stronger with such challenges. It is the finished product; their romantic love had been only the molten ore.

To sum it up in Dr. Shostrom's words: "Mature love requires serious study, so that we may know what it is. Too many people perceive it as something which one 'falls into' and which can be defined rather simply. In reality, love is a compound thing and has many elements.

"It also requires practice, just as becoming a good doctor or violinist requires practice."

They recognize that marriage is a contract.

They may never have put it in so many words but they accept certain obligations and rights. They realize that marriage isn't a license to do as you please without regard for the other one, but that it is a merging of interests, a mutual satisfying of needs, a give-and-take that results in the maximum of happiness to each.

It is an agreement between two parties, and they need a knowledge of all the facts they can get. Most of these facts are about themselves. They have to know and understand each other. They have to discern not only how the other fellow is thinking but, more important, how he is feeling. So they do research—research into their emotional lives as well as into their thinking processes. With most couples, this is accomplished without conscious effort. It comes naturally. Others, though, who are beset with problems in their relationship, have to dig up the facts in earnest fashion. They have to think their way through situations to learn about each other.

This business of marriage calls for ferreting out other information as well. They learn more than the biological facts about their marital relationship. They learn the needs and responses of each other, all the emotional phases that the act takes them through. They learn a lot of other things in time, how to rear children, how to juggle the weekly pay check so there will be a minimum of conflict, how to manage a household.

They consider themselves partners.

They consult each other about everything. They keep no secrets one from the other. They never consider themselves in competition, nor does one try to show up the other.

They plan together for their children. They plan for owning a new home or buying a new car. They believe that their money and everything they own belongs to each and that each must have a say in how it is handled. They decide together on their vacations, on the movies they see, on the friends they will invite over to dinner.

Like partners in any undertaking, they appreciate that they will differ on many matters and that in so doing each will maintain his individuality and freedom.

As partners, they sustain each other. They support each other before the criticism of the neighbors or the boss. If one makes a mistake, they are quick to overlook it and go on to new undertakings.

As partners, too, they take stock from time to time—of their marriage, their physical goods, and their children. They talk about whether they are living as they want to live.

Their partnership develops until they move "like stars united in their spheres."

Each is willing to make sacrifices for the other.

They never ask, "What's in it for me?" They realize that with that kind of an attitude, their marital days may be few. Instead, they ask themselves, "Does the word 'love' as I live it require sacrifice on my part?"

The wife gives up new clothes so they can get together the down payment on a new home. She works so her husband can go to school or can get ahead faster in his business. He forgoes a fishing trip because she has her heart set on seeing her folks. He takes a lunch to the office to save dollars needed for a winter coat for her. She does her own house cleaning to buy him tools for his home workshop for Christmas. And so on.

Sacrifice may take on a grim note. He may be forced by economic necessity to give up a career when she falls into a long illness. Or she may take a job for the first time in her life to pay his medical bills. Suffering comes, but they manage without histrionics. They experience no misgivings, either expressed or silent, because it never occurs to either that they could live otherwise than by sacrifice when misfortune happens on them.

A professional friend told me that people don't like the word "sacrifice." He suggested we remove it from the Reconciliation Agreement. He contended that people were not interested in giving up anything, but only in gaining something, that the term was discouraging. But to those who have found oneness in marriage, sacrifice poses no burden. They sacrifice every day of their lives without thinking once about it.

They have understanding.

Neither one is ever without concern for his mate. If he's in trouble at the office, she sympathizes. If she is too exhausted for the marital act, he understands.

Each tries to see things as the other does and to know the other's feelings. They ask themselves, "How does she feel about this?" or "Is he thinking as I am?" They struggle to climb out of their own thought and feeling processes—to empathize. To requote Dr. Shostrom, this is a matter of "getting into the frame of reference of another person." It means a sincere and genuine effort to think not *for* or *about* the other person, but to think *with* him.

Such understanding goes to the heart of a matter. The husband knows now why his wife seems frigid and how he can help her. She fathoms the how and why of his uncontrollable temper, and what she must and must not do.

A couple comprehends mental illnesses as well as physical ones. If one is mentally ill, the other treats him as if he were suffering from tuberculosis or heart trouble. They recognize mental sickness when it develops, and they look for the best professional counsel they can find.

Their understanding includes forgiveness. They never

condemn each other, never hold grudges, never sulk or apply the silent treatment to the other. They are forgiving in small things as well as in the major ones. They forgive because they understand, and they forgive in the same way that they themselves would want forgiveness. It is a forgiveness of love, not a forgiveness that comes from doing what one thinks is the right thing, or from being big about it.

They supply each other's needs.

Their needs are as complex as human nature, ranging from the physical to the spiritual. They recognize that they must supply these needs in the other if their marriage is to grow and bring them a full measure of happiness.

They need love and affection, and they give it to each other in a hundred little ways, knowing that otherwise they would dry up and become only a shell of a human being. They need attention, and they notice what the other is doing, the new dress she bought that day, the polish job he did on the car. They need encouragement because even the strongest of us experience moments of depression.

They need to know that no matter what problems come up, neither is alone in the struggle, that the other is there at all times, ready to help, and with confidence and faith.

Each recognizes the sexual needs of the other and realizes that these may not be the same as his or her own. Therefore, they are considerate one of the other, and conceive of their marital relationship as a union of affection and tenderness and an expression of love as well as a physical meeting.

They understand that their needs may vary greatly, that she may hunger for music and he for golf, and that they must never attempt to mold the other into something he is not. They understand, too, that their needs may change with the years, that she now prefers an apartment instead of a house, that he would rather look at television than play canasta.

Above all, they need a feeling of security, for this is elemental. They needed it as babies, they need it even more as adults so they may impart it to their children. They recognize many kinds of security. She may feel a strong need for economic security for herself and the children. He must feel secure in his ability as a wage earner. He needs a feeling of adequacy and competence, nourished by his wife's expressed faith and encouragement.

They know that sometimes the other's need is so obscure as to be hidden completely from those closest to him, and that when this occurs, the "eyes" of a third party, be it confidant, relative, or professional, are necessary.

Finally, they know that when one no longer needs the other, love is through. Therefore, they know that though they devote a lifetime to it, they will never successfully bring to a conclusion this wonderful task of supplying the other's needs.

They share mutual interests and friends.

They begin their married life with a variety of interests and friends, not all of them compatible. Some of the wife's may bother her husband, and vice versa.

Slowly, so that it won't jar either of them, they work toward a goal of sharing as many interests and friends as possible. They don't give up the sports, hobbies, or avocations that each feels a need to continue. He still takes his fishing treks and she goes with friends to the travel club lectures.

They are always on the lookout, though, for interests

that will bind them together, that will provide the closeness, the camaraderie, that supports a marriage. They go to football games together, take hikes and picnics, work in the yard week ends, paint a room or two, listen to the same television shows, and when the children start growing up, they find themselves attending Parent-Teachers Association meetings and helping out with community projects.

Before they were married, they decided they would cultivate new friends. Many of their old ones were single and didn't fit in. They shied away from persons having marital troubles, from those who were generally downbeat, and from those of doubtful morals or obscene speech. Their new friends were happily married couples with responsibilities and problems akin to their own.

They are relaxed and easy with each other and the world in general.

They have come by a secret that many never acquire: that the human being needs moments of quiet and relaxation; at times he needs to get away from it all; and he needs to live the day as though they were hours to be enjoyed rather than chased constantly.

They accept each day as it is. They plan how to accommodate it to their way of thinking and doing, to make it come out the kind of a day they want. But they don't drive too hard, they don't let their ambitions inflame them.

Perhaps it is because they are adjusted to their world, and feel easy and comfortable around each other, that they are relaxed. Even when the going turns rough, they manage to take the days in stride, knowing full well that one too intent, too full of tensions, converts himself into an automaton devoid of any deep, honest feelings.

When the day ends, they put a period to it. When they shut the door to their room at night, they shut out the turbulent, frenetic world.

To me, this was the most surprising of all the sailing rules we found. Many, many of the people coming before the Court were possessed with an intensity that was frightening. The man with his drive night and day had forgotten those around him. The woman had been so busy, wrapped up in her individual purposes, that she had ignored her loved ones. Their personalities had gradually changed and they had lost the qualities that had endeared them to each other.

They face up to their personal troubles.

Because they are mature people, they realize they will get into arguments. They anticipate serious differences arising between them from time to time, differences that, if allowed to run will become cancers eating away at their love and marriage.

They may do some shouting, since few can control their responses in times of emotion, but eventually they sit down to discuss the matter calmly. They may postpone the talk for a few hours so they can enter into it more rationally. They never, though, permit it to become well rooted, and never bury it as a cat would a piece of rotten meat, for they have learned not to fear strong emotion. They realize that negative feelings, if given expression, turn into positive feelings. They know, too, that expression of strong feeling does not mean that the other partner must necessarily think the same way. Rather, they recognize the importance of building a tolerance for differences.

They have built their marriage on a love that is frank and honest. If they harbor secret ill will, they know they will destroy it.

They hold fast to another precept: They will leave the past where it belongs—in the past. "Each of us agrees to start afresh . . . we realize that love deepens because it has survived a crisis in which it might have perished."

They have a healthy relationship.

They are husband and wife to each other in every meaning of the words. He is not a boy to be mothered, nor she a girl to be fathered. They respect each other as grownups who have no need for the emotional props of childhood—grownups who take an adult view of life.

They hold a basic respect for the dignity of man and woman as human beings created by God in His own likeness and image. Each behaves toward the other, both by word and physical act, as he would want to be treated if he stood in the other's place. Neither ever thinks he owns or possesses the other in any manner. Neither is the boss of the household, nor the doormat to be trod over. Their love in itself precludes any such conception of possession.

They maintain the same healthy attitude toward their children, knowing that their own happiness and that of their children are bound inextricably. They don't try to "project" their own childhoods or their own idiosyncrasies on their children. They recognize that children are not adults and cannot behave or be held accountable as such. They consider them in the light of their years and expect of them accordingly. They think of them as individuals with their own rights and duties and their own needs that must be satisfied. They give fully of their time and love.

In other words, they are normal, mature people, adjusting each day to each other and their world. They never reach the port of complete adjustment but rather, as Seneca admonished, consider each day a new life.

Finally, their objective determines the set of the sails.

Happiness in itself is not their goal, for it rarely comes to those who seek it. Love is pure when the thirst for happiness gives way to the passion for direction and unity. They trim their sails and set a course that will take them to their ultimate objective, which is God. They do not expect that happiness will shadow them step by step; they are content to heed the prophecy that when their love attains its goal, eternal joy will be theirs. Until then, they sail hand in hand, looking in the same direction, confident that they will reach their goal if they but follow the instructions that prayer and religion supply.

chapter twenty-three

The Visitor

Husband and wife possess Nature's most valued treasure—the loyal love of a human heart.

—RECONCILIATION AGREEMENT

Friends have asked why I subsequently volunteered for a tour of duty in the criminal courts when I had found the conciliation work so rewarding. A good question. I have asked it of myself.

A number of considerations entered into my decision. My interest hadn't waned. I continued to handle a large volume of correspondence, mostly from professional people, both in this country and abroad. As a member of the committee of judges appointed to act in an advisory capacity to the Court, I followed its work very closely. Too, I felt both honored and gratified at being appointed to membership on a committee of the American Bar Association dealing with the problems of marriage and divorce.

No, the reason was not lack of interest. For one thing, I sought to prove that the Court's program was sound and did not depend for its success upon my own particular views and beliefs. I was succeeded by Judge Lewis Drucker, and later by Judges John Gee Clark and Roger Alton Pfaff. All three effectively carried on the judicial functions of the court and provided leadership in their supervision of the work of the counselors. The percentage of reconciliations, although varying from month to month, remained constant.

Veteran judges maintain that a judge's education is not complete until he has served on the criminal side of the bench. I sought this experience, but like that of serving in the Army, I will be glad to get it behind me.

One day recently, nearing the end of my Probation and Sentence Calendar, I reached "People *v.* John Tolan Moore, III. Charge: Forgery, six counts, with two prior felonies." I had circled it with red pencil instead of my usual abbreviations showing intended disposition. The young man had come from an excellent family background and had had a good education. The report of the probation officer showed the immediate cause of his trouble to be alcoholism. His family had been overindulgent. The success of brothers and sisters had accentuated his own failures. He had become estranged from his father through the embarrassment his repeated transgressions had caused.

Only his wife had stayed by him. That must be she, I thought, sitting tense and nervous on the edge of her seat, almost kneeling, with her eyes darting from John Moore to the bench. For her, each second must be an eternity, and yet the answer of what to do with him came hard. The telltale red line indicated I had failed to reach even a tentative conclusion from my review of the file.

He was young—only twenty-eight—with a sensitive face, high forehead, somber eyes, and fine mouth. It was a face that asked nothing and expected nothing. For him the die had already been cast. It was as though he would welcome the anonymity and security of prison.

Two terms of prison had accomplished nothing. Eighteen months, the first trip; two full years, the second. True, society would be protected from him. His friends and family would be freed from the continuing worry and embarrassment. But what would we be doing for him?

It had been a long, hard morning. One wife had fainted, and another had bolted the courtroom to carry her hysterics into the corridors. One defendant had silently mouthed me to the lower regions upon the pronouncement of sentence. Another had laughed, a mirthless laugh that chilled.

Perhaps a short recess would help. I ordered it, and young Moore was returned to the detention room.

Scarcely had I thrown off my robe and begun pacing my chambers when Jim Taylor, clerk of the court, entered to say there was a man outside anxious to see me.

The man entered, and a warm, engaging smile greeted me. He offered me his hand, and a vibrant clasp followed, the grip of a person who is glad to be there. Eyes that were blue and clear took hold of mine.

"You don't remember me, Judge, but that's understandable. The name's Morrow, Jim Morrow. The missus and I were before you in the Conciliation Court. I had been drinking a lot and . . ."

Recognition flooded in. I remembered him . . . his wife, Carol . . . their daughter, Nancy . . . his struggle as an alcoholic.

His voice sifted through. "I've been on the Alcoholics Anonymous program for three years, Judge. I'd of never made it without their help. Carol and Nancy have stood by me and we have done well. I'm trying to pay it back by working with other alcoholics. We have a unit here in the county jail—I started it."

He hesitated. "Fact is, I met young Moore there last week, and after the meeting had a long talk with him. I came up today to find out what disposition was to be made of his case, so that I could follow him up. I really believe

AA could do a lot for him. When I told Carol you were the judge on the case, she wanted to come in, too, just on the off-chance we might get to talk with you for a minute. I hope you won't mind, but when you seemed to pause in your disposition of the case I just wondered if I could offer any help."

Again he paused, and I asked him what he had in mind.

"Could you continue final disposition for sixty or ninety days, with his consent of course, and release him on bail to our AA group? We've done it with several others. We would get him a place to stay, a job, and give him plenty of moral support. He looks like an excellent prospect, but if I'm wrong we would promptly surrender him to the court. If he makes good for the sixty days, perhaps probation would be indicated with a state prison sentence suspended."

"It's worth a try," I said.

As I mounted the bench to complete the calendar, I spotted Carol Morrow when her husband resumed his seat alongside her. She slid her arm under his. She was proud of him, that was clear. Her composure was in striking contrast to the state of the distraught, little wife in the first row, and to that of the young man at the bar, sitting without will or emotion, staring into nothing. If we could transform those two to look like the Morrows...

Later, in my chambers, Carol Morrow radiated happiness. "Jim has such a fine position. He's with a firm whose general manager is a member of Jim's AA group. We've moved into a new home and just as soon as we have the second mortgage paid off I'm going to quit my job."

Big Jim Morrow pulled out a picture of Nancy. "Little Sober Sides," I thought, but the picture of health. She was a beautiful child, and pride and love shown out of their eyes as they spoke of her.

Jim paused in the doorway. "You know the thing that helped the most, Judge?" he said. "It was knowing we couldn't do it ourselves." As we shook hands, the cares of the morning dropped away. All the nights I had trudged downhearted from my old chambers in the Conciliation Court, all the stings of disappointment I had suffered in hours so black I can still feel the hurt—they went with them. If the Conciliation Court could recapture the happiness Jim and Carol Morrow had known when they repeated "With this ring I thee wed," and keep love unspoiled for Nancy, and do this for others like them . . .

As I sank back in my big leather chair, I thought of St. Francis of Assisi.

> Lord, make me an instrument of your peace; where there is hatred, let me sow love; where there is injury, pardon; where there is doubt, faith; where there is despair, hope; where there is darkness, light; and where there is sadness, joy.

Appendix

Typical Reconciliation Agreement of the Los Angeles Conciliation Court

IN THE SUPERIOR COURT OF THE STATE OF CALIFORNIA

IN AND FOR THE COUNTY OF LOS ANGELES

Conciliation Court

Jane Rollins Petitioner	No. C.C. *129876*
vs.	No. D– *4785896*
Jonathan Rollins Respondent	RECONCILIATION AGREEMENT

The aid of the court having been requested to effect a reconciliation, or an amicable settlement of the controversy existing between the above named husband and wife, and a court conference having been held thereon in which it was indicated that certain conduct is deemed necessary to preserve the marriage or to implement the reconciliation of the parties, the parties hereby agree, each with the other and with the court, as follows:

MARITAL COUNSELING The ability of a husband and wife to meet each other's basic needs as human beings is important to a successful marriage. When these needs are not being met some of the results are unhappiness, resentment, frustration and arguments. Instead of being united in marriage, each party begins to pull in the opposite direction. The marriage has become sick.

When we are sick, most people go to a doctor for help to get well. When a marriage is sick we should go to a professionally trained person for help. In this County there are many excellent agencies with professional counselors who specialize in helping people with marriage problems. Many of these agencies are partially supported by the Community Chest. Usually, these agencies charge a fee but the amount is scaled down to the person's income and ability to pay.

Every effort is made to arrange appointments so that time off from work is not necessary. Some agencies have evening as well as Saturday appointments. Appointments are usually once a week.

Marriage counseling is most effective when both husband and wife attend. Each party is given the opportunity to speak to the counselor alone....

Many people believe that only they can really understand and do something about their marital problems. This is not true. One has but to ask himself this question: "If I can solve my own problems, why haven't I done so?" By understanding himself as well as the needs of his spouse, a person becomes a better marriage partner. To admit that there is a problem and ask for help with it, is a sign of strength, not weakness.

If an agency is selected the name of such agency will be typed below and our signature to this agreement authorizes such agency and the Court to release to each other such information as each may require in the consideration of this case:

FAMILY SERVICE OF FERNDALE
102 South Broadway
Telephone MAin 09652

"HUSBAND" AND "WIFE" Wherever in this agreement the word "husband" or "wife" is used it shall mean the petitioner or respondent as indicated in the caption of this agreement.

FORGETTING THE PAST We agree that the most important job ahead of us is the carrying out of our responsibility to raise our children in a proper home. We realize, however, that this cannot be done if we do not bury the past. We agree that we will not accuse, blame or nag each other about things which have happened in the past. Each agrees to start afresh and to do his very best to carry out the promises he makes in this agreement....

DIVISION OF RESPONSIBILITY We know that in maintaining a home there must be a division of responsibility between us.

The home Generally speaking, the care of the inside of the home, the preparation of meals, the care of the physical needs of the children and the family clothing are the responsibility, mainly, of the wife.

Support of the family The financial support of the family and the care of the outside of the home are the responsibility, mainly, of the husband.

Welfare of the children The supervision of the children is the joint responsibility of the parents in which each must support the other.

Where wife works outside the home Where the wife works on the outside then the husband must share to a larger extent in the work of the home.

We agree to the above division of responsibilities, with whatever changes we have inserted. Where the main responsibility is something that belongs to one of us, the other agrees not to interfere with it or to belittle that one's efforts but, on the contrary, agrees to help the other in any reasonable way.

HUSBAND'S ROLE IN THE FAMILY As individuals, men and women have been endowed by God with an equality in dignity and potential. They do not, however, have the same functions to perform in society. In marriage they are joined together to attain a common goal, and it is then that one must be able to depend on the other. Sometimes men forfeit this right of having their loved ones depend upon them by active brutality or passive weakness, and, upon the happening of either event, women refuse to accept a dependent role. In either case women are robbed of their full dignity.

It will always be true in marriage that the greatest giving will be required on the part of the wife. Through pregnancy and child-raising she loses the independence which the man continues to retain. When today we find a woman who is reluctant to face the loss of such independence, it is generally because she does not trust the man to be loving, confident and considerate, particularly at the times when she must, of necessity, depend solely upon him. Generally speaking, a good woman is happy to go through a great amount of sacrifice for her husband and family, as long as his step is firm, his love tender and his faith in her and in himself is strong.

The husband agrees to do everything in his power to merit his wife's confidence in him. The wife agrees to respect her husband and to encourage him in his efforts.

A NORMAL MARRIED LIFE Many people who feel aggrieved at the state of their marriage lament the fact that they do not have a "normal" married life. In determining the cause for this unhappy state, these people should first ask themselves "what do I put into the marriage?"; "does the word 'love,' as I live it, require 'sacrifice' on my part?" If it does not, then it generally means that such a person gets little out of the marriage because that's exactly what he puts into it. Marriage, to be a success, is a school for sacrifice.

FALLING OUT OF LOVE When people say they are "falling out of love" they usually mean out of romantic or passionate love. Often it is just the beginning of real love. In the first stage of love, the joys, the journeys, the pleasures, the presents, the holidays were necessary to help build it up. Now, it is the illnesses, the obstacles, the sorrows, and the sacrifices which sustain and strengthen it....

WORK, HOBBIES, ETC. Each party should make a deliberate effort to become interested in the work, hobbies and activities which the mate enjoys. Usually, this requires some "giving and taking" on the part of each. Married people should resolve to spend at least one-half of their leisure time together, but still allow each other some freedom.

Successful marriages are those in which husband and wife plan together, work, play and laugh together, and suffer, sacrifice and pray together.

PRIVACY The parties agree to respect each other's right of privacy in such matters as personal mail. The return of either partner from an outing or visit should never be made the signal for a suspicious quizzing bee. Let each do the other the honor of reposing implicit trust in him; and let each so behave as to deserve that loyal trust by never doing anything to violate it. The parties should also learn to give each other freedom to be alone on occasions.

MUTUAL FRIENDS When a man marries he must cease to be one of "the boys." His interests and responsibilities are no longer the same as theirs. Likewise, the married woman soon finds that she lives in her own little world, one entirely different from that of her single friends.

Early in their marriage the young couple should seek new friends among happily married people of their own age and circumstances. Unhappy persons, particularly divorced people or those who are in the throes of domestic strife of their own, are usually poor companions for the ordinary married couple.

We agree to strengthen our marriage through the making of mutual friends, new ones, if necessary, among happily married couples with responsibilities and problems akin to our own.

ALCOHOLIC BEVERAGES—MODERATION *Husband* agrees not to partake of any alcoholic beverages except beer and only in the family domicile, or on social occasions when spouse is present.

FIGHTING Neither party shall strike, slap, molest, harass or threaten the other in any manner.

The parties acknowledge that it takes at least two to make a fight and that when one is obviously angry, or "out of sorts," it is agreed that the other shall refrain from any action which may aggravate such condition.

SPEAKING IN A NORMAL TONE OF VOICE Both parties agree that they will speak to each other in a normal tone of voice, and specifically agree not to speak in a loud or boisterous manner, or swear at, or call the other foul or obscene names, or use profane language in the presence of the children, or say anything derogatory of the members of the other's family.

SARCASTIC, BELITTLING REMARKS *Wife* admits using sarcastic, cutting and belittling remarks to spouse and agrees to make every effort to avoid doing so in the future.

SILENT TREATMENT Each party agrees not to give the other the "silent treatment" by refusing to engage in normal conversation with the other for extended periods of time.

RELIGION We have indicated that fundamentally we are religious people. We acknowledge that religion can become a very important factor in the preservation of our home. We agree to attend the services of our church regularly.

LOVE AND AFFECTION Each party agrees to exert every effort to treat the other with consideration, love and understanding at all times.

CONSIDERATION FOR THE OTHER PERSON'S FEELINGS *Wife* admits having been inconsiderate of spouse and has completely disregarded the wishes, desires and needs of such spouse. Therefore, such party agrees to be more understanding and considerate of the feelings, wants, wishes and desires of such spouse.

RECOGNITION OF ACCOMPLISHMENTS Human beings are often in need of encouragement and recognition for their efforts, work and accomplishments. *Wife* agrees to give spouse such credit and encouragement; and, in return, such spouse agrees to accept suggestions without taking exception to them.

NAGGING The mere fact that fault finding may be done for some justifiable reason does not excuse it. A nagging wife or husband is a most difficult person to live with. As a rule, nagging accomplishes nothing constructive; if anything, it merely gives the person being nagged an excuse for a very negative attitude.

Wife admits having "nagged" spouse and agrees to make every effort to avoid doing so in the future. In return, spouse agrees to listen to the suggestions of the other and to discuss matters calmly, thereby doing away with any excuse for nagging.

MEALTIMES Mealtimes should be times of great peace and calmness. They should never be the times for fault finding or the occasions for unloading upon one another the unhappy events that have transpired during the day.

Some people with a background of religious training have found that the pausing of the family at the start of each meal for the invoking of God's blessing serves as a great deterrent to discord at mealtimes and as a reminder that with God's blessing each meal can be a time of peace and contentment.

Sometimes one or the other of the parties requires a brief pause to relax before commencement of the evening meal. In such instances the children should be fed and the mealtime for the husband and wife deferred until both are ready in order that the mealtime may be a time of leisure and contentment for both.

TOLERANCE OF FRIENDS AND RELATIVES *Wife* admits having been very intolerant of spouse's relatives and friends. Therefore, such party agrees to accept such persons into the family home in a gracious manner; to carry on a natural and normal conversation with them; and to treat them with respect, consideration and courtesy.

SOCIAL ACTIVITIES *Husband* agrees to take out the *wife* for dinner, entertainment, for a drive or outing, or for other social activities within the financial means of the family at least *once a week.*

LATE HOURS *Husband* agrees not to maintain late and unusual hours or to stay away from home without advising the other of the necessity therefor in advance and of the place where such party may be reached in the event of emergencies.

THIRD PERSONS IN THE HOME Generally speaking, the home of the modern family is not designed for the constant presence of an outsider or third person. The lengthy intrusion of such a person into the home life of a family cannot occur without real danger. Such presence has a direct bearing upon the relationship of husband and wife and often has a very adverse effect. Detrimental comparisons are likely to be made and "taking sides" becomes inevitable. It is also true that the more inoffensive and "innocent" the third person, the more dangerous is the possibility of attachments being formed which may result in jealousy and misunderstanding, if not worse. We will avoid endangering our home by permitting unnecessary and continuing intrusions of third persons in our home.

CHILDREN Children bring life to a marriage. There are no dull moments in parenthood. With children a "house" becomes a "home"; the "married couple" becomes a "family." Each parent taken on a new dignity and new responsibility. Teamwork between the parents becomes a necessity.

The coming of children must not be permitted to disturb the warm relationship between husband and wife. One must not neglect the other.

When parents hold their newly-born for the first time—they must ask themselves—Is it possible that we, alone, are responsible for this perfect little bundle of humanity? The answer is obvious to most. They see in the child the handwork of God.

God entrusts in the parents a new life, a body, and a soul. The child is His child and theirs. They become God's agents in the upbringing of the child. And what an awesome responsibility it is! It is estimated that 80 per cent of what a child is, or turns out to be, is attributable directly to his parents, or to those in whom his upbringing is entrusted.

We realize that a child is the outgrowth of the love of its parents and just as his conception required their joint act so will each step in his training and development require the love, attention, and self-sacrifice of each parent. We agree that neither of us can do the job alone.

ESSENTIALS FOR NORMAL CHILDHOOD We agree that if a child is to attain full stature, physically, mentally and spiritually, he will need many things, including:

1. The love and active interest of each parent.

2. A home, however humble, where harmony prevails.

3. The good example and leadership of his parents in his moral and spiritual development.

4. The assurance that he and each other child in the home is treated fairly and impartially and that no one is loved more than any other.

PARENTS' CONDUCT TOWARD CHILD We agree that each child has his own individuality and that his training must be planned with his particular needs and abilities definitely in mind.

We agree that our conduct toward our child, or children, shall include the following:

1. We will think and speak of our child as "our" child, never as "my" child or "your" child. The responsibility is joint and will always be that way.

2. We will maintain a united front on matters of policy and discipline. We won't interfere with one another in the administering of discipline. We will settle any differences of opinion out of the presence of the child.

3. We will try to reduce the number of commands or orders which we issue to our child. (A flood of orders turns to "nagging" and becomes meaningless. Their number can be reduced by establishing regular rules and sticking with them and by making use of suggestions, requests, hints, praise, etc. Orders should be based on reason, and most children will profit by a simple statement of the reason. Modest praise for obedience usually helps.)

4. We will try to get the child's full attention before giving an order. His mind may be miles away. We will strive to give orders calmly, in a tone which indicates we expect them to be carried out.

5. We agree never to administer physical punishment while in anger.

6. We will always administer punishment in privacy; we will try not to humiliate the child in front of "the fellas."

7. We will try to answer our child's questions; encourage him to grow up with a wholesome respect for himself, his body, and for others.

8. We will teach him the proper care of his own property and to respect the property of others.

9. We will develop his sense of responsibility by assigning him responsibilities suitable to his age and development.

10. We will help him to develop sound judgment in the choice of companions. We won't do all the judging for him or impose our own prejudices on him. We realize that some day he will have to rely on his own judgment—that ours won't be available.

11. We will not quarrel in the presence of the child.

12. We will not speak ill of one another in his presence; if it happens inadvertently—we will explain later that we did not mean it.

13. We promise not to unload on him the worries and troubles of adults—he will be a child only once.

SOUND FAMILY RELATIONSHIP Finally—we will strive to remember that the best discipline is the disapproval of whatever wrongful act the child has done by a *loved* and *loving* parent. We know that obedience through fear is short-lived—the child will outgrow the fear and long before that he will have lost respect. We acknowledge that obedience through love endures and that just as love between husband and wife must be mutual to be effective, so the love of parent and child must be reciprocal—must be earned by both. We have stressed that the disapproval should be of the wrongful act and not of the child because the distinction is important. It is not the child that it bad, but rather *what he has done* that is inappropriate in the eyes of the parent.

We will strive for patience, gentleness, understanding, firmness, ingenuity and love in dealing with our child or children. We recognize that these are some of the principal ingredients for a happy relationship.

SEXUAL INTERCOURSE Sexual intercourse provides a safe and healthy outlet for passion and preserves each party from temptations to infidelity, or to self-abuse. Moderation and considerateness should be observed in sexual relations. Moderation is simply the ability to manage one's self wisely, not allowing one's self to be carried away with passion; whether for food, drink, sex, or other pleasures.

The amount of sexual activity that constitutes moderation differs with persons, just as the amount of food they require likewise differs. To show selfishness in sexual matters brings on the offender the punishment of forfeiting respect and love. Love and consideration for the other partner will operate to find the right balance.

The parties have agreed that *twice a week* on an average, under normal conditions, should not be considered excessive. They further agree that it should not be necessary for one to urge or insist that the other shall indulge in an act of sexual intercourse; because the other does not have the right to refuse, except for serious reasons. They further agree that it would be quite selfish and unjust for one to manufacture excuses or put difficulties in the way of granting the other's request. Mere inconvenience or disinclination are not sufficient reasons for refusing. The attitude of continual unwillingness or of reluctant and uncooperative acquiescence is a common cause of marital unhappiness. On the contrary, to anticipate the other's wishes—while sparing the other having to request—is proof of a love that is thoughtful, as well as genuine.

The importance of lovemaking The importance of "lovemaking" in the first stages of intercourse must not be ignored. Unfortunately, this occurs quite often between husband and wife after a few years of marriage. "Lovemaking," consisting of all those tender and gentle acts which are utilized to show affection and to give delight of mind and body, should not be rushed, but should be prolonged. The attentions given, however, must be such as to be agreeable and welcome—else they would repress desire, instead of arousing it.

"Lovemaking" as a prelude to sexual intercourse takes into account the difference in the nature of love in man and woman. In man, the physical or passion side is generally quickly and strongly aroused by the slightest stimulation and desire and by appropriate actions he quickly reaches the climax of physical satisfaction. In woman, it is the emotional and mental side that is most in evidence; for her, love is meaningless unless it be manifested in a profusion of loving attentions. Consequently, her passion side is slow to make its appearance, generally speaking; nor will it become strongly enough aroused except after an abundance of appropriate lovemaking. Physical union for her is out of the question until her physical desire is sufficiently aroused and her glandular processes have prepared her body for such union. Unless she has been properly prepared for it, the few minutes of union will not be sufficient to bring her to the necessary climax and consequent release of nerve tension.

Repeated acts of intercourse which do not result in satisfaction for the wife become unpleasant. Under such conditions the evident satisfaction of the husband and his repeated requests must inevitably give the wife the impression of male selfishness. All the while, the ill-advised husband will come to blame her for not being interested in him—he will complain bitterly of her reluctance and her refusal—never realizing that he is himself responsible because of his own ineptness.

The wife agrees to respond to the husband's efforts in lovemaking and not to act like a patient undergoing a physical examination. For the husband to acquire proficiency in making intercourse pleasurable to the wife, he must learn to relax physically and to take his time. To do so, he should not be absorbed in himself, but rather in seeing to it that his wife is duly responding. The ultimate in his pleasure should be the realization that his wife also has enjoyed complete satisfaction.

In the event that any phase of intercourse is a cause of pain or discomfiture to either one, the parties agree to discuss the matter jointly with a competent physician; rather than to allow such a condition to continue until it becomes a real threat to the success of the marriage.

PERSONAL APPEARANCE During the years when persons are courting one another, and generally speaking for a few years thereafter, each is very careful about his own personal appearance. However, as time goes on, husband and wife tend to take each other for granted and to assume that the love of one for the other is permanent. As a result, quite often one or the other allows his personal appearance to take a very secondary place to the other cares and responsibilities of married life.

Sometimes one or the other will give gentle hints that something should be done to rectify the situation, but these hints are usually not taken very seriously until real trouble has developed. Such things as uncleanliness, over-weight, vulgarity or carelessness in dress, can become so offensive to the other party as to lead to the breakup of the home.

The parties recognize that the passing years carry with them a definite toll, and that some things result over which the parties have no control—such as baldness, wrinkles, denture difficulties, arthritis, the physical results of all types of illnesses, etc.—and it would be sinful for one to blame the other for such failings. However, this does not apply to many conditions which are simply the result of carelessness or of a lack of real effort to remedy.

HOUSEHOLD EXPENSES Parties agree that the *wife* shall be the treasurer of the family partnership and that all pay checks shall be properly endorsed promptly upon receipt and delivered to said party. Said party shall apply the funds from such checks in payment of regular monthly bills and installment payments when due and provide necessary food, clothing and other necessities for the family. Any remaining balance shall be applied by said party only as agreed upon by husband and wife. Said party, as the family treasurer, shall maintain an accurate account of all receipts and payments in a permanent notebook which shall be available for inspection by the other party and by the court upon demand.

POCKET MONEY Parties further agree that there is to be deducted from each *weekly* check the sum of *$10.00* as "pocket money" for the husband and *$10.00* as "pin money" for the wife. Out of these sums parties are to bear their own expenses for the following enumerated items as well as for the general purpose implied by the terms "pocket money" and "pin money."

ITEMS TO BE PAID OUT OF POCKET MONEY	ITEMS TO BE PAID OUT OF PIN MONEY
Golf Expense	*Beauty Parlor*
Snacks	*Cosmetics*

CHARGE ACCOUNTS The parties acknowledge that a substantial part of their difficulty has resulted from the opening of charge accounts and from the purchasing on credit in amounts beyond the financial means of the parties. The parties agree to exert every effort to arrange for a pooling of their credit payment items and obligations in order to reduce the monthly total required for such purpose.

A PARTNERSHIP AGREEMENT Habits formed over a long period of time are not easily altered. Undoubtedly some of the provisions in this agreement will require considerable effort of the parties to this agreement. Many of the matters referred to in it may be forgotten unless it is used to refresh the memories of the parties from time to time. In times of stress, particularly, the parties should refer to it and calmly discuss it with one another, in an effort to see if its provisions are being fully complied with.

Business partnership agreements between individuals have provided the means whereby people of very different temperaments, experience and abilities have joined hands to accomplish a common objective. When difficulties arise between such partners they resort to the partnership agreement for the solution of those difficulties. If the problem is one which is new and has not been provided for in the agreement, and if they are unable to settle it between themselves, then the matter is referred to a third party or to the court to settle the dispute.

If the parties to this agreement will consider it in the nature of a partnership agreement between them and resort to it for the settlement of such disputes as may arise, it is believed that it will be of inestimable aid to them in preserving their marriage and in enabling them to discharge the obligations to one another and to the children of the marriage, which they assumed through the entering into of the marriage contract.

AN END TO THE DAY'S PROBLEMS Married people should acquire the habit of ending each day by calling a definite halt (as definite as the factory whistle) on the day's work and problems. Perhaps that halt might be when they close the door of their room at night. Once this time has been reached, they must resolutely keep out everything unpleaasnt (for their retirement hour is no place for such things). From then until sleep overtakes them, they should gladly give to each other the comfort, encouragement, and loving solace they daily need, so that with strengthened hearts they can both face cheerfully the tasks and troubles of the morrow. That daily measure of mutual interest, support and love, is just as necessary for their happiness and welfare as their food and drink; and given this daily portion, they will be much less likely to forget and wound each other.

Such love, between husband and wife, is so strong a force for developing all that is good in human nature, that wise couples will not suffer their mutual attachment to become casual and commonplace under the spell of monotony, or to languish with neglect, or to degenerate into mere selfish passion; for they will realize that in this life they possess nature's most valued treasure—the loyal love of a human heart.

We promise that we will do our utmost to give each other the daily measure of interest, support, and love required for a happy marriage and for a happy home for our children.

FAMILY PRAYER We have indicated to the Court that we believe in the existence of a Supreme Being and in the efficacy of prayer. We believe that the saying "The family that prays together stays together," has real merit and that the daily recitation of a family prayer would aid us in keeping uppermost in our minds our responsibilities to God, to our children and to each other.

We agree that we will make every effort to recite a daily prayer together, asking the Blessings of Almighty God upon our family. Such prayer will be couched in words in conformity with our own religious beliefs.

It is agreed that the provisions of this agreement may be incorporated by the Court in a court order. In making this agreement we and each of us hereby acknowledge that should either of us willfully fail to comply with any such court order, we shall be subject to being brought into court on a proceeding to show cause why we should not be found in contempt of court. We further understand that in the event we are found to be in contempt of court we shall be subject to the payment of a fine or to imprisonment, or both, as provided by law.

Term: We, and each of us, hereby agree that this agreement and any order of the Court made pursuant hereto shall remain in full force and effect until further order of Court.

Dated: *October 25, 1956*

Jane Rollins
Petitioner

Jonathan Rollins
Respondent

About the Authors

LOUIS H. BURKE has been a judge of the Superior Court in Los Angeles since 1951, when Governor Earl Warren appointed him to the bench. Born in Montebello, California, in 1905, he attended local schools and in 1922 enrolled with his brother in Loyola University, studying arts and sciences by day and law by night, and graduating in 1926 with both the Bachelor of Philosophy and Bachelor of Law degrees. Appointed city attorney of Montebello in 1928, Judge Burke served for twelve years as general counsel to the League of California Cities, and as a charter consultant drafted the city and county charters of such California communities as Arcadia, Compton, and Santa Monica.

In 1943 Judge Burke volunteered for service with the United States Army and was sent overseas for two years. He served as a United States Army government judge in Germany, establishing the first military government court in Cologne during the occupation of the city. Upon his return to the States he resumed the practice of law and was appointed to the California Veterans Board, on which he served until his appointment to the Superior Court. He was recently named by his fellow jurists as presiding judge of the widespread 90-judge Los Angeles Superior Court.

He and his wife, Ruth, live today in Montebello, on the site of his original home. They are the parents of five children, two sons and three daughters.

MILDRED AND GORDON GORDON, who worked closely with Judge Burke in the writing of this book, met while students at the University of Arizona and thereby made possible one of the most successful husband-and-wife writing teams in America. After working separately for the United Press, *Arizona Magazine*, International News Service, and Twentieth Century–Fox, they decided to pool their talents, and a delighted reading public has been grateful ever since. To date, their carefully researched, soundly constructed suspense novels have sold over four million copies and have been made into such movies as *Case File: FBI* and the forthcoming *Captive*.

The Gordons live at Sherman Oaks, California, where they work on a regular schedule, blue-penciling, as they put it, "each other's best material." Despite the problems of such a collaboration, it has been, in their case, extremely successful. "People are always surprised that we don't have violent quarrels collaborating," Mildred writes. "Perhaps it's because we're married."

DR. EVERETT L. SHOSTROM, psychological consultant of *With This Ring*, is a clinical psychologist in private practice in Southern California. A member of the American Psychological Association and president-elect of the Southern California Psychological Association, he is co-author, with Dr. L. M. Brammer, of *The Dynamics of the Counseling Process* and the forthcoming *Therapeutic Psychology*. He was formerly head of the department of psychology of Pepperdine College, Los Angeles.

On the assumption that family problems are many times both legal and psychological in scope, Dr. Shostrom, with Dr. Richard Hogan and Mark F. Joseff, founded and today co-directs the Institute of Juridical Psychotherapy, an organization whose function is to counsel people in marital difficulties and to consult with lawyers and psychologists regarding interprofessional cooperation in the solution of family problems. He brings unique qualifications, therefore, to his role as consultant in the preparation of this volume.